BLUE LIVES MATTER

IN THE LINE OF DUTY

Former LAPD Reserve Officer and LA District Attorney

HON. STEVE COOLEY

Career Prosecutor & Office Historian

ROBERT SCHIRN

BLUE LIVES MATTER: IN THE LINE OF DUTY
Steve Cooley & Robert Schirn

For information, bulk orders, or to use this as a part of your training programs, please contact:

TitleTown Publishing
P.O. Box 12093 | Green Bay, WI 54307-12093
920.737.8051 | www.titletownpublishing.com

Edited by Kylie Shannon & Cathy Hawks
Front cover design by Erika Block
Interior design and layout by Euan Monaghan
Design & Layout Editor | Travis J. Vanden Heuvel

Contact Publisher Tracy Ertl for all review, media, reprint inquires at (920) 737–8051 | tracy@titletownpublishing.com

Represented for Film and Television by
Intellectual Property Group
Office of Joel Gotler | (310) 402–5154 | joel@ipglm.com
12400 Wilshire Blvd., Suite 500, Los Angeles, CA 90025

PUBLISHER'S CATALOGING-IN-PUBLICATION DATA
Cooley, Steve; Schirn, Robert
BLUE LIVES MATTER: IN THE LINE OF DUTY / Cooley & Schirn.
– 1st edition. Green Bay, WI : TitleTown Pub., c2017.

ISBN: 978-09-96295-16-1

10 9 8 7 6 5 4 3 2 1

In valor there is hope.

— Tacitus

PUBLISHER'S NOTE

In addition to leading a mainstream publishing company and working on wonderful projects like *Blue Lives Matter*, I've dedicated more than 25 years of my professional life to public safety communications. Through my service as a 911 dispatcher (supervisor) at Brown County Public Safety Communications and my mission with the world's largest public safety education organization (APCO) as an instructor and presenter, I've deepened my appreciation for – and respect of – all men and women who wear the badge. *Blue Lives Matter: In the Line of Duty* has given me the opportunity to take my vocation as a public servant and combine it with my entrepreneurial spirit and passion for storytelling in a way that honors the fallen and teaches valuable lessons about officer safety.

One of my favorite lines from scripture comes from Jeremiah, "Before I formed you in the womb, I knew you." (Jeremiah 1:5) It's extremely unlikely that you – our reader – and I will ever meet, yet I feel like I know you intimately. We are connected to one another through our blue family. You are police officers and sheriff's deputies, dispatchers and records professionals, parents, spouses and children. And we've been brought together because we have a common mission: We want to do everything in our power to ensure that every member of the law enforcement community is able to safely return home at the end of their tour.

This book is my best attempt to convey admiration, respect, and appreciation for the risks and work of our blue family. It is my hope that this book and series has the ability to impact and save lives by humanizing officers and their families, while creating deeply needed, effective conversation. I am humbled to be part of the blue family and this project.

Respectfully,
Tracy C. Ertl

Chief Executive Officer & Publisher
TitleTown Publishing

CONTENTS

PROLOGUE

(COMMENTARY OF STEVE COOLEY)

INTRODUCTION

Throughout my career, I have been exposed to officers killed in the line of duty. My first recollection was when I was a reserve LAPD officer working in Newton Division in the mid-seventies when an officer was shot and killed during a routine traffic stop. Finally it dawned on me how potentially dangerous it is to be a police officer.

During my time as District Attorney, I went to many active crime scene investigations where police officers had been shot and killed or seriously wounded. I strongly supported efforts to place special emphasis on the prosecutions of those responsible for the murder of police officers.

When I joined the District Attorney's Office as a brand new prosecutor, I became emotionally involved in many of my cases. I was unprepared to being exposed to the large number of persons committing murders, rapes, robberies, serious assaults, and selling large amounts of narcotics. Gradually a certain acceptance and cynicism set in as I was prosecuting these cases on a regular basis. I became hardened to these crimes. I prosecuted all these cases thoroughly and professionally but without becoming personally or emotionally involved, with one exception.

The exception involves the murder of a police officer. To this day, I have a strong emotional reaction when I hear about the murder of a police officer. I have known and worked with many peace officers during my career as a prosecutor. When the job is done right, there is not a more admirable nor noble profession, to protect and to serve the public.

"LESSONS LEARNED"

One purpose in writing this book was to memorialize and honor police officers who have given their lives in service to their community and to their profession. Although this book contains eight chapters involving the death of eight officers and one police canine, it is dedicated to all officers who made the ultimate sacrifice in the line of duty.

Although there is nothing positive about the death of a police officer, the authors have included a "Lessons Learned" segment at the end of each chapter. Former LAPD Captain Greg Meyer is one of the nation's foremost experts on police tactics and on officer safety, having lectured and provided expert testimony on these topics throughout the country over the years. He has contributed his opinions and expertise in the preparation of these "Lessons Learned" segments. It is hoped that police officers in the future can benefit from this component of the book to enhance their safety and awareness of potentially dangerous situations.

I remember a bit of advice that my father, a former FBI agent, gave me when I told him how excited I was to be an LAPD reserve officer. "Fine, Steve. Just don't get your ass shot off."

CAPOS (Crimes Against Peace Officers Section)

In my view, the murder of a police officer is a crime that attacks the very fabric of our society. A strong police presence is in the public interest because it maintains public safety. Without the police to maintain law and order, there would be anarchy. The prosecution of persons who have murdered police officers is one of the most important functions performed by a prosecuting agency.

To that end, the Los Angeles County District Attorney's Office maintains a special unit called the Crimes Against Peace Officers Section (CAPOS) to handle these cases.

In 1978, District Attorney John Van de Kamp hired private attorney Johnnie Cochran to be the Assistant District Attorney, one of the two highest positions in the office below the District Attorney. He remained in this position for about two years before returning to private practice. Cochran had already established a reputation handling high profile cases and police brutality cases. One of his responsibilities was oversight over cases involving police misconduct, and he oversaw a rollout program in which a deputy district attorney and a district attorney investigator would go to the scene of a shooting by a police officer involving injury to a civilian.

Law enforcement officials suggested to District Attorney John Van de

Kamp that if he was allocating resources to investigate police officers who fire their weapons, it was only fair to allocate similar resources when a police officer was the victim of a violent assault. In 1980, Van de Kamp created CAPOS. As written in my 2003–2005 Biennial Report, the mission of CAPOS was described as follows:

> *Prosecutors assigned to the Crimes Against Peace Officers Section (CAPOS) play an integral role in the investigation and prosecution of cases in which police officers are victims. CAPOS deputies are always on call and respond to the scene whenever an officer is seriously injured or killed in the line of duty. The deputies work closely with the investigating agency. They advise agency personnel on legal issues; assist in the preparation of search warrants and other legal tools; and aggressively prosecute those criminally charged.*

CAPOS is considered a highly desirable assignment, and the unit attracts some of the most talented prosecutors in the District Attorney's Office. Many of the prosecutors from CAPOS have become judges or have been promoted to high-level positions in the office. CAPOS did not lose a case during my twelve years as District Attorney.

One of the goals of this book is to encourage other prosecuting agencies to establish and maintain special units or assign specially trained prosecutors to assist in the investigation and handle the prosecution of cases involving the murder and serious assault of police officers.

DEATH PENALTY

The current law in California makes first degree murder punishable by death or by life imprisonment without the possibility of parole when "special circumstances" of the crime have been charged and proven in court. Existing state law identifies 22 special circumstances that can be alleged, such as cases when the murder was carried out for financial gain, when more than one murder was committed, or when the victim of the murder was a peace officer in the performance of his or her duties.

The first phase of a murder trial where the prosecution seeks a death sentence is a guilt phase that determines whether the defendant is guilty of first degree murder with special circumstances. If the defendant is found guilty of first degree murder and a special circumstance has been found true, then the second phase, or penalty phase, involves determining whether the death penalty or life without the possibility of parole should be imposed.

Whether to seek the death penalty in an appropriate case is one of the most difficult decisions that a district attorney's office must make. The Los Angeles County District Attorney's Office has a Special Circumstances Committee chaired by a top executive in the office who determines the cases in which the death penalty will be sought. After the preliminary hearing has been completed in a murder case in which special circumstances are alleged, the prosecutor assigned to the case prepares a lengthy Capital Case Memorandum and makes a presentation to the Special Circumstances Committee. The defense attorney may submit materials to the committee in mitigation of punishment. The committee then determines the penalty that will be sought.

Between January 1, 2001 and January 1, 2011, the Special Circumstances Committee considered a total of 1,213 defendants for penalty recommendations. The committee selected death for 146 defendants. Of these, 62 received death, 59 received life without parole or less (either due to a verdict or through a change of the People's recommendation), while 25 were still pending.

My personal view is that I generally favor the death penalty in cases involving multiple murders including sexually motivated murders, murder of a child, murder of a public official (including a peace officer), and murders that are especially cruel and depraved.

This preference for the death penalty for the murder of peace officers in the performance of his or her duties is reflected in the seven chapters in this book involving the murder of a police officer. In four of the chapters, the jury voted for the death penalty for the defendant. In Chapter One, the death penalty statute at the time of the crime no longer existed when the case went to trial. In Chapter Five, the defendants did not know that the murder victim was a police officer; and, in Chapter Six, an extradition treaty precluded the seeking of the death penalty.

Despite the number of cop killers on death row in California, none of them has been executed since the death penalty was reinstated in California in 1978.

PROLOGUE

ACKNOWLEDGMENTS

First and foremost, I want to acknowledge my co-author Robert (Bob) Schirn, the unofficial historian for the District Attorney's Office. He shares my appreciation for the contributions and sacrifices that police officers have made in the line of duty, and we both wanted to prepare a book that portrays police officers in a positive and accurate manner. Bob spent countless hours locating files, transcripts, reports, and photographs and collected documents from various sources including case files, police agencies, clerks' offices, and newspapers. Bob and I then spent many hours collaborating on and organizing each chapter in this book.

Both Bob and I are career prosecutors, and we have written this book in the manner and style of a lawyer. We are direct and straightforward in our approach, and we have attempted to lay out the facts and the court proceedings without undue embellishment. We have avoided literary devices that would overly dramatize the deaths of the officers. The death of an officer and its impact on family, friends, and society is dramatic enough that additional emphasis is not necessary. This book is written primarily in the third person, but certain segments are in the first person when I have been personally involved in the case or have personal comments to make about the case.

I want to acknowledge the contributions of Deputy District Attorney Darren Levine not only to this book but also for his successful prosecutions of cases involving murdered police officers. Darren also should be credited for helping develop and advance many of the techniques, procedures, and protocols utilized by CAPOS (Crimes Against Peace Officers Section) in the earliest levels of investigations and successful prosecutions in court. CAPOS has been blessed with some of the best lawyers in the office. However, Darren Levine clearly has distinguished himself as perhaps the best in CAPOS' history. Out of eight chapters in this book, four involve cases handled by DDA Darren Levine.

I also want to acknowledge the contributions of former LAPD Captain Greg Meyer, who provided the authors with his insightful expertise on police tactics and officer safety. I hope that police officers can benefit from the "Lessons Learned" segments and use them as a training device to increase their awareness and response to potentially dangerous situations.

Bob Schirn and I interviewed numerous individuals involved in the prosecution and investigation of the cases set forth in this book. They provided us with valuable insights, anecdotes, information, and materials. In particular, we received information from current and former prosecutors who were involved in prosecuting each of the cases. They include Ellen Berk, Sheldon Brown, Judge Maureen Duffy-Lewis, Judge Dino Fulgoni, Richard Jenkins, Daniel Lenhart, Darren Levine, and Janice Maurizi.

Current and former law enforcement officers who made valuable contributions to this project include John Hall, Chief Dan Hughes, Glynn Martin, Michael Thies, Jimmy Trahin, and Joe Vita. I also want to thank my good friend John March, the father of Deputy David March, for his input.

Typing and computer services were provided by Joyce Irving, Sylvia Nuñez, William Marcus, and my good friend and personal secretary, Cathy Hawks.

Bob Schirn and I received the support and encouragement of our families in this project. I am indebted to my wife of 43 years Jana and my children Michael and Shannon. Bob wants to thank his wife of over 50 years Zanda and his sons Brian and Jason.

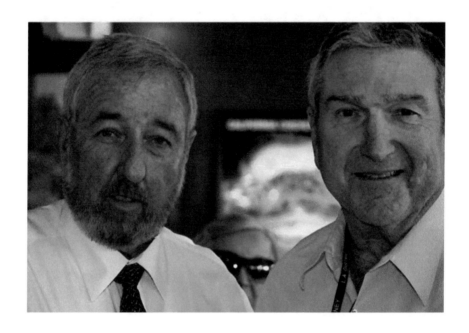

STEVE COOLEY

BOB SCHIRN

High School: Pater Noster High School
College: Cal State L.A. (1970)
Law School: U.S.C. School of Law (1973)
Deputy District Atty: 1973–1982
Head Deputy D.A.: 1982–2000
District Attorney: 2000–2012

High School: Beverly Hills High School
College: Princeton University (1963)
Law School: U.C.L.A. Law School (1966)
Deputy District Atty: 1967–1978
Head Deputy D.A.: 1978–2005
Part Time D.A.: 2005–Present

December 2, 2003

Bob Schirn receives a commemorative clock from
District Attorney Steve Cooley for 35 years of service

CNOA President Rudy Tai presents District Attorney Cooley with the CNOA Prosecutor of the Year award for 2008.

Previous winners of the award from Los Angeles County attended the California Narcotic Officers' Association Conference: Robert Schirn, Curt Hazell, Barbara Turner, Steve Cooley, Joseph Esposito, Scott Collins, and John Allen Ramseyer.

On December 1, 2008, District Attorney Steve Cooley is sworn into office for a third term by Superior Court Judge Ruth Ann Kwan. His wife, Jana, looks on.

Steve Cooley was a reserve officer for the Los Angeles Police Department from 1972 to 1977

CHAPTER 1

Officers Richard Phillips and Milton Curtis

El Segundo Police Department

"We Do Not Forgive;

We Do Not Forget; We Do Not Give Up"

INTRODUCTION

On July 22, 1957, Officer Bernie Bangasser of the El Segundo Police Department had the morning watch at the station's police radio desk. At approximately 1:30 a.m., he heard a desperate voice over the police radio: "Ambulance!" it gasped. "Rosecrans... Sepulveda!" And then silence.

The next voice Officer Bangasser heard over the police radio was that of Officer James Gilbert, who yelled, "Send an ambulance fast, Bernie! Rosecrans, just west of Sepulveda! It's Unit 35! Both boys have been shot! It's bad!"

JULY 21, 1957—JUST BEFORE MIDNIGHT

The events leading to the frantic phone calls began on the late evening of July 21, 1957. Two teenage couples were parked in a secluded lovers' lane behind the Western Avenue Golf Course in Hawthorne, California. They were four high school students—the boys were ages 16 and 17, and their dates were 15 years of age. The 17-year-old was driving a car registered to his father, a 1949 Ford four-door sedan, metallic blue in color. They had been to a party that evening, and on the way home they had turned off the main road and parked at this secluded location.

One of the girls looked at her wrist watch, saw that it was 11:40 p.m., and stated that she had to be home by midnight. At approximately 11:50 p.m., they were getting ready to leave. Suddenly, a man appeared at the right rear window of the vehicle. He was described as a white male, approximately 25–30 years old, 6 feet, 190 pounds, his hair combed back, pompadour-style in the front, wearing a white and light red sport shirt and khaki pants. He spoke with a southern drawl. He was holding a chrome-plated revolver and stated, "This is a robbery. All I want is your money. Take it easy and I won't hurt you."

The man opened the car door and ordered the 17-year-old driver into the back seat and to kneel down. He then got into the front seat next to the petrified girl. He reached into his pocket and produced a roll of adhesive tape and a pocket knife and began cutting lengths of tape from the roll. He ordered the two boys and the girl in the back seat to tape their own eyes and mouths. Then he ripped off the boys' shirts, tore them into strips, and tied the boys' hands behind them. He removed two wrist watches from the victims—one boy's and one girl's. He also took the boys' wallets, which only contained a few dollars. Then, he directed the two boys and the girl in the back seat to lie on the floor.

The man then directed his attention to the 15-year-old girl in the front seat. He started the 1949 Ford and drove about 500 yards to a more secluded area. There he forcibly began undressing the girl in the front seat. He removed her brassiere and tied her hands behind her back with the brassiere. He proceeded to remove the rest of her clothing and then forcibly raped her on the front seat of the car as the young victim sobbed and prayed.

At the conclusion of the rape, he ordered the four teenagers to disrobe. At his direction, one of the girls removed the strips binding the boys' hands. All took off their clothes with the two boys and one girl still with tape over their eyes and mouths. The man then ordered the four victims out of the car, leaving their clothes in the vehicle.

The man re-entered the 1949 Ford and drove off, leaving the four teenagers stranded. It was not until 1:30 a.m. that they were able to hail down a vehicle driven by a guard at the Northrup plant at the nearby airport. The four victims told the guard what had happened to them, and he called the Hawthorne police. By 2:00 a.m. the police had obtained the full story from the four teenagers, and a radio dispatch of the stolen 1949 Ford and license number were broadcast over police frequencies.

OFFICERS MILTON CURTIS AND RICHARD PHILLIPS

On the early morning of July 22, 1957, Milton G. Curtis and Richard A. Phillips were police officers for the El Segundo Police Department. They had come on duty at midnight and left the police station on Main Street at about 12:15 a.m. They were in uniform and in a marked police vehicle, Unit 35, assigned to patrol the southern sector of town.

Officer Richard Phillips was 28 years of age and had been with the police department just under two years. Previously he spent four years with the air police during the Korean War. He and his wife Carole lived in El Segundo and had three children, daughters Carolyn age four, Patricia age three, and son Dick Jr. age 20 months.

Officer Milton Curtis was 25 years of age and had been on the force only two months. He had been a member of the Hawthorne police reserve for several years and had taken police science classes. Becoming a full-time police officer was a fulfillment of his lifetime ambition. He and his wife Jean lived in Hawthorne. They were the parents of a five-year-old son, Keith, and two-year-old daughter, Toni.

JULY 22, 1957 – EARLY MORNING

At approximately 1:25 a.m. on July 22, 1957, the 1949 Ford was driving westbound on Rosecrans Avenue and Sepulveda Boulevard when it ran a red light at this intersection. Officers Richard Phillips and Milton Curtis were on patrol in Unit 35 and observed the traffic violation. They initiated a stop of the 1949 Ford sedan (which had not yet been reported as stolen by the four teenage victims).

Officer Bernie Bangasser was working the El Segundo police radio desk. At 1:29 a.m., he received a radio call from Officer Curtis requesting a check of the license number of a 1949 Ford against the automobile registration and traffic warrant files.

A second El Segundo police car designated as Unit 33 containing Officers Charles Porter and James Gilbert drove by the scene shortly after the traffic stop. They observed Unit 35 stopped on the road shoulder of Rosecrans Avenue behind a dark blue 1949 Ford sedan. Both cars were facing west. Officer Phillips was standing by the right front fender of the patrol car holding his traffic book. A tall man wearing a red-and-white checkered sports shirt, apparently the driver of the 1949 Ford, was standing behind him. Officer Curtis was in the front seat of the police car, apparently in conversation with the police dispatcher. Unit 33 stopped briefly in the middle of the street to determine whether the detaining officers needed any assistance. Officer Phillips waved them on, indicating that this was a routine traffic stop and that everything was under control. Unit 33 then drove away from the scene.

In the meantime, Officer Bernie Bangasser was checking the license number and automobile registration information of the 1949 Ford. Suddenly he heard the frantic call for an ambulance over the police radio. Officer Bangasser called Unit 35 but there was no response.

Officers Porter and Gilbert in Unit 33 recognized the quavering voice of the "Ambulance" call as being from Officer Phillips. They raced back using their red light and siren to the scene of the traffic stop. After returning to the scene, Officer Gilbert immediately yelled over the police radio to Officer Bangasser for an ambulance.

Officers Porter and Gilbert observed that Unit 35 was still in the same location with its lights on. The 1949 Ford was no longer there. The right front door of the police vehicle was fully open. Officer Curtis was slumped in the front seat with Officer Phillips lying across him, halfway in and halfway out of the car. Both were unconscious and bleeding from gunshot wounds. Phillips' gun lay outside the car, its six chambers having been fired. Curtis' gun was still in its holster.

After radioing for assistance and an ambulance, the officers attempted to render aid. However, Officer Curtis died at the scene, and Officer Phillips died on his way to the hospital.

CRIME SCENE INVESTIGATION

The blue 1949 Ford sedan was located on Rosecrans Avenue on the wrong side of the street just four blocks from the scene of the shooting. It was abandoned, and its lights were off. Apparently the driver had seen Unit 33 racing back to the location with its lights flashing and siren on; he turned his lights off and pulled over to the other side of the road. After the police car had passed him, he left on foot. The rear window of the 1949 Ford had been shattered by two bullets, and there was another bullet hole in the trunk deck. The clothes of the four teenage robbery-rape victims were in the back seat.

At the crime scene, Officer Phillips' book of traffic tickets was on the right front fender of the police car with only the date of "7/22/57" written at the top of the ticket. The registration for the 1949 Ford and a ball point pen were on the ground nearby.

Police investigators were able to surmise what happened and recon-structed the sequence of events, as follows: After Unit 33 had driven away from the location of the traffic stop, the man driving the 1949 Ford knew that his identity did not match the vehicle registration. He also did not know whether the four teenage victims had told police officials about the robberies, rape, and car theft. Officer Phillips was just beginning to prepare a traffic ticket by writing the date of "7/22/57" at the top of the ticket when the man took out his gun and shot Officer Phillips three times in the back at point-blank range. Then he moved quickly to the open front passenger door of the police car and fired three shots at Officer Curtis, who was sit-ting in the front seat attending to the police radio. The shooter then ran to the 1949 Ford sedan and drove off. Officer Phillips was lying on the ground mortally wounded, but he was able to unholster his gun and fire six rounds at the fleeing sedan. Then he somehow managed to lift himself over his fatally wounded partner and make his desperate call over the police radio for an ambulance.

ADDITIONAL INVESTIGATION

A massive manhunt of the area of the shooting did not result in the loca-tion of any suspects or in any useful information.

The four teenage victims assisted police investigators with the descrip-tion of the suspect and the preparation of a composite sketch. Circulars of the composite sketch were widely distributed to other law enforcement agencies. Some composite sketches containing a description of the watches taken from the teenagers were distributed to pawnbrokers and second-hand dealers in case the suspect attempted to dispose of the watches.

Two partial fingerprints were lifted from the steering wheel of the 1949 Ford sedan. Since they could not be matched to anyone with access to the vehicle, the prints were believed to belong to the suspect. A palm print believed to belong to the suspect was lifted from the hood of the police car.

On July 22, 1957, autopsies were performed on the bodies of Officer Richard Phillips and Officer Milton Curtis. The cause of death for Officer Phillips was ascribed to "Gunshot wounds of the back with massive hemor-rhage in the chest." Three .22 caliber bullets were recovered from his body during the autopsy. As to Officer Curtis, the cause of death was ascribed to

"Gunshot wounds of the chest, abdomen, and forearm with massive hemorrhage." One of the bullets had passed through his heart. Three .22 caliber bullets were recovered from the body of Officer Curtis during the autopsy. All six bullets had distinctive markings and were fired from the same gun.

Detective Bruce Clements of the El Segundo Police Department and Detective Raymond Hopkins of the Los Angeles Sheriff's Office were assigned full time to investigating the case. Hundreds of guns were checked against the death slugs, hundreds of fingerprints were compared, and thousands of booking photographs were compared with the composite sketches. Numerous leads were investigated, but the identity of the killer of the officers was not identified. It would be many years before the case would eventually be solved.

RECOVERY OF MURDER WEAPON

In March 1960, law enforcement officers went to the residence of Douglas Tuley at 555 3rd Street in Manhattan Beach. This residence was approximately one-fourth mile from the location on Rosecrans Avenue where the 1949 Ford sedan had been abandoned. Mr. Tuley gave the officers two watches and a chrome-plated Harrington and Richardson .22 caliber revolver. He stated that the watches and the firearm were found in the rear yard and alleyway of his home on different dates between July 1957 and March 1960.

The two watches were positively identified by the teenage victims as the watches taken during the robbery-rape, prior to the murder of the officers.

Inside the cylinder of the Harrison and Richardson .22 caliber revolver were six expended shell casings and one live cartridge. The ammunition recovered inside the gun was consistent with the ammunition used to kill the El Segundo police officers. The gun was tested, and there was a "consistent" match to the projectiles recovered from the bodies of the officers. However, the tests were not conclusive because of the poor condition of the gun.

A check of the firearm's serial number revealed that it was purchased at a Sears Roebuck and Company in Shreveport, Louisiana on July 18, 1957, four days prior to the shooting deaths of the two police officers. Records from the Sears store indicated that the weapon was purchased by an unidentified male who gave the name of "G. D. Wilson" with an address of

2831 NW 37th Avenue, Miami, Florida. This address was later determined to be a gravel pit. Officers investigated the surrounding area near Sears and determined that a man using the name "George D. Wilson" had checked in and signed the guest registry on July 17, 1957, at a YMCA located two blocks from the Sears store. Investigators took possession of the registration card containing the suspect's handwriting from the YMCA.

Sheriff's Homicide and El Segundo Police investigators requested the assistance of the Federal Bureau of Investigation in an attempt to identify the person who purchased the .22 caliber revolver from the Shreveport Sears store. Numerous individuals using the name of, or identified as a, George D. Wilson were investigated. However, all these individuals were cleared by photo show-ups (viewed by victims), print comparisons, and handwriting comparisons.

The murder case in the death of Officers Richard Phillips and Milton Curtis remained unsolved.

BREAKTHROUGH

The case remained open but inactive for over 40 years. In September 2002, the El Segundo Police Department received a tip regarding the possible identity of the killer. The tip proved false, but it resulted in a review and re-examination of the evidence in the case.

Investigators contacted Los Angeles Sheriff's Crime Lab personnel, who re-examined the fingerprints lifted in 1957 from the stolen 1949 Ford sedan. The two partial fingerprints were put together to make a composite fingerprint. This composite fingerprint was processed through a new FBI fingerprint data base called "Universal Latent Workstation". This was a nationwide computerized fingerprint data base that included fingerprint records from police agencies over the entire United States. It became operational in February 2002. A hit was made on the fingerprint, which was positively identified as belonging to a Gerald F. Mason. The fingerprint that provided the critical link was a digital composite constructed from the two partial fingerprints.

Investigators determined the following about Gerald F. Mason: He was born on January 31, 1934 in Richland County, South Carolina. He had owned several service stations before retiring in the mid-1990s. He was currently living in a fashionable suburb in Columbia, South Carolina with Betty, his wife of over 40 years. They had two daughters—Maria, age 39, and Terry, age 37—and five grandchildren. His criminal record consisted of just one arrest for burglary in January 1956 in South Carolina for which he served a prison sentence from April 1956 to December 1956. It was the fingerprints from that arrest that were matched to the fingerprints lifted from the stolen 1949 Ford.

Deputy District Attorney Darren Levine of the Crimes Against Peace Officers Section (CAPOS) was assigned to work with the investigating officers and put together a prosecutable case against Gerald Mason. However, Levine was concerned whether a 45-year-old fingerprint would be enough to convict Mason of murdering the two El Segundo police officers, especially when Mason had lived an apparently productive and law-abiding life since 1956.

Prosecutor Levine directed the investigating officers to conduct a further investigation and develop additional evidence connecting Gerald Mason to the murders. First, the investigators obtained the booking photograph taken at the time of Mason's burglary arrest in 1956. The photograph strongly resembled the composite sketch prepared of the rape/robbery suspect in July 1957. Also, Mason's physical description at the time of his 1956 arrest of 6'3", 195 pounds, and brown hair matched the description of the rape/robbery suspect.

Between September 2002 and December 2002, the investigators obtained several handwriting exemplars of Gerald Mason without his knowledge from public records in South Carolina. These included a 1999 South Carolina drivers' license application and social security records from 1954 and 1993. Questioned document examiner Paul Edholm compared these records with the guest registry from the Shreveport YMCA and concluded that Gerald Mason wrote the name George D. Wilson in the YMCA registry.

By January 2003, Deputy District Attorney Darren Levine was prepared to file charges against Gerald Mason for the 1957 murders of the two El Segundo police officers.

ARREST

On January 24, 2003, Deputy District Attorney Darren Levine filed a 12-count complaint in Los Angeles Superior Court charging Gerald Fit

Mason with two counts of murder, one count of rape, five counts of kidnapping, and four counts of robbery. A no bail arrest warrant was issued for Mason's arrest.

On the morning of January 28, 2003, a team of United States marshals and law enforcement officers from Los Angeles County and from South Carolina arrested Gerald Mason at his home in Columbia, South Carolina. Mason seemed shocked when told that he was being arrested for the murder of two police officers in Los Angeles in 1957. Three days after his arrest, Mason turned 69 years of age.

Mason was held in custody without bail. He was extradited to Los Angeles to face the charges against him.

GUILTY PLEA

On March 23, 2003, Gerald Mason appeared in Department 100 of the Los Angeles Superior Court. He pleaded guilty to two first degree murders in the killings of El Segundo police officers Richard Phillips and Milton Curtis. He was sentenced to consecutive life terms in state prison. Mason was not eligible for the death penalty since the death penalty law in existence in 1957 had been declared unconstitutional by the California and United States Supreme Courts.

Pursuant to a plea agreement, the remaining counts involving the rape, kidnappings, and robberies of the four teenage victims were dismissed. It was agreed that Mason could serve his prison sentence in South Carolina so he could be close to his family.

Mason offered a tearful apology. He stated in court, "I don't understand why I did this. It makes no sense. It's contrary to everything I believe. At no time in my life have I intentionally harmed anyone."

FAMILY IMPACT STATEMENTS

Under California law, the family members of a murder victim have the right to be heard in court at the time of sentencing. I was in attendance in the court at the time of the guilty plea and sentencing along with Sheriff Lee Baca, El Segundo Police Chief Jack Wayt, about a dozen officers from the El Segundo Police Department and family members of the murdered officers. Two children of the slain officers spoke of the grief on their families of growing up without their fathers.

Carolyn Phillips Stewart was four years old when her father Richard Phillips was murdered. She stated, "Your cowardly act shattered our lives forever. You caused his beloved wife, our mother, to become a widow with three babies to raise alone. She grieved for him her entire life and cried whenever we mentioned his name. For all of this we cannot and will not forgive you!"

Keith Curtis expressed gratitude that the killer of his father had been caught but expressed disappointment that his sister, Toni, had passed away before seeing him brought to justice. He spoke of the devastation Mason had brought to two families and four teenage victims.

I spoke at a press conference after the proceedings. I noted the interagency cooperation among the Los Angeles Sheriff's Department, the El Segundo Police Department, and the District Attorney's Office in solving the case. I pointed out that the two Sheriff's detectives who solved the case were born two years after the El Segundo killings occurred. Deputy District Attorney Darren Levine was born three years after the killings. I concluded by stating, "The message is, when it comes to killing a peace officer, we don't forgive, we don't forget, we don't give up."

GERALD MASON ADMISSIONS

Over time, Gerald Mason gave his version of what happened. He stated that after his release from custody for burglary at age 23, he hitchhiked to California. On the way, he stopped in Shreveport, stayed at the YMCA, and purchased a revolver using a false name. He said that he purchased the weapon for protection while hitchhiking.

He claimed that he was intoxicated when he stumbled upon the four teenage victims. When asked why he had raped a 15-year-old girl, he responded that he no longer remembered. He admitted that he shot the officers to avoid being arrested for the rape, robberies, and car theft. After shooting the officers, he dumped the car and fled through some backyards and got rid of the gun and stolen watches. He hitchhiked away from the area and eventually hitchhiked back to South Carolina.

EPILOGUE – PAROLE HEARING

Gerald Mason was sentenced to two consecutive sentences of life in prison for the first degree murders of Officers Richard Phillips and Milton Curtis. However, under the applicable California law at the time of the crimes in 1957, the sentence of life in prison was subject to the possibility of parole after seven years. The law allows a parole hearing for prison inmates to be scheduled one year prior to the seven-year period.

Gerald Mason at age 75 had his first parole hearing on March 20, 2009, six years into his life sentence. The hearing took place in a Sacramento conference room before a parole board consisting of three members. Present at the hearing were Deputy District Attorney Darren Levine, family members of the slain officers, and representatives from law enforcement. Mason was represented by an attorney. Mason was not personally present but communicated to the parole board through a speaker phone from South Carolina where he was imprisoned.

The parole board was presented with the details of the brutal and heartless acts committed by Mason in July 1957. Mason's attorney presented to the parole board a photo album that purported to show that he lived a productive and law-abiding life as a family and business man.

Officer Phillips' children also addressed the board, pointing out that the only time they could spend with their father was when they visited his grave at the cemetery. Mason, on the other hand, was able to enjoy raising a family and spending time with his children and grandchildren.

After conferring for about forty minutes, the three-member board denied Mason's request for release on parole. They described his crimes as "heinous" and "atrocious" and stated that he continued to minimize his crimes and failed to show any remorse. They stated that Mason should not have another parole hearing for the maximum period of 15 years.

Undoubtedly, Gerald Fit Mason will die in prison.

LESSONS LEARNED

The murders of Officers Richard Phillips and Milton Curtis took place in 1957 when officer safety and survival were not something for which officers received much training. Officers Phillips and Curtis treated the detention of Gerald Mason as a routine traffic stop. They did not coordinate their actions and cover for one another. Officer Phillips was standing by the right front fender of the police car starting to write a citation for Mason, who was standing behind him. Officer Curtis was in the front seat of the police car, apparently communicating with the police dispatcher. Mason shot Officer Phillips three times in the back at point blank range. Mason then quickly moved to the open front passenger door of the police car and fired three shots at Officer Curtis. It was not until the officers were shot that the mortally wounded Officer Phillips was able to unholster his gun and fire six rounds at Mason, who was fleeing in the stolen sedan. Officer Phillips then crawled into the police car to make a last desperate call for help.

Officer Phillips exhibited commendable bravery and fortitude when, after being fatally wounded by multiple gunshots, he returned gunfire and crawled back to the police car to report the emergency. This will to "finish the fight" despite being badly hurt comes from the mental attitude of "never give up". Tragically, Officer Phillips suffered fatal wounds. But not all gunshots are fatal, and officers need to train their minds and bodies to keep going, even when experiencing unspeakable adversity.

The proper deployment of officers during a vehicle stop and strategies for officer safety and survival will be discussed in ensuing chapters. The lesson to be learned in this case can be summarized by my comments at the press conference after Gerald Mason was sentenced for the murders of the two officers: "When it comes to killing a peace officer, we don't forgive, we don't forget, we don't give up."

Officer Richard Phillips 28 *Officer Milton Curtis 25*

Murder of two El Segundo Police Officers
July 21, 1957

Murderer of Police Officers !
WANTED
Also Wanted for Rape, Robbery, Kidnapping and Auto Theft

MODUS OPERANDI: At approximately 11:45 PM - 7-21-57, four teen-age victims, (2 Girls & 2 Boys) were parked on a "Lovers Lane" when suspect approached carrying a chrome plated .22 caliber revolver, 2" to 4" barrel, a small flashlight and a roll of 1 inch adhesive tape.

Suspect forced victims to tape their own mouths and eyes with strips of tape which he cut from the roll with a pocket knife. He then tied the male victim's arms behind them, with pieces torn from their shirts and then robbed the victims of their wallets and wrist watches. Suspect then raped one of the girls while the two boys and the other girl were forced to lie down in the back of the car. He then forced all the victims to disrobe, after which he drove away with their car with their clothing on the rear seat, leaving them nude.

Approximately twenty minutes later at 1:29 AM - 7-22-57, suspect murdered two police officers when he was stopped for a minor traffic violation while driving the stolen car.

During Robbery - Rape & Kidnapping suspect was very polite, used no profanity and at times was apologetic for his actions. Several times he used the expression "fella" or "fellas". He also referred to police as "policemen." Suspect's opening statement was, "This is a robbery. All I want is your money. I won't hurt you." Suspect spent considerable time with the victims before the rape and at times seemed to be indecisive as to his next moves.

The recovered slugs are .22 caliber, short or longs with a right hand twist, 6 lands and grooves. It is possible that they were fired from a .22 caliber Harrington & Richardson revolver, 2" or 4" barrel.

DESCRIPTION: WM, 25 to 30 years old, 190 lbs., 6' to 6'2", light brown hair, combed back in pompadour style, parted on left side, has receding hairline both sides of forehead; medium complexion with clear skin; sharp clear voice with a slight drawl; muscular build with broad shoulders and slim-waist; was dressed in khaki trousers with short-sleeved sports shirt with red and white squared check pattern, worn outside the trousers.

This print was found in the stolen car and is believed to belong to the suspect. All known persons who had access to the stolen car have been eliminated.

NOTE: The above print is a composite made from two lifts. This print is most likely a fingerprint but may be a section of palm print.

All police departments are requested to check this print against all robbery-rape suspects known to your personnel.

White metal Wittnauer lady's wrist watch, 17 jewel, white face, white gold numerals. Case number unknown. No repair scratch marks. White metal expansion band with white metal crucifix and blue enamel 'Miraculous

White metal Tower boy's waterproof wrist watch, white face, black numerals and hands. No second hand. No movement or case numbers. No repair scratch marks. New clear crystal. White metal expansion band.

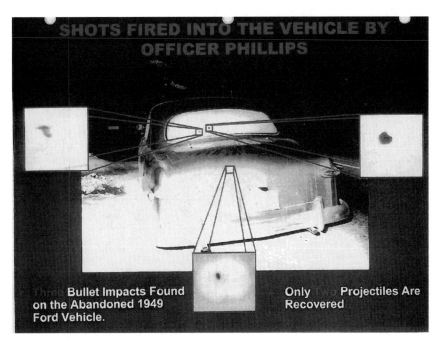

SHOTS FIRED INTO THE VEHICLE BY OFFICER PHILLIPS

Three Bullet Impacts Found on the Abandoned 1949 Ford Vehicle.

Only Two Projectiles Are Recovered

MASON'S FINGERPRINTS LIFTED FROM INSIDE STOLEN VEHICLE

Stolen Vehicle

Steering Wheel

Partial Print

Partial Print

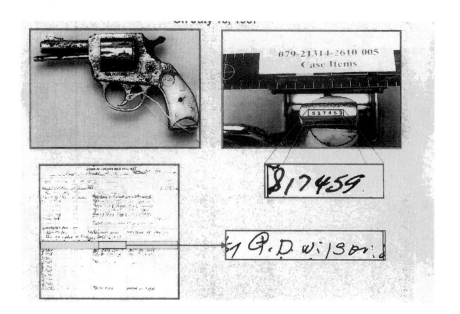

Gun purchased at Sears in Shreveport, LA
by G.D. Wilson on July 18, 1957

Photograph of Gerald Fit Mason after his arrest in
South Carolina on January 28, 2003

CHAPTER 2

Officer Ian Campbell

Los Angeles Police Department

"Don't Give Up Your Gun"

THE PROTAGONISTS

Ian James Campbell

Outside the Los Angeles Police Station in Downtown Los Angeles is a memorial wall honoring the over-200 officers of the Los Angeles Police Department who have given their lives in the line of duty. Among the names of the fallen officers is "Police Officer Ian J. Campbell, March 9, 1963."

Ian James Campbell was born on August 21, 1931, in Valley City, North Dakota. He was the son of William and Chrissie Campbell. William Campbell was a doctor with an active practice in Valley City. In 1944, he died of cancer. After his death, Chrissie and Ian Campbell moved to Los Angeles.

Ian Campbell was proud of his Scottish heritage, and he began playing the bagpipes when he was about 12 years old. He took lessons and became quite skilled at it. At age 17, he competed in the Scottish Highland Games held in Southern California and won best piper in the "novice" category.

Campbell attended Fairfax High School in Los Angeles. After his graduation from high school in 1950, he joined the Marine Corps and served in the Korean War. He completed two combat tours and received an honorable discharge as a staff sergeant. He was awarded the Marine Corps Good Conduct Medal, National Defense Medal, Korean Service Medal with four bronze stars, and the United Nations Korean Service Medal.

After his military discharge, he went to college. He eventually dropped out of college and joined the Los Angeles Police Department on May 5, 1958. He was initially assigned to the West Los Angeles Division and then to the Hollywood Division.

He married his wife Adah in 1958 and, at the time of his death, had two young daughters, Valerie, age three and a half, and Lori, age two.

Karl Hettinger

Karl Hettinger was born in 1934. He attended Pierce Junior College in the San Fernando Valley of Los Angeles County. He was a good student with an interest in agriculture, and he was elected student body president. He attended Fresno State College but dropped out his senior year. He joined the Marines and was stationed at Twenty-nine Palms, California for most of his enlistment. He joined the Los Angeles Police Department in 1958 and was the valedictorian of his police academy class. He was assigned to the Central Division for two years and then to the Hollywood Division where he worked the vice detail and then a plain-clothes felony car. He married Helen Davis in December 1962, and she was pregnant with their first child at the time of the crime on March 9, 1963.

Gregory Ulas Powell

Gregory Ulas Powell was a poster boy for a career criminal. He was born on August 29, 1934, and grew up in Cadillac, Michigan. He had a juvenile record of car theft and escape. At age 18, he was convicted of car theft and sentenced to state prison in Michigan. For the next ten years he was in and out of custody. He was almost 29 when he was paroled from Vacaville in California in May 1962, having spent ten of the past thirteen years in penal institutions. On the date of the murder of Officer Ian Campbell, he was on parole and had committed over 30 armed robberies of grocery and liquor stores in the Hollywood Division.

Jimmy Lee Smith

Jimmy Lee Smith was born in 1931 in Texas. He was raised by his maternal great-aunt. When he was age 16, he ran away to Los Angeles where he was sent to Juvenile Hall for burglary. He became a heroin addict and was in and out of custody for burglary and narcotics offenses.

In February 1963, Jimmy Lee Smith was paroled from Folsom Prison after a five-year term. He was on parole only two weeks before the murder of Officer Campbell. He came to Los Angeles and met Gregory Powell, who recruited Smith to be his wheel man for the robberies that he was committing. Smith and Powell committed about five robberies together before March 9, 1963.

Jimmy Lee Smith was a strong contrast from Gregory Powell. He was African American and Powell was white. Powell was a psychopath who did not feel an obligation to follow society's rules. Smith was a heroin addict, and his criminal record when he met Powell had been for theft-related offenses to support his narcotics habit and for narcotics violations. Powell was the dominant person in their relationship.

Both Gregory Ulas Powell and Jimmy Lee Smith were inmates in the California State Prison in 1960. In that year, Caryl Chessman was executed in the gas chamber at San Quentin for a violation of the "Little Lindbergh Law". This law was enacted in response to the kidnapping of the Lindbergh baby as California Penal Code section 209. The statute provided for a sentence of death or life in prison without the possibility of parole, in the discretion of the jury, for kidnapping for the purpose of robbery or extortion, when the kidnapping victim suffered death or bodily injury. Under the statute, a person could receive a death penalty sentence even if the kidnapping victim was not killed, as long as the victim sustained bodily injury. Caryl Chessman had been convicted of a series of crimes in which he would rob couples parked in vehicles late at night on so-called "lovers' lanes". On two occasions, he forcibly removed the female victim from the vehicle, took her to his car, and forced her to commit an act of oral copulation before releasing her. Although neither female victim received a visible bodily injury, Caryl Chessman received the death penalty in his jury trial. Chessman was convicted in 1947, and he remained on death row for thirteen years while he received eight stays of execution. A ninth stay was granted in May 1960, just minutes before his death in the gas chamber, but it was not communicated to the warden in time to halt the execution. While on death row, Chessman authored four books, including a best-selling autobiography, "Cell Block 2455". Chessman's battle to avoid the death penalty drew international attention, most of which supported his position. Every state prison inmate in California knew about Caryl Chessman and that he had been executed pursuant to a conviction under the Little Lindbergh Law.

THE CRIME

On March 9, 1963, a Saturday evening, Officers Ian Campbell and Karl Hettinger were assigned to the Hollywood Division working in plain clothes in an unmarked 1960 Plymouth. It was their ninth day as partners. Officer Campbell was driving the police car. The officers were aware that numerous robberies of markets and liquor stores were being committed in the Hollywood area.

At approximately 10:00 p.m., they observed a 1946 maroon Ford with Nevada license plates. There were two occupants in the Ford – a white driver and a black passenger. They were wearing matching leather jackets and leather caps. Gregory Powell was driving the vehicle and Jimmy Lee Smith was the passenger.

The officers decided to investigate the vehicle and its occupants, and they stopped the car for "rear plate illumination." The stop took place on Gower Street near Carlos Avenue in Hollywood, a location approximately one block off Hollywood Boulevard without much vehicular traffic. Officer Hettinger radioed the traffic stop and the location to police communications.

Officer Campbell parked the unmarked police car directly behind the 1946 maroon Ford. The officers were unaware that the occupants of the Ford were both on parole and armed with handguns. Both Gregory Powell and Jimmy Lee Smith knew that they would be sent back to prison if the guns in their possession were observed and seized by the officers. During the vehicle stop, Smith quietly dropped his gun to the floorboard and pushed it with his foot to the driver's side in the hope that the officers would attribute possession of the gun to Powell should they recover it from the driver's side of the vehicle.

Officer Campbell exited the police vehicle and approached the Ford from the driver's side while Officer Hettinger approached on the passenger side. The officers were holding flashlights and did not have their guns drawn. Jimmy Lee Smith got out of the Ford from the passenger side and raised his hands. Officer Hettinger sensed something was amiss, so he drew his gun and pointed it at Smith. In the meantime, Gregory Powell exited on the driver's side and pulled a gun on Officer Campbell. Powell got behind Officer Campbell with his gun placed against the officer's back. He maneuvered Officer Campbell to the back of the car and told Officer Hettinger to give up his gun. Officer Campbell told his partner, "He's got a gun in my back. Give him your gun."

Officer Hettinger was faced with a dilemma that he had to resolve in just a few seconds. This was a situation for which the officers had not received any training. Should Hettinger keep his gun and maintain the *status quo* while Gregory Powell had a gun on Officer Campbell? Powell was using Campbell as a shield, while Hettinger was standing next to the Ford with no cover and was vulnerable to being shot by Powell. In 1963, law enforcement officers did not wear bulletproof vests, so Officer Hettinger was in a defenseless position if Powell decided to open fire. Officer Campbell was the senior officer, and he had told his partner to give up his gun. Of course, if Officer Hettinger gave up his gun, he was putting himself and his partner at the mercy of two apparently dangerous criminals, who were armed and threatening two police officers with a firearm. Officer Hettinger did not know whether the passenger had exited the vehicle with his hands up to distract him while the driver got the drop on Officer Campbell.

With just a few seconds to make a decision, Officer Hettinger reluctantly handed his gun to Jimmy Lee Smith. Powell then ordered the officers into the 1946 Ford. Officer Campbell was told to sit in the driver's seat, Powell sat next to him, and Smith sat in the right front passenger seat. Officer Hettinger was made to lie down on the floor of the back seat. The unmarked 1960 Plymouth remained parked by the curb on Gower Street near Carlos Avenue.

Gregory Powell placed his gun in Officer Campbell's side and directed him to drive from the location. Powell told Campbell not to do anything that might attract attention. Following Powell's instructions, Officer Campbell drove to a nearby onramp of the Hollywood Freeway and eventually traveled north toward Bakersfield in Kern County. During the drive, Powell assured the officers that they would not be harmed and that they would be released at a location where Smith and Powell could get a sufficient head start before the officers could get help. After traveling a distance of approximately 90 miles, Powell told Officer Campbell to exit Highway 99 at the Mariposa Highway turnoff. Powell directed Officer Campbell to stop the vehicle at an onion field where a lighted farmhouse could be observed in the distance. Powell told the officers that they could go to the farmhouse and use a telephone to call for help. Powell said that they were now going to let them go and ordered the officers to exit the car. Everyone got out of the car, with the two officers standing side by side with their hands up. Both Smith and Powell were armed with both their own guns and the guns that they had taken from the officers.

While Officers Campbell and Hettinger were being kidnapped, other officers had begun a frantic search for them. At the time of the traffic stop of the 1946 Ford, Officer Hettinger had radioed in their location. When Officers Campbell and Hettinger did not call in after announcing the traffic stop, other officers went to the location of Gower Street and Carlos Avenue where they observed the unmarked 1960 Plymouth used by the now-missing officers parked at the location. An intensive search was made to locate either witnesses or the officers, including a house-to-house search that produced no results.

It was just past midnight on March 10, 1963, when Officers Campbell and Hettinger were being held at gunpoint by Gregory Powell and Jimmy Lee Smith next to the 1946 maroon Ford in an onion field in Kern County. Powell asked Officer Campbell, "We told you that we were going to let you guys go, but have you heard of the Little Lindbergh Law?" Officer Campbell said yes, and Powell then raised his gun and shot Officer Campbell once in the mouth at close range.

Gregory Powell apparently believed that the Little Lindbergh Law applied to the kidnapping of Officers Campbell and Hettinger, and that he was already subject to the death penalty. Since he believed that he was subject to the death penalty, he could kill the two officers and eliminate the witnesses without being subject to any greater penalty. Thus he had nothing to lose by killing the officers and something to gain by eliminating the eyewitnesses.

Gregory Powell, of course, was wrong in concluding that the Little Lindbergh Law applied prior to the time that he shot Officer Campbell. Until Officer Campbell was shot in the face by Powell, neither officer had sustained bodily injury, so prior to that time the Little Lindbergh Law did not apply. At most, Powell and Smith were guilty of kidnapping for the purpose of robbery. A kidnapping of the officers had clearly occurred, and the officers were robbed when their guns were taken by force. But the lack of bodily injury precluded the application of the Little Lindbergh Law.

As soon as Officer Hettinger saw Powell shoot Officer Campbell in the face, he let out a scream and ran for his life into the darkness. As he was running he looked back and saw both Smith and Powell firing guns. There were round flashes from one gun that were fired at the fleeing Officer

Hettinger. There were oblong flashes from another gun that was fired at the prone Officer Campbell.

Officer Hettinger dove through a barbed wire fence while Powell chased him on foot and Smith went down the road in the Ford in an attempt to cut off the fleeing officer. Hettinger, running through the fields in terror, managed to elude his pursuers. He came across a farmer, Emmanuel McFadden, who had just finished plowing a field by moonlight with a tractor. Hettinger quickly told McFadden what was happening and they got in the tractor. However, Hettinger could see the front lights of the Ford in the distance, so they abandoned the tractor and ran to a nearby farmhouse on foot. Hettinger banged on the door of the farmhouse, waking Jack Fry, his wife, and teenage son. Hettinger was out of breath, his pants were torn, and he was covered with blood and mud. He excitedly explained the situation to Mr. Fry, who got his shotgun and allowed Hettinger to use the phone.

At approximately 12:30 a.m. on the morning of March 10, 1963, Officer Hettinger called the Kern County Sheriff's Office from the farmhouse and gave a remarkably accurate description of the events and of the suspects, considering what he had just experienced. Hettinger identified himself as a Los Angeles police officer and stated that he and his partner had been kidnapped from Hollywood Division and that his partner had been shot. He described the vehicle as a 1946 maroon Ford with Nevada plates. He described one suspect as a male Caucasian, age thirty-one, five feet nine inches, one hundred fifty pounds with light brown hair and blue eyes, wearing a dark leather jacket and dark pants. He described the other suspect as a male Mexican, age twenty-five, five feet ten inches, one hundred fifty pounds, black curly hair, brown eyes, wearing a brown leather jacket and dark pants. He also mentioned that the suspects were armed with a .45 automatic and the officers' .38 specials. When asked how badly his partner was hurt, Hettinger stated that his partner was dead.

THE ARRESTS

In the meantime, Gregory Powell realized that he had not chosen the most reliable crime partner. While Powell was chasing Officer Hettinger on foot, Jimmy Lee Smith pursued the officer in the maroon Ford. Instead of returning to the onion field after a futile effort to catch the fleeing officer, Smith just kept on driving, leaving Powell stranded in the onion field. Powell was forced to go by foot to a nearby farm where he used his skills as a long-time auto thief to steal a Plymouth car. The occupants at the farm heard their car drive off, so they called the police to report the theft of the car. At about 1:30 a.m., two California Highway Patrol officers who were aware of both the shooting of a police officer and of the theft of the Plymouth stopped the vehicle with Gregory Powell, the driver and sole occupant. A 32-caliber revolver was found under the front seat, and a flashlight with the name "Hettinger" printed on it was found on the front seat. It was later determined that this 32-caliber revolver was fired once at the onion field, probably at the fleeing Officer Hettinger, with no one being struck by this bullet.

After Powell's arrest, he was not advised of his right to a lawyer or his right to remain silent. The *Miranda* case and its progeny had not yet been decided, so it appeared that officers were in compliance with the law as it existed in 1963 with regard to admonishments before an arrestee could be questioned. Powell was very talkative and gave at least eight separate statements to law enforcement officers after his arrest on March 10, 1963, through March 12, 1963.

Powell made his first statement on March 10, 1963 to Deputy Chief Fote of the Kern County Sheriff's Department, given partly at the scene of the arrest and partly en route to the Bakersfield County Jail. Los Angeles Police Department Detective Pierce Brooks was the lead investigator in the case, and he went to Bakersfield and transported Powell back to Los Angeles. At police headquarters he interviewed Powell on six separate occasions between the afternoon of Sunday, March 10, 1963, and the morning of Tuesday, March 12, 1963. Initially, Powell admitted kidnapping the officers but blamed Jimmy Lee Smith for the shooting of Officer Campbell. Eventually, he admitted firing the first shot into the mouth of Officer Campbell, but claimed that it was Smith who fired the four shots into the chest of the prone officer.

At the time of Gregory Powell's arrest, Jimmy Lee Smith was driving the 1946 Ford away from the scene of the shooting. In the vehicle with Smith were Powell's four-inch Colt, Officer Campbell's 38-caliber revolver, and Officer's Hettinger's 38-caliber revolver. Smith kept driving the 1946 Ford until it ran out of gas in Lamont, California. He abandoned the vehicle, taking Hettinger's gun with him. When police later located the abandoned 1946 Ford, they found Powell's four-inch Colt and Campbell's 38-caliber revolver inside the vehicle. Ballistics tests later confirmed that the 4-inch Colt had fired the bullet into Officer Campbell's mouth, and the 38-caliber revolver had fired the four bullets into Officer Campbell's chest.

When Smith abandoned the 1946 Ford, he took with him Officer Hettinger's gun, the only gun that was not fired at the onion field.

Jimmy Lee Smith was arrested on Sunday evening, March 10, 1963, at 10:50 p.m. in a rooming house in Bakersfield. Officer Hettinger's gun was found in a jacket on the bed. At the time of the arrest, Smith made a spontaneous statement, "It's that detective's gun."

Smith was also very talkative and made at least eight statements to police officers between the time of his arrest in Bakersfield and his arraignment in Los Angeles on the morning of Wednesday, March 13, 1963. He was not advised of his right to a lawyer and his right to an attorney prior to questioning. He admitted to kidnapping the officers but denied shooting Officer Campbell, laying the entire blame on Gregory Powell. LAPD Detectives Pierce Brooks, Glen Bates, and Danny Galindo went to the Bakersfield police station to transport Smith back to Los Angeles. On March 11, 1963, at 7:00 a.m., the three LAPD detectives took Smith to the scene of the shooting, where Smith re-enacted the events for the officers.

Gregory Ulas Powell and Jimmy Lee Smith were both arrested on Sunday, March 10, 1963. They were brought to court in Los Angeles for arraignment on the morning of Wednesday, March 13, 1963. The arraignment involved being taken to a magistrate where they were formally charged with one count of murder, advised of their rights, and provided with counsel.

Although Powell and Smith had been arraigned and provided with counsel, LAPD detectives continued to question them without their attorneys present. Smith was questioned twice on March 15, 1963, and Powell was questioned on March 15 and 18, 1963. Both admitted participating in robberies, with Smith the getaway driver in robberies committed by Powell.

Officer Karl Hettinger reported for work on Monday, March 11, 1963, at Hollywood Station, less than 48 hours after the kidnapping of both officers and the murder of his partner. He did not receive any counseling for the horrible experiences that he had undergone. Instead, he was asked to talk to numerous roll calls about the events of the evening of March 9, 1963.

On Friday, March 15, 1963, the Los Angeles Police Department issued Patrol Bureau Memorandum Number 11. This Memorandum was a cover letter for a series of four training bulletins discussing officer survival. The first sentence stated the following:

The brutal gangland style execution of Officer Ian Campbell underlines a basic premise of law enforcement. You cannot make deals with vicious criminals, such as kidnappers, suspects who have seized hostages, or those who assault police officers with deadly weapons.

This was the basic premise of the cover letter and the four subsequent training bulletins. Although Officer Karl Hettinger was never mentioned by name, it was clear that the bulletins were criticizing Officer Hettinger's decision to surrender his weapon and impliedly blaming him for the death of his partner. Patrol Bureau Memorandum Number 11 became unofficially called the "Hettinger Memorandum."

THE TRIAL

Below is listed the names of the key participants in the trial against Gregory Ulas Powell and Jimmy Lee Smith and a general overview of the case.

PEOPLE V. GREGORY ULAS POWELL AND JIMMY LEE SMITH

JUDGE:	Mark Brandler
PROSECUTOR:	Marshall Schulman, Deputy District Attorney
DEFENSE ATTORNEYS:	Deputy Public Defenders John Moore
	and Kathryn McDonald for Gregory Ulas Powell
	Attorney Ray Smith for Jimmy Lee Smith
CHARGE:	One Count of First Degree Murder
LOCATION OF TRIAL:	Los Angeles County Superior Court
DATES OF TRIAL:	July 7, 1963 to September 12, 1963

The trial began on July 7, 1963, less than four months after the murder of Officer Ian Campbell.

The only charge filed against both defendants was one count of first degree murder. This may have been a tactical mistake, since the case was filed in Los Angeles County even though the murder was committed in Kern County. A second count alleging an aggravated kidnapping with bodily injury under the Little Lindbergh Law could have been filed for several reasons. First, it also provided for the death penalty, and it eliminated any jurisdictional issues since the kidnapping clearly took place in Los Angeles County. Second, the punishment for a violation of the Little Lindbergh Law was the death penalty or life imprisonment without the possibility of parole, in the discretion of the jury. Therefore, if either defendant did not receive the death penalty after a conviction, he would receive the alternative sentence of life without the possibility of parole and serve a true life sentence without being eligible for parole. In 1963, a first degree murder conviction carried a possible sentence of the death penalty or a life sentence with the possibility of parole. Therefore, if Smith or Powell were convicted only of first degree murder and did not receive a death sentence, he would be eligible for parole. On top of this, Gregory Powell believed that he and Jimmy Lee Smith had violated the Little Lindbergh Law even before the shooting of Officer Campbell, and this would provide the prosecution with a powerful closing argument to the jury (and ironic justice) in convicting the defendants of this crime.

However, there was a concern that if the aggravated kidnapping with bodily injury were filed as a second count, the jury would learn that the punishment for this crime was life imprisonment without the possibility of parole. This could give the jury an incentive to vote against the death penalty, knowing that the defendants would spend the rest of their lives in prison.

No robbery counts were filed, even though Smith and Powell had committed several robberies together. The prosecution proceeded to trial alleging only one count against both defendants, the first degree murder of Officer Ian James Campbell.

The trial lasted slightly over two months. Officer Karl Hettinger was the key prosecution witness. Prosecutor Marshal Schulman was very thorough and introduced all the evidence at his disposal, including the numerous statements made by Smith and Powell.

The ballistics evidence established that Officer Campbell was shot with two different guns. Gregory Powell had used his four-inch Colt to fire one shot into Officer Campbell's face. Officer Campbell's 38-caliber revolver had fired the four shots into his chest. However, it was unclear at the trial which defendant had fired Campbell's gun. Neither defendant ever admitted firing Campbell's gun and, in fact, each blamed the other defendant. Officer Hettinger had initially believed that Jimmy Lee Smith had fired these four shots into Officer Campbell's chest, but at the time of the trial he was unsure as to which defendant had fired these shots.

On September 4, 1963, the jury convicted both defendants of first degree murder. On September 12, 1963, the jury imposed the death penalty on both defendants. November 13, 1963, was the date that Judge Brandler was to sentence the defendants. He had the authority to impose the death sentence imposed by the jury, or he could reduce the sentence to life imprisonment.

Prior to sentencing, Jimmy Lee Smith wrote a letter to Judge Mark Brandler begging for mercy. In this handwritten letter, Smith said in part that, "I have never had a profound fear of death, but to end one's life in such a grim, ghastly, and unjustified way frightens me."

On November 13, 1963, Judge Brandler imposed the death sentence on both Gregory Ulas Powell and Jimmy Lee Smith. He made the following comments at the time of sentencing:

Sadistically, Gregory Ulas Powell led Officer Campbell to believe that his life would be spared up to the very moment that he took deliberate aim and cold bloodedly executed Officer Campbell by firing one shot into the officer's mouth. While Officer Campbell, unconscious but writhing on the ground, was in the throes of death, Jimmy Lee Smith standing over the body of Officer Campbell, with revolting, inhuman savagery, pumped four more additional fatal shots into the prostrate officer.

Then these two defendants continued their barbarous attack by stalking the fleeing Officer Hettinger, who miraculously escaped from being likewise cruelly executed by these defendants.

The evidence in this case overwhelmingly justified the death verdict by the jury. It is the order of the court that you shall suffer the death penalty and that said penalty be inflicted within the walls of the State

Penitentiary of San Quentin, California, in the manner and means prescribed by law at a time to be fixed by this court in the warrant of execution.

Judge Brandler had presided over the trial and had heard all the evidence. Based on his comments at the time of sentencing, he clearly believed that Powell had fired the shot into Officer Campbell's mouth and that Jimmy Lee Smith had fired the four additional fatal shots into the prostrate officer and that the death penalty was the appropriate punishment for both defendants.

At this point, the case against Gregory Powell and Jimmy Lee Smith appeared to have reached an appropriate conclusion. LAPD investigators had put together a strong case clearly establishing the guilt of the defendants. There was an eyewitness, the guns had been recovered, and the defendants had made multiple confessions. The investigators had complied with existing rules for admissibility of the evidence. The defendants were convicted by a jury and received the death penalty. This was an appropriate resolution for two felons on parole who had kidnapped two police officers at gunpoint and executed one of them. All that was left was the appeal.

THE APPEAL

Under California law, any defendant who is sentenced to death has a direct appeal to the California Supreme Court. Gregory Ulas Powell and Jimmy Lee Smith had two main issues on appeal. First, were the numerous statements obtained by law enforcement officers in violation of the defendants' rights? Second, was there jurisdiction to hold the trial in Los Angeles County even though the murder took place in Kern County?

With regard to the statements made to law enforcement officers by Smith and Powell after their arrests, the officers had complied with the law in existence at the time. A defendant's extrajudicial statements to law enforcement were admissible against him in court without a requirement of informing him of his rights.

Gregory Powell and Jimmy Lee Smith were sentenced to death on November 13, 1963, and they filed an appeal to the California Supreme Court. While the appeal was pending, the United States Supreme Court decided the case of *Escobedo* v. *Illinois* [(1964) 378 U.S. 478] on June 22, 1964. *Escobedo* held that statements of an in-custody defendant were admissible only if the defendant was informed of his right to counsel and his right to remain silent and waived those rights.

Escobedo was the forerunner to *Miranda* v. *Arizona* [(1966) 384 U.S. 436], which was decided two years later on June 13, 1966. *Miranda* set forth more detailed guidelines for the admissibility of confessions and required a four-part admonition in addition to a waiver of the right to counsel and the right to remain silent.

The United States Supreme Court in *Escobedo* and *Miranda* did not state in those decisions whether the new rules set forth in those cases applied retroactively or just prospectively. If they applied prospectively, only crimes committed after these decisions would be impacted, and Powell and Smith would not benefit from these decisions. If these new rules were retroactive, then the decisions in *Escobedo* and *Miranda* could result in the reversal of Powell and Smith's convictions and death sentences.

On June 20, 1966, in the case of *Johnson* v. *New Jersey* [(1966) 384 U.S. 719], the United States Supreme Court issued its decision on the retroactivity of *Escobedo* and *Miranda*. The high court held that the application of *Escobedo* and *Miranda* was required only to trials which began after the respective dates of these decisions. Since the trial of Powell and Smith had been completed well before the decisions in *Escobedo* and *Miranda*, it appeared that the new rules would not apply to their case.

However, the United States Supreme Court stated in *Johnson* v. *New Jersey* that states were free to apply *Escobedo* and *Miranda* to a broader range of cases. This is what the California Supreme Court did in the case of *In re Lopez* [(1965) 62 Cal. 2d 368] by holding that *Escobedo* applied to any case in which the judgment of conviction was not final before June 22, 1964 (the date of the *Escobedo* decision).

If a case is on appeal, the judgment is not final. Since Powell and Smith's appeal was pending on June 22, 1964, the judgment was not final and the *Escobedo* holding applied to their case.

On July 18, 1967, a unanimous California Supreme Court reversed the convictions and death sentences and ordered a new trial for both Gregory Ulas Powell and Jimmy Lee Smith for violation of their rights during police interrogations and the introduction of their statements during the trial.

The California Supreme Court did rule that since preliminary arrangements (i.e., the kidnapping of the two officers) leading up to the murder of Officer Campbell in Kern County took place in Los Angeles County, the murder retrial could take place in Los Angeles County.

In late 1967, the case of the People v. Gregory Ulas Powell and Jimmy Lee Smith was sent back to the Los Angeles Superior Court for retrial.

THE RETRIAL (I)

Below is listed the initial judge and the original attorneys for the retrial of Gregory Ulas Powell and Jimmy Lee Smith. These parties were to undergo substantial change before the start of jury selection in the trial.

PEOPLE V. GREGORY ULAS POWELL AND JIMMY LEE SMITH

JUDGE:	Alfred Peracca
PROSECUTORS:	Phil Halpin, Deputy District Attorney
	Pat McCormack, Deputy District Attorney
DEFENSE ATTORNEYS:	Deputy Public Defender Charles Maple
	for Gregory Ulas Powell
	Irving Kanarek for Jimmy Lee Smith
CHARGE:	First Degree Murder (One Count)

Of the persons listed above, defense attorney Irving Kanarek had by far the greatest impact on the case than any other lawyer. He became involved with the case when he represented Jimmy Lee Smith at the time of sentencing before Judge Mark Brandler on November 13, 1963. He remained on the case during the appeal and successfully represented Smith on his appeal before the California Supreme Court. When the case was sent back to the Los Angeles Court for retrial, Kanarek stayed on as Smith's attorney.

Irving Kanarek was considered the most obstructionist lawyer in the history of Los Angeles County. He filed motion after motion, and he objected to almost every question. Trials that should have been completed in a few days dragged on for weeks when Irving Kanarek was the defense attorney. One Superior Court Judge, Raymond Roberts, described his *modus operandi* as follows:

> *You take interminable lengths of time in cross-examining, on the*
> *most minute, unimportant details; you ramble back and forth with*
> *no chronology of events, to just totally confuse everyone in the court-*
> *room, to the utter frustration of the jury, the witnesses, and the judge.*

Many judges and prosecutors were delighted that Kanarek was in-volved in the retrial of Powell and Smith, since that meant that they would not have any trials with him while he was an attorney on the case. Judge Peracca was not so fortunate, since he had a heart condition and had to be removed from the case. He was replaced by Judge Arthur Alarcon, a no-nonsense judge.

On January 28, 1968, Judge Alarcon removed Irving Kanarek as the attorney for Smith on the grounds that Kanarek was not competent to ef-fectively represent Smith in such a serious case. Both Irving Kanarek and Jimmy Lee Smith objected to Kanarek's removal as Smith's attorney, but to no avail. Judge Alarcon appointed private attorney William Drake as the new lawyer for Smith.

Irving Kanarek appealed his removal as Smith's attorney to the California Supreme Court. In May 1968, the California Supreme Court reinstated Kanarek as Smith's attorney, reasoning that the unlimited au-thority of a trial judge to remove a defense attorney in a criminal case could have a chilling effect on the attorney's effective representation of a client. An attorney concerned about being removed from a case might be more concerned in not antagonizing the judge than in effectively and fully representing his client.

With Irving Kanarek back on the case, no judge wanted to preside over the trial. The case was finally assigned to Judge Thomas LeSage, a recent appointee to the bench with little seniority. Kanarek filed motion after mo-tion, delaying the start of the trial because a judge must resolve pending motions before a trial can begin. Kanarek lost almost every one of his mo-tions, but sometimes after he lost a motion he would give it a new title and resubmit it. For example, a motion to sever (the trials of the defendants) later became a motion for separate trials.

Deputy District Attorney Phil Halpin was the lead prosecutor on the case assisted by Deputy District Attorney Pat McCormack. Halpin was frustrated by Kanarek's tactics and wanted the jury trial to begin. At least he had another prosecutor assigned to the case to share his pain. The pre-trial proceedings dragged on into 1969. On March 2, 1969, Pat McCormack was appointed a Court Commissioner, and he resigned from the District Attorney's Office. Phil Halpin was now the sole prosecutor on the case.

On the morning of March 5, 1969, things came to a head in the court-room of Judge Thomas LeSage. Prosecutor Halpin was addressing the court when he was interrupted by Irving Kanarek. Below is a partial transcript of what transpired in the courtroom that morning.

> *Kanarek: I object to* inter se *remarks---.*
>
> *Halpin: I am addressing my remarks to the court.*
>
> *Kanarek: He was directing his face at Mr. Maple, and he just said, "Fuck you."*
>
> *Halpin: I didn't say any such thing. I did not say any such thing. I will not permit this man to say this about me. I didn't say any such thing. I never have said such thing, and I won't tolerate it. [Grabs and shakes Kanarek].*
>
> *Kanarek: He said it just before he grabbed me.*
>
> *Smith: He struck him.*
>
> *Judge: Just a moment.*
>
> *Smith: The bailiff, the judge, Mr. Maple, everyone in the courtroom wit-nessed it.*
>
> *Halpin: And I want this man instructed to keep quiet. [Releasing Kanarek]*
>
> *Judge: All counsel sit down.*

After some more yelling, Judge LeSage declared a recess. Fifteen min-utes later, proceedings resumed.

> *Kanarek: Your honor, if I may, I would ask that Mr. Halpin be ar-rested immediately for a misdemeanor committed in the presence of the court in violation of the Penal Code of the State of California. In the presence of peace officers he committed an assault.*

Judge LeSage denied Irving Kanarek's request to have Phil Halpin arrested. However, for Halpin it was the last straw, and he submitted his resignation from the District Attorney's Office. The case had claimed another victim, and the trial had to be reassigned to another prosecutor.

In a final bit of irony, Irving Kanarek and his client Jimmy Lee Smith had a dispute shortly thereafter. On April 1, 1969, Smith asked that Kanarek be removed as his attorney and that he be appointed another lawyer. Judge Thomas LeSage quickly took advantage of this opportunity and relieved Kanarek as Smith's attorney. This time Kanarek could not appeal to be reinstated, since Smith had requested a new attorney. Defense Attorney Charles Hollopeter was appointed to represent Jimmy Lee Smith, and he remained Smith's attorney for the duration of the court proceedings.

Since Kanarek had been court-appointed to represent Jimmy Lee Smith, he was entitled to be compensated by the court for the legal services that he had rendered. Kanarek had been on the case for approximately fifteen months, during which he had prepared and filed numerous pre-trial motions and made numerous court appearances. Kanarek asked the court for $200,000 in fees, but he was awarded only $4,800. By contrast, attorney William Drake, who represented Smith for about three months while Kanarek appealed his 1968 removal from the case to the California Supreme Court, received $4,500 in fees from the court.

THE RETRIAL (II)

Charles Hollopeter was appointed the attorney for Jimmy Lee Smith on April 2, 1969. The trial for both defendants was scheduled to begin in early April 1969, but Hollopeter needed time to review the numerous transcripts and documents in order to prepare and get ready for trial. As a result, separate trials were ordered for each defendant.

The Retrial of Gregory Powell

Judge Thomas LeSage kept the trial of Gregory Powell, which began on April 7, 1969. Deputy District Attorney Joseph P. Busch had been Phil Halpin's supervisor and was familiar with the case, so he became the lead prosecutor in Powell's retrial. Below is a summary of the parties and of the result of Gregory Powell's retrial.

CHAPTER 2

PEOPLE V. GREGORY ULAS POWELL

JUDGE: Thomas LeSage

PROSECUTORS: Joseph P. Busch, Deputy District Attorney

                    Raymond Byrne, Deputy District Attorney

DEFENSE ATTORNEY: Charles Maple

START OF TRIAL: April 7, 1969

CHARGE: Murder in the First Degree (One Count)

RESULT: Guilty of First Degree Murder

After Gregory Powell was again convicted of first degree murder, all that remained was a short penalty phase to complete the trial. Prosecutor Joseph Busch could then return to his duties as the Chief Deputy District Attorney. However, the penalty phase resulted in an 11 – 1 hung jury in favor of the death penalty, as one juror held out for a sentence of life imprisonment. There would be a retrial of the penalty phase against Powell, but it would not be handled by Joseph Busch.

Deputy District Attorney James Kolts was scheduled to travel to Italy to handle an extradition. However, he had applied to be a judge and was anticipating a telephone call from the Governor's office confirming his appointment to the bench. He wanted to be in town if the call arrived, so he was looking for someone to go to Italy on the extradition. Deputy District Attorney Sheldon Brown was in Kolts's office and expressed interest in handling the extradition. Joseph Busch overheard the conversation, and he stated that he was finishing the Powell trial and would like to go to Italy for the extradition. After the hung jury in the penalty phase, Busch resumed his duties as Chief Deputy but not before going to Italy with his wife to handle the extradition.

Sheldon Brown was then selected as the lead prosecutor in the retrial of the penalty phase against Gregory Powell. He was assisted by Deputy District Attorney Raymond Byrne who had been the second chair to Busch. Since a new jury was hearing the case, the prosecution had to present all the evidence in the retrial of the penalty phase, including the testimony of Karl Hettinger. This time, the jury reached a unanimous decision and returned a verdict of death.

Each prosecutor benefitted from this scenario. James Kolts received the phone call and was appointed judge of the Superior Court. Joseph Busch went to Italy, and Sheldon Brown obtained a death penalty verdict against Gregory Powell.

The Retrial of Jimmy Lee Smith

Deputy District Attorney Dino Fulgoni was selected to prosecute the retrial of Jimmy Lee Smith. Fulgoni had joined the District Attorney's Office in April 1962, and he was eventually assigned to Central Trials where he obtained convictions in several difficult trials and earned a reputation as an outstanding trial lawyer. In the summer of 1969, he was assigned by Chief Deputy Joseph Busch to prosecute the retrial of Jimmy Lee Smith. Fulgoni would be the sole prosecutor, and he had about two months to prepare for the trial.

The retrial of Jimmy Lee Smith began on October 2, 1969. Below is a summary of the parties in the retrial:

PEOPLE V. JIMMY LEE SMITH

JUDGE:	Harold Shepherd
PROSECUTOR:	Dino Fulgoni, Deputy District Attorney
DEFENSE ATTORNEY:	Charles Hollopeter
CHARGE:	Murder in the First Degree

Once again, Karl Hettinger was the key prosecution witness. Prosecutor Dino Fulgoni noted that Hettinger was subdued but cogent during his testimony. On cross-examination, defense attorney Charles Hollopeter brought out that Gregory Powell was the dominant person in the relationship between Smith and Powell. Powell did all the talking in the car on the way to the onion field and after the car stopped there. Powell asked Officer Campbell about the Little Lindbergh Law and fired the first shot into the officer's mouth. It was apparent that Hollopeter's strategy was to use the guilt phase to set the stage for the penalty trial argument that his client did not deserve the death penalty. In the guilt phase, the jury convicted Jimmy Lee Smith of first degree murder.

During the penalty phase of Smith's trial, Hollopeter called Gregory Powell as a defense witness. By this time, Powell had been convicted in his trial and sentenced to death. When Powell entered the courtroom, he sneered at the judge and the jury. Case law prevents a witness from asserting his Fifth Amendment right not to testify in front of the jury. Prosecutor Dino Fulgoni attempted to prevent Powell from claiming his right not to testify in front of the jury, but the trial judge denied the prosecutor's request. Hollopeter asked Powell just three questions. First: "Mr. Powell, how many times did you shoot Officer Campbell?" Second: "On the evening of March 9, 1963, did you decide to kidnap two officers in the vicinity of Carlos and Gower?" Third: "Did you retain Officer Campbell's gun in your possession until after the shooting?" To each of these three questions Powell stated that he refused to answer on the ground that the answer may tend to incriminate him. Although Powell had refused to answer any questions, the jury was left with the impression that Powell had fired all the bullets into Officer Campbell's body, making Smith's culpability in the crime greatly mitigated. The jury came back with a verdict of life imprisonment for Jimmy Lee Smith.

POST CONVICTION

On February 18, 1972, the California Supreme Court voided the death penalty in California on the grounds that it constituted "cruel and unusual punishment." The 107 persons on death row in California had their death sentences reduced to life imprisonment with the possibility of parole. Among the state prison inmates who benefited from this decision were Sirhan Sirhan, Charles Manson and five of his followers, and Gregory Ulas Powell.

On June 26, 1974, the Court of Appeal in California affirmed the first degree murder convictions (and life sentences) of Gregory Ulas Powell and Jimmy Lee Smith. Since the alternative sentence for murder was life with the possibility of parole, both Powell and Smith were entitled to parole hearings in which they could request an eventual release on parole. Had they been charged with, and convicted of, a violation of aggravated kidnapping under the Little Lindbergh Law, they would not have been eligible for parole. The Little Lindbergh Law had provided for a punishment of death or life in prison <u>without</u> the possibility of parole for persons convicted of violating that law. However, Powell and Smith had not been charged with a violation of the Little Lindbergh Law, so they never received a sentence of life without the possibility of parole. However, few people believed that the persons who kidnapped and executed a police officer would ever be paroled.

In January 1975, Edmund G. (Jerry) Brown became Governor of California. After he became Governor, several notorious murder inmates who had previously received a death penalty verdict were granted parole dates. In 1977, both Gregory Ulas Powell and Jimmy Lee Smith were granted parole dates; Powell was scheduled to be paroled in 1983, and Smith was scheduled for parole in 1982. The California Attorney General appealed Powell's parole, and it was rescinded by the California Supreme Court.[1] However, Jimmy Lee Smith was paroled in 1982, having served less than 20 years for his role in the kidnapping and execution of Officer Ian Campbell.

Jimmy Lee Smith reverted to his use of heroin, and he was a chronic parole violator. He died of a heart attack on April 6, 2007, at the age of 76 while in custody on a parole violation.

Gregory Ulas Powell's latest bid for parole was denied in January 2010. Powell later requested a "compassionate release" on the grounds that he was dying of prostate cancer and had six months or less to live. At a hearing on October 19, 2011, before the entire parole board, several of Ian Campbell's family members and relatives provided statements opposing Powell's release. A Los Angeles police officer read a statement from Campbell's daughters asking the board to end the decades of parole hearings, court appeals, and media coverage that had forced them "to rearrange our lives to fit the schedule of the beast" who took their father's life. As young children, they could only learn about their father through other people.

Campbell's great-niece, Stephanie LiPilusa, tearfully told the board how she worked on petitions opposing Powell's release while in junior high school. She stated, "He was sentenced to death and, in order for justice to be served, that death needs to happen behind bars." Campbell's niece, Pat Corral, stated that "the only way Gregory Powell should leave prison is in

---

1   See <u>In re Powell</u> 45 Cal. 3rd 894 (1985)

a body bag."

The parole board denied Powell's request for a compassionate release in a 10–1 decision. Powell remained in custody. He died on August 12, 2012, at age 79 of prostate cancer at the California Medical Facility, a men's prison in the city of Vacaville. He had remained in continuous custody for over 49 years, since his arrest on March 10, 1963.

EPILOGUE – PIERCE R. BROOKS

Pierce R. Brooks was the Los Angeles Police Department detective who headed the investigation into the kidnapping and murder of Officer Ian Campbell. He had a remarkable career and has achieved legendary status.

Pierce Brooks was born in 1922. He was a United States Navy Pilot during World War II. He joined the Los Angeles Police Department on June 28, 1948, and his assignments included Patrol, Vice, Narcotics, and Homicide. He retired on July 30, 1969, with the rank of Captain of the Robbery-Homicide Division.

Although he was involved in the investigation of hundreds of homicides while an LAPD detective, he is best remembered for two cases that he investigated: one was the case against Gregory Powell and Jimmy Lee Smith. The second case involved Harvey Glatman, Los Angeles' first identified serial killer.

Glatman was a serial killer arrested in 1958 when the concept of serial killers was just beginning to be recognized. Glatman was convicted of the murders of two women and executed in California's gas chamber in 1959. Since Glatman received the death penalty, charges in other counties (including another murder) were not filed against him.

Because of the Glatman case, Detective Brooks became interested in developing a system to identify serial killers by common characteristics in the crimes they committed. Harvey Glatman had come to Los Angeles in 1957, and he had committed the three murders to which he confessed in 1957 and 1958. Detective Brooks believed that Harvey Glatman had committed other crimes before coming to Los Angeles. He spent many hours in the library reviewing old newspapers from the other cities where Glatman had resided. He found an article on "Boulder Jane Doe", involving an unsolved murder in Boulder, Colorado in 1954 he believed could have been committed by Harvey Glatman.

Legend has it that in 1960, Pierce Brooks went to the LAPD brass and inquired about creating a computer system to track murder cases around the country. He was turned down because the computer would have been too expensive and would have occupied most of a city block.

After Brooks retired from the LAPD, he was Chief of Police of the Springfield (Oregon) Police Department from 1969 to 1971 and Director of Police Safety for the Lakewood (Colorado) Police Department from 1971 to 1976.

Pierce Brooks was concerned about officer survival and officer safety. He wrote a book titled "...officer down, code three" that was published in 1975. The book discussed ten deadly errors that contributed to the deaths of many law enforcement officers. For many years it was the main book on officer survival, and he lectured throughout the country on this topic.

Pierce Brooks was also an expert on serial murders, and he acted as a consultant on investigations of the Atlanta child killer, Chicago's Tylenol murders, and the Green River killings. In 1982, he submitted a concept paper to the Justice Department for the use of computerized databases to identify and apprehend serial killers. This led to the creation of the Violent Criminal Apprehension Program (VICAP) at the FBI Academy in Quantico, Virginia. In 1985, at the age of 63, Pierce Brooks was named the first director of VICAP. He remained in this position for about one year and helped get the program off the ground.

Pierce Brooks died in 1998 at age 76.

EPILOGUE – PHIL HALPIN

Phil Halpin, the original prosecutor in the retrial of Gregory Powell and Jimmy Lee Smith, resigned from the Los Angeles County District Attorney's Office in March 1969. He rejoined the District Attorney's Office one year later.

He had a distinguished career in the office after his return, highlighted by the successful prosecution in 1989 of Night Stalker Richard Ramirez of 43 counts, including 13 counts of first degree murder. Ramirez was sentenced to death, and his convictions and death penalty sentence were affirmed by the California Supreme Court.

Phil Halpin retired in March 2001, and died on July 25, 2003, from cancer on his sixty-fifth birthday.

EPILOGUE - JOSEPH P. BUSCH

Joseph P. (Joe) Busch was the lead prosecutor in the 1969 retrial of Gregory Powell. He was the Chief of Trials and Phil Halpin's supervisor when Halpin resigned from the District Attorney's Office in March 1969. Since Busch was familiar with the case, he took over the prosecution of Gregory Powell and convicted him of first degree murder.

He was captain of the District Attorney's slow-pitch softball team that was nicknamed the "Busch Leaguers." He served as Director of Special Operations, Assistant District Attorney, and Chief Deputy District Attorney. He was appointed District Attorney in 1971 when then-District Attorney Evelle Younger was elected State Attorney General. Busch was elected to a full four-year term in 1972.

Joe Busch died suddenly of a heart attack in the summer of 1975 at the age of 49.

EPILOGUE - CHANGES IN LAWS AND PROCEDURES

The following changes in laws and procedures have resulted since the death of Officer Ian Campbell in 1963.

1. Law enforcement agencies now provide counseling to officers who have undergone a traumatic experience or event. This is recognition that peace officers are not superhuman and often need help in coping with the stress of the job.
2. There was a great public outcry when Jimmy Lee Smith was paroled in 1982 and Gregory Powell was given a parole date (that was later rescinded). In California, the prosecuting agency and other interested parties can now attend the parole hearing of a prisoner serving a life sentence and present reasons why the prisoner is not suitable for parole. The Los Angeles County District Attorney's Office has a Lifer Hearing Unit that attends lifer hearings, either in person or by tele-conference, and provides input and recommendations

regarding the inmate's suitability for parole.

3. The death penalty for a conviction under the Little Lindbergh Law was repealed in 1973. The United States Supreme Court has since ruled that the death penalty is unconstitutional for a crime which has not resulted in the death of a victim.

4. Law enforcement officers now receive training to handle situations in which an officer is taken hostage but his partner is still armed.

5. Many prosecution agencies have created special units that handle cases involving murder or serious assaults against peace officers. The Los Angeles County District Attorney's Office has a Crimes Against Peace Officers Section (CAPOS) staffed with skilled prosecutors who handle these types of cases exclusively, and it has an impressive record of successfully prosecuting these cases.

EPILOGUE – KARL HETTINGER

Officer Karl Hettinger, severely affected by the events of March 9 and 10, 1963, suffered from survivor's guilt. Less than a week after the incident, the Los Angeles Police Department issued a training bulletin that officers should not surrender their weapons. Many officers blamed him for the death of his partner. He was forced to relive the incident every time he testified in the court proceedings.

Officer Hettinger first testified in court proceedings against Gregory Powell and Jimmy Lee Smith at their preliminary hearing on March 19, 1963. He also testified at their first trial in July and August 1963. He was assigned to the Homicide Division during the trial so that he would be available for court proceedings.

After the trial, he became the driver for LAPD Chief William Parker. He was subsequently assigned to Detectives and later to the Pickpocket Detail.

In May 1966, Hettinger was observed stealing cigars from a supermarket. He was called to Internal Affairs and resigned from the Los Angeles Police Department. After leaving the LAPD, he stayed home and watched his three children while his wife, Helen, worked as a bookkeeper.

He and his family desperately needed money, so he applied for a disability pension at a time when they were rarely granted. He was examined by several doctors who concluded that he was deeply affected and damaged by the events of March 9, 1963, but he had never received counseling or treatment. He was awarded a seventy percent disability pension.

In 1969, Hettinger testified again in the retrials of Powell and Smith. Prosecutors observed that he appeared to have deteriorated mentally and emotionally, and they were concerned how he would perform as a witness. However, he held together sufficiently on the witness stand and both defendants were convicted.

After the retrials, Karl Hettinger made a comeback. In 1971, he enrolled at UCLA night school and took three agriculture classes. He received two A's and one B. In 1972, he returned to Kern County, where his partner had been murdered, accepting a job managing a plant nursery in Bakersfield.

For ten years, Hettinger worked as an administrative assistant to Kern County Supervisor Trice Harvey. When Harvey was elected to the State Assembly in the November 1986 General Election, Governor George Deukmejian appointed Hettinger in March 1987 to serve the remaining 21 months of Harvey's term.

Karl Hettinger died in 1994 in Bakersfield at age 59 from an assortment of ailments, including cirrhosis of the liver. Although Hettinger physically survived the events of March 9 and 10, 1963, he never recovered emotionally.

LESSONS LEARNED

Officer Karl Hettinger had only a few seconds to make a life/death decision – i.e., whether to surrender his weapon to a pair of suspects, one of whom had taken his partner Officer Ian Campbell as a hostage, or not. Hettinger had not received any training on how to handle such a situation, and he reluctantly gave up his gun. His decision resulted in the execution-style slaying of Officer Campbell. Historically, about 20 percent of officers murdered in the line of duty were killed with their own guns.

More recently, because of weapons-retention training, police handgun holsters feature safety mechanisms that make it harder for a suspect to take away their gun. The number is now down to around 10 percent. There is training to physically resist and overcome a suspect who has a gun pointed at an officer at close range, whether from in front or behind. Officers need to take advantage of weapons-retention and gun-takeaway training, practice it, and wear holsters that offer the greater safety features.

Officer Hettinger was criticized for his decision. Less than a week after the kidnapping of the officers and the death of Officer Campbell, the Los Angeles Police Department issued Parole Bureau Memorandum Number 11, unofficially called the "Hettinger Memorandum". The memorandum made it clear that a police officer must not surrender his weapon to "... vicious criminals, such as kidnappers, suspects who have seized hostages, or those who assault police officers with deadly weapons."

Law enforcement officers now receive training on how to handle a situation in which an officer is taken hostage while his partner remains armed. When I attended the Police Academy prior to becoming a reserve police officer, I received training on how to handle such a situation. One of the officers would call out, addressing his partner in "reverse name calling." The officer being held hostage would call his partner using the hostage officer's name, or vice versa. This "reverse name-calling" would alert the officers that the officer held hostage would make a sudden move to give the officer with the gun a clear shot at the suspect. Although not foolproof, it did give the officers a reasonable plan to end the threat to the officers.

Pierce Brooks. After his retirement from the Los Angeles Police Department, Pierce Brooks became a leading spokesperson on officer safety and officer survival. He lectured to law enforcement groups throughout the United States. He wrote a book that was published in 1975 called "... officer down, code three." For many years, this was the main book on officer survival.

Until Pierce Brooks wrote his book, police agencies did not dwell on mistakes made by a victim officer that may have contributed to his death. By ignoring mistakes made by the officer, the agency protected itself from errors that may have been made in the victim officer's training or deployment, as well as to provide respect and avoid damaging the reputation of an officer who died in the line of duty.

By writing his book, Brooks hoped to greatly increase an officer's chances of survival in the street. Brooks broke the silence by identifying and discussing the "ten deadly errors" as the causes for police officers unnecessarily killed in the line of duty. They are as follows:

1. Failure to Maintain Proficiency and Care of Weapon, Vehicle, and Equipment
2. Improper Search and Use of Handcuffs
3. Sleepy or Asleep
4. Relaxing Too Soon
5. Missing the Danger Signs
6. Taking a Bad Position
7. Failure to Watch Their Hands
8. Tombstone Courage
9. Preoccupation
10. Apathy

Note that six of the "ten deadly errors" involve the officer's cognitive processes of mental awareness and preparation; these were the predominant elements of officer survival.

In his book, Brooks stressed that staying alert, along with using good judgment and common sense, combined with a little bit of good luck, was the key to officer survival.

Ian James Campbell

Date of Birth: August 21, 1931
Date Appointed: May 5, 1958
End of Watch: March 9, 1963

Gower Street

*Ian Campbell
Square at Gower
Street near
Carlos Avenue in
Hollywood*

The 1946 maroon Ford containing Gregory Powell and Jimmy Lee Smith stopped by Officers Campbell and Hettinger

*The unmarked 1960 Plymouth used by Officers
Campbell and Hettinger that was left parked on
Gower Street near Carlos Avenue*

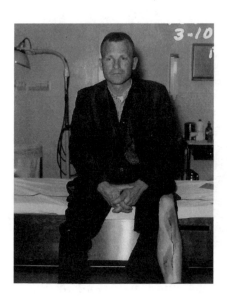

*Officer Hettinger
in hospital getting
medical treatment
in early morning of
March 10, 1963*

Bob Schirn holding the 32 caliber Spanish Star Echeverria automatic recovered from Powell at time of his arrest

Jimmy Lee Smith re-enacting the crime with LAPD detectives Pierce Brooks, Glen Bates, and Danny Galindo

*Detective Pierce Brooks and other LAPD detectives escort Jimmy
Lee Smith and Gregory Powell to court for arraignment*

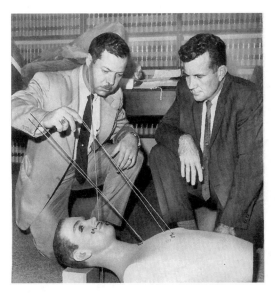

*Dr. Harold Kade of Coroner's Office with LAPD investigator Pierce
Brooks using mannequinn to show trajectory of the bullets*

CHAPTER 3

Officer Kenneth Scott Wrede

West Covina Police Department

"Sometimes You Have to Shoot"

INTRODUCTION

Kenneth Scott Wrede was born in Chicago, Illinois on February 12, 1957. He was the second of four children born to Kenneth C. and Marianne Wrede. His three siblings were sisters Nickie, Karen, and Kerry. The family moved to Southern California in 1965 and eventually settled in the Orange County area. Wrede graduated from Katella High School in 1975, and he received his AA degree in criminal justice from Fullerton Community College. He was preparing to pursue his BA degree at the time of his death.

Wrede graduated from the Orange County Peace Officers Academy on August 1, 1980, and he was hired by the West Covina Police Department.

He married his wife, Denel, a medical social worker, in October 1982. They bought a condo and were planning to eventually start a family.

West Covina Police Officer Kenneth "Ken" Wrede, #203, died in the line of duty on August 31, 1983.

AUGUST 31, 1983

The facts surrounding the death of Officer Kenneth Wrede are not in dispute since the event was observed by several eyewitnesses and corroborated by several radio calls made by Officer Wrede during the incident.

On Wednesday, August 31, 1983, Officer Wrede was working as a patrol officer for the West Covina Police Department. He was in his police uniform working a one-man marked police vehicle.

Shortly after noon, a motorist named Lucinda Ann Smith told Officer Wrede about an intoxicated person who was walking nearby and acting strangely. He told her, "Ma'am, thank you. I'll take care of that." Officer Wrede located Michael Anthony Jackson in a residential neighborhood walking toward the corner of Glenview Road and Francisquito Avenue. Jackson was barefoot and disheveled and walking aimlessly. Officer Wrede pulled his police vehicle to the curb at an angle. He broadcast his location, saying that the suspect was "possibly dusted" (i.e., under the influence of phencyclidine – P.C.P.) and requested backup.

Officer Wrede exited the police car, asked Jackson where he was going, and told him to sit on the curb. Jackson began to walk away, and the officer used his walkie-talkie to again request backup. Officer Wrede approached Jackson and again told him to sit on the curb, but he continued walking. The officer then hit Jackson in the back of his legs with his baton. Jackson turned around and started fighting with the officer, and they both fell to the ground. As they got up, Jackson was punching and kicking Officer Wrede. The officer tried to defend himself and struck Jackson several times in the midsection with his baton and sprayed mace in his face several times, to no apparent effect. During the altercation, Jackson ripped the officer's badge from his uniform.

Jackson went to the adjacent yard and attempted to pull a sapling from the ground. He did remove two support sticks (six and nine feet long) that he threw at the officer.

Officer Wrede ran to the driver's side of the police car and reached for the radio. Jackson could have run off and left the scene. Instead, he ran to the passenger side of the police vehicle, opened the door, and reached for the shotgun located in a rack at the front of the patrol car. Jackson pulled the gun and the rack from the vehicle and tried unsuccessfully to cock it by pulling the chamber back.

The shotgun was kept in the rack at "patrol ready," so that there were four rounds of ammunition in the magazine and the safety was on. To fire the shotgun, the safety had to be off and a round had to be moved to the firing chamber by sliding the pump action. Each shotgun shell contained nine pellets.

Officer Wrede, for the first time, drew his gun and moved to the left rear of the police car while Jackson remained on the passenger side and pointed the shotgun across the top of the car toward Officer Wrede. After some difficulty (because the rack was still attached to the shotgun), Jackson managed to pump a round into the chamber.

Jackson pointed the now-loaded shotgun toward the officer, who now was crouched near the driver's door. Officer Wrede yelled to Jackson to put the shotgun down, still pointing his gun at him. Jackson then laid the shotgun on the roof of the police car and placed his hands on the roof of the vehicle, appearing to give up. Officer Wrede then lowered his gun and began to walk around the vehicle when Jackson suddenly picked up the shotgun and fired at the officer. Only one of the nine pellets from the shotgun shell struck Officer Wrede, but it penetrated the left cheek area, causing a fatal injury. He fell to the ground mortally wounded.

Three or four of the pellets were later found in the light bar on the top of the police car. The encounter between Officer Wrede and Michael Jackson lasted less than four minutes.

Officer Wrede's body remained on the ground at the scene of the shooting for several hours. Eventually his body was transported to the Los Angeles County Coroner's Office. On September 1, 1983, an autopsy was performed on Officer Wrede's body by Dr. Lakshmanan Sathyavagiswaran, an autopsy surgeon for the Coroner's Office since 1977. He observed contusions and bruises on the officer's body, indicating that the officer had been in a physical struggle prior to his death. The doctor ascribed the cause of death to a buckshot injury with the projectile entering the left cheek area and penetrating the brain. The wound resulted in bleeding into his respiratory tract. Officer Wrede was rapidly incapacitated and unconscious. Death would have resulted within minutes from the nature of the brain injuries and from the officer choking on his own blood. The shotgun pellet was recovered from Officer Wrede's head during the autopsy.

ARREST OF MICHAEL ANTHONY JACKSON

Three police officers arrived at the scene in separate police vehicles just after Officer Wrede was shot – Deputy Sheriff Stephen Vine, West Covina Police Officer Arthur Marinello with his police dog, and Officer Christopher Mohler.

Deputy Vine placed his vehicle next to Officer Wrede's police car and observed Officer Wrede's body on the ground. Michael Jackson was still behind Officer Wrede's police vehicle and pointed the shotgun at Deputy Vine. The deputy quickly backed up his police vehicle several hundred feet and exited the car with his gun drawn. Jackson was now walking toward Deputy Vine pointing the shotgun at him while attempting to pull the trigger and move the slide to load a round into the shotgun.

Deputy Vine did not fire his weapon because Officer Marinello and his police dog were behind Jackson in the line of fire. Deputy Vine yelled to Officer Marinello, "Release your dog, do something," and, "Shoot him, shoot him!" Officer Mohler later testified that he heard Jackson yell, "Now I'm going to kill all you fucking pigs!"

The dog was unleashed to attack Jackson, who hit the dog with the shotgun. Though stunned, the dog was able to bite Jackson causing him to drop the shotgun. Officer Mohler ran up and kicked away the shotgun. The three officers had a fierce struggle with Jackson, during which he attempted to grab the handguns of Officer Mohler and Officer Marinello. Finally, they were able to subdue Jackson and handcuff him.

TRANSPORTATION TO HOSPITAL

After his arrest, Michael Anthony Jackson was initially taken to the West Covina Police Station; but at approximately 1:30 p.m., he was transferred to the Queen of the Valley Hospital for treatment. Jackson was not responsive when admitted to the hospital. His arms and legs were restrained because he was a suspected user of P.C.P., and it was difficult to maintain an intravenous connection because he was uncooperative and "thrashing around." Hospital records described him as incoherent, in shock, and semi-conscious. He had a low blood pressure of 90 over 40. A blood sample was taken that was later determined to be positive for P.C.P. in the amount of 176 nanograms per milliliter.

Jackson finally became verbally responsive after receiving intravenous fluids. At about 3:00 p.m., a nurse questioned him, and he made his first lucid response, stating his name and that he had taken P.C.P.

Deputy Sheriff Sabrino Muñiz was at the hospital with Jackson. Muñiz later testified that, after Jackson received treatment, Jackson asked him, "Why am I under arrest? Am I being charged for killing a cop?" To the knowledge of Deputy Muñiz, no one had mentioned in Jackson's presence that a police officer had been killed.

INTERROGATION OF MICHAEL ANTHONY JACKSON

Shortly after 4:00 p.m. on August 31, 1983, Michael Jackson was transferred to the jail ward of the Los Angeles County Medical Center. There, Sheriff's

Homicide Detective Michael Lee and his partner Detective Michael Bumcrot visited Jackson at approximately 5:50 p.m. on that date. Jackson was advised of his *Miranda* rights, which he waived. Jackson asked why he was being arrested, and Detective Lee answered, "Murder." Jackson replied, "I killed a policeman?"

Detectives Lee and Bumcrot returned the next day at around noon to further interrogate Jackson. Jackson said that he remembered the officers from the previous day, stating that they were "the cops who say I killed that officer with a shotgun." Detective Lee later testified that, to his knowledge, no one had told Jackson that Officer Wrede had been killed with a shotgun. When Detective Lee asked Jackson how he knew that Officer Wrede had been killed with a shotgun, he replied that he had read it in the newspaper. However, newspapers were not available in the jail ward, and Jackson's wrists were secured to the sides of his bed.

This was the last time Jackson spoke to law enforcement officers. He was visited by an attorney who advised him not to talk to anyone.

TRIAL OVERVIEW

Michael Anthony Jackson was charged with first degree murder with a special circumstance allegation that Officer Kenneth Wrede was a peace officer intentionally killed in the performance of his duties. If the special circumstance allegation were found true, Jackson would be eligible for the death penalty.

Jackson's preliminary hearing was conducted on October 17, 1983. The preliminary hearing lasted less than an hour as the prosecution called only one witness. Nineteen-year-old Robert Durham testified that he observed Jackson shoot Officer Wrede, and no other witness was necessary. Judge Robert Young found the evidence sufficient and bound Jackson over for trial.

There was no dispute that Michael Anthony Jackson shot and killed Officer Kenneth Wrede. The only real issue for the jury would be determining whether or not Jackson had the necessary mental state for first degree murder, which requires premeditation and deliberation and an intent to kill. The prosecution was seeking the death penalty for Jackson, which only applied if he was first convicted of first degree murder with special circumstances.

In preparation for the trial, defense attorney William Klump requested the trial court to appoint two psychiatrists to examine his client. Dr. Blake Skrdla and Dr. John Mead were appointed by the court to examine Jackson and determine his mental state at the time he shot and killed Officer Wrede.

TRIAL

The trial of the case was assigned to Judge Loren Miller, Jr. in the Pomona Branch of the Los Angeles Superior Court. The selection of the jury began on February 28, 1984. Since the prosecution was seeking the death penalty, the jury selection process involved questioning prospective jurors to determine whether they had an open mind about the death penalty and would not automatically reject it in any case. On March 8, the trial jury and four alternates were impaneled and sworn to try the case. The jury was "death qualified" in that its members had stated that they could impose the death penalty in an appropriate case.

Below is an overview of the case and its main participants:

PEOPLE v. MICHAEL ANTHONY JACKSON
CASE A530714

JUDGE:	Loren Miller, Jr.
PROSECUTOR:	John Ouderkirk, Deputy District Attorney
DEFENSE ATTORNEY:	William Klump, Deputy Public Defender
CHARGES:	First Degree Murder with Personal Use of a Firearm
	Special Circumstance Allegation of Peace Officer
	Intentionally Killed in the Performance of His Duties
LOCATION:	Los Angeles Superior Court
	Pomona Courthouse, Department E

Deputy District Attorney John W. Ouderkirk, who was assigned to prosecute the case, had a remarkable professional career. He graduated from the Los Angeles Police Academy in 1965 and served as a police officer for the City of Santa Monica from 1965 to 1970. From 1970 to 1978, he was an investigator for the Los Angeles County District Attorney's Office. He went to Loyola Law School in the evenings, graduating in 1977. He passed the California bar examination and became a deputy district attorney for the County of Los Angeles. He tried over 30 cases to verdict, including the Michael Anthony Jackson murder trial. In 1989, he was appointed to the bench by Governor Pete Wilson and served with distinction in both the Criminal Division and Civil Division until his retirement in 2000.

Defense attorney William Klump graduated from Southwestern University School of Law in 1960. He worked in private practice and for NASA before being hired by the Los Angeles County Public Defender's Office in 1964. In 1966, he was transferred to the Pomona Branch of the Public Defender's Office where he remained until his retirement. In 1983, he was a Grade IV deputy, the highest classification for a trial deputy; and he had represented clients in hundreds of felony jury trials. Before being assigned to Jackson's case in September 1983, Klump had represented seven defendants in death penalty cases, although none had gone to a penalty phase.

In his opening statement, defense attorney William Klump conceded that Michael Jackson shot and killed Officer Wrede, but he asserted that his client did not have the requisite intent for first degree murder and was guilty only of a lesser offense such as second degree murder or manslaughter.

The presentation of evidence began on March 8, 1984. In its case in chief, the prosecution clearly proved that Michael Jackson shot and killed Officer Wrede.

DEFENSE CASE

The defense presented evidence that Michael Anthony Jackson was a regular user of phencyclidine (P.C.P.) and that he was under the influence of P.C.P. at the time that he shot and killed Officer Wrede. This evidence consisted of the following:

Defendant's testimony

Michael Jackson testified in his own behalf. He stated that he was a chronic user of P.C.P., having used it since 1977. In the summer of 1983, he used P.C.P. three or four times a week. He had been arrested and convicted of using or being under the influence of P.C.P. four or five times.

On the morning of August 31, 1983, he went to the home of a friend, James Butler. There he shared with some women friends "super cools," cigarettes that were dipped in P.C.P. The last thing he remembered was passing around the third "super cool" with the others. The next thing he remembered was waking up in the hospital. He claimed that he had no memory of the events involving the shooting of Officer Wrede.

Witnesses at the crime scene and hospital

The defense called witnesses who had been at the scene of the shooting. Defense attorney William Klump directed the bulk of his questions to Jackson's bizarre behavior before the arrival of Officer Wrede, to Jackson's angry response to Officer Wrede, and the physical strength exhibited by the defendant. Witnesses at the hospital testified to Jackson's lack of responsiveness and to his apparently being under the influence of an unknown substance. A blood sample taken from Jackson at the hospital confirmed that he had a large amount of P.C.P. in his system at that time.

Dr. Orm Aniline

During the guilt phase of the trial, the only medical expert whom the defense called was Dr. Orm Aniline. He was an expert on the effects of P.C.P., and he was the Ward Chief in Psychiatry at the Los Angeles County Medical Center. He had not examined Michael Jackson, but he had been furnished with the "murder book" containing all the police reports and witness statements, with toxicological reports, and with daily reports of the trial testimony.

Dr. Aniline testified to the effects of P.C.P. He pointed out that because P.C.P. is stored in the system of a chronic user, a slight amount of P.C.P. may "set off" a chronic user as compared to a first-time user. There is no agreed-upon level of P.C.P. which indicates when a person is under the influence of P.C.P. or which predictably will result in unusual behavior. Some persons under the influence of P.C.P. will behave normally, while other persons with similar intoxication levels of P.C.P. will engage in distorted or bizarre behavior.

Dr. Aniline was of the opinion that Jackson was under the influence of P.C.P. when he fatally shot Officer Wrede. However, he was equivocal of the full impact of the defendant's intoxication on his mental state. He could not say whether Jackson had deliberated, premeditated or had the specific intent to kill when he committed the fatal act because of the uncertainty of the effects of P.C.P. on an individual. He did conclude that some of Jackson's ability to think may have been impaired by his usage of P.C.P.

FAILURE TO CALL DR. BLAKE SKRDLA AND DR. MEAD

Dr. Blake Skrdla and Dr. John Mead were the two psychiatrists appointed by the court to examine Michael Jackson. Defense attorney William Klump instructed them to determine whether Jackson had the mental capacity to form a specific intent to kill, to deliberate or premeditate, or to harbor malice.

Dr. Skrdla prepared a report which stated his opinion that Jackson was intoxicated but legally sane at the time of the offense. He believed that Jackson "possessed the mental capacity to form the specific intent to kill and actually formed such intent." Skrdla added that "(b)ecause of his drug induced state of intoxication, he is not believed to have actually deliberated, premeditated, nor meaningfully or naturally reflected upon the gravity of his contemplated acts. However, he is believed to have been capable of harboring malice aforethought."

Dr. Mead's report contained four brief opinions: (1) At the time of the commission of the alleged offense, Mr. Jackson was sane. (2) Mr. Jackson is able to understand the nature and purpose of the proceedings against him. (3) He is able to cooperate in a rational manner with counsel in presenting a defense. (4) At the time of the commission of the alleged offense, Mr. Jackson was grossly intoxicated with P.C.P. He has little recollection of the day's proceedings. Dr. Mead's report also contained information about Jackson's background, including his lengthy use of P.C.P. and that he had not lost consciousness on a P.C.P. trip until the date of Officer Wrede's death.

Neither Dr. Skrdla nor Dr. Mead was called as a defense witness because defense attorney Klump believed that their testimony would have been more damaging than helpful to the defense.

JURY VERDICT

After both sides rested, prosecutor John Ouderkirk and defense attorney William Klump each argued his case to the jury.

Premeditation is usually difficult to prove when a homicide results from an unplanned encounter between a victim and a suspect who is heavily intoxicated. In this case, however, the prosecution had presented a persuasive case that Jackson had acted with deliberation and premeditation, as follows: Jackson had chosen tree stakes as his first weapon that he threw at Officer Wrede; Jackson then followed the officer to the police car where he selected a shotgun as his weapon; he released the shotgun's slide action, cocking the weapon; Jackson laid the shotgun on the roof of the police vehicle, appearing to surrender; then, with Officer Wrede off guard, Jackson quickly picked up the shotgun and fired at the officer; Jackson threatened other officers with the shotgun; and he reached for the guns of other officers during the arrest struggle.

After being instructed on the law by Judge Miller, the jury retired to deliberate. The jury returned a guilty verdict after less than one day of deliberation, finding Michael Anthony Jackson guilty of murder in the first degree with personal use of a firearm. The jury found true the special circumstance allegation that Kenneth Wrede was a peace officer who was intentionally killed while engaged in the performance of his duties. This made Jackson eligible for the death penalty, and the same jury that found him guilty would now decide whether Jackson would receive the death penalty or be sentenced to life imprisonment without the possibility of parole.

PENALTY PHASE

Four days after the jury returned its verdict, the penalty phase began. Both the prosecution and the defense introduced evidence of the defendant's background and character to assist the jury in determining the appropriate sentence for the defendant.

Prosecution evidence

The prosecution introduced evidence that, in 1975, Jackson had been tried and convicted of second degree burglary; in 1976, he committed forcible sodomy on a 17-year-old soldier while he was in the Army; and that on July 5, 1983, he committed an assault on a West Covina police officer while he was under the influence of P.C.P.

Defense evidence

Defense attorney William Klump called only two witnesses during the penalty phase: Jackson's wife and his mother.

Defendant's wife, Sabrina Jackson, testified that she was married to him for ten years and that they separated three years before his arrest for shooting Officer Wrede. The defendant's use of drugs was the reason for their separation. She testified that Jackson was a good father to their three children and provided financial support when he was able to do so. She said that he was a good and unselfish person.

Defendant's mother, Lillian Williams, testified that his natural father had no interest in his son. When the defendant was age 14, she divorced his father and married a man with six children. Her son began sniffing glue around this time. He later joined the United States Army but received a dishonorable discharge. She described her son as "two different people" depending on whether or not he was on drugs. She acknowledged that her son had a lengthy criminal history and blamed her son's problems to his involvement with drugs.

The testimony of these two defense witnesses covered less than 30 pages of the trial transcript. There was no medical testimony during the penalty phase. However, the jury was instructed that, in determining the penalty, they could consider the evidence from the guilt phase of the trial, which included the testimony of Dr. Orm Aniline.

The jury returned a verdict of death on April 19, 1984, and Judge Miller imposed the death sentence for Michael Anthony Jackson on May 21, 1984.

CALIFORNIA SUPREME COURT DECISION

Under California law, a defendant who is sentenced to death receives an automatic appeal to the California Supreme Court. (California Constitution,

Article VI, section 11; California Penal Code section 1239, subdivision (b)).

On December 18, 1989, the California Supreme Court issued its decision in *People v. Michael Anthony Jackson,* which appears in the official California reports at 49 Cal. 3rd 1170. A unanimous court affirmed the conviction and death sentence of Michael Jackson. The opinion, written by Judge Panelli, rejected all the defense claims of error and found the evidence sufficient to support the conviction for first degree murder and death sentence.

WRIT OF *HABEAS CORPUS*

After the California Supreme Court affirmed Michael Jackson's conviction for first degree murder and the death sentence, his lawyers filed a petition for *habeas corpus* relief in the federal district court. The petition alleged that Jackson received ineffective assistance of counsel in his state trial in both the guilt phase and penalty phase.

In *Strickland v. Washington,* 466 U.S. 668 (1984), the United States Supreme Court ruled that to prevail under a claim of ineffective assistance of counsel, the defense must establish the following: (1) that the defense attorney's performance was unreasonable in light of prevailing professional norms, and (2) that there was a reasonable possibility that, but for counsel's unprofessional errors, the result of the proceeding would have been different. A reasonable probability is a probability sufficient to undermine confidence in the outcome.

Federal District Judge Manuel Real held an evidentiary hearing and denied the petition for *habeas corpus.* Jackson's lawyers appealed the denial of the petition to a three-judge panel of the United States Court of Appeal for the Ninth Circuit.

On May 8, 2000, the Court of Appeal in a 2–1 decision ruled that Michael Jackson's attorney did such a poor job during the penalty phase of the trial that the death sentence had to be set aside. The conviction for first degree murder was affirmed; only the death penalty was affected by the Court's decision. The majority opinion pointed out that Jackson's defense attorney had called only the defendant's mother and estranged wife during the penalty phase of the trial. The defense failed to present potentially mitigating evidence that Jackson was choked by his mother as a boy, that he once had been diagnosed as schizophrenic, and that his use of P.C.P. might have made him unable of knowing that he killed Officer Wrede.

The dissenting judge argued that the defense had failed to establish the second prong as required by *Strickland v. Washington*, i.e., that the result would have been different. As stated in the dissenting opinion:

> *Trial counsel's decision fell well within the wide range of professional conduct and there is no 'reasonable probability' that any errors he may have made affected the outcome of the proceeding. Thus, I must dissent from that portion of the opinion vacating Jackson's capital sentence.*

RETRIAL

On April 24, 2001, the case returned to the Los Angeles Superior Court from the Court of Appeal for a retrial of the penalty phase. The public defender declared a conflict of interest, and private attorney Anthony Robusto was appointed as Michael Jackson's attorney. Deputy District Attorney Steven Ipsen of CAPOS was assigned to prosecute the case.

Ipsen made all the court appearances, including on November 8, 2001, when January 16, 2002, was set for a pretrial conference and March 19, 2002 was selected as the trial date. However, after this date, Ipsen told his supervisors that he did not have the confidence or desire to try the case, and he asked to be removed as the prosecutor. Deputy District Attorney Darren Levine, the workhorse and premier lawyer in CAPOS, was asked to take over the prosecution of the case. Although he already had a substantial caseload, he agreed to take over the case.

Upon his initial review of the case, Levine discovered that nothing had been done in preparation of the case. There were no follow-up interviews, no subpoenas, no further investigation, and no expert witnesses to testify on the mental issues. Darren Levine told me that it looked like the file had not been touched by human hands. Ultimately, my promise to Ken Wrede's parents that justice would be done was kept, but only through the heroic efforts of Darren Levine.

The penalty retrial was scheduled in 2002, approximately 19 years after the murder of Officer Wrede. Such a passage of time can create problems in locating witnesses. To assist in the preparation for the retrial, prosecutor Levine obtained the assistance of District Attorney Investigator Joe Vita. Wrede and Vita became friends in 1980 when Vita was a Los Angeles police officer and Wrede was a West Covina police officer. Vita planned Wrede's bachelor party and was a member of the wedding party. He was a pallbearer at Wrede's funeral. Over the years, Vita maintained contact with Wrede's parents, who became activists for families of deceased law enforcement personnel. Vita located the witnesses and assembled the evidence that Darren Levine needed to conduct the penalty retrial.

When the Jackson case next reconvened on January 16, 2002, for the pretrial conference, Darren Levine made his first appearance as the prosecutor on the case. The trial was assigned to Judge Charles Horan. Some pretrial motions were litigated, and jury selection began on July 1, 2002. Below is an overview of the main participants in the retrial.

PEOPLE v. MICHAEL ANTHONY JACKSON
CASE A530714

JUDGE:	Charles E. Horan
PROSECUTOR:	Darren Levine, Deputy District Attorney
DEFENSE ATTORNEY:	Anthony Robusto, Private Attorney
ISSUE:	Death Penalty Retrial
LOCATION:	Los Angeles Superior Court
	Pomona Courthouse

Penal Code section 190.3 states in part the evidence that can be introduced at a penalty phase hearing, as follows:

In the proceedings on the question of penalty, evidence may be presented by both the people and the defendant as to any matter relevant to aggravation, mitigation, and sentence including, but not limited to, the nature and circumstances of the present offense, any prior felony conviction or convictions whether or not such conviction or convictions involved a crime of violence, the presence or absence of other criminal activity by the defendant which involved the use or attempted use of force or violence or which involved the express or implied threat to use force or violence, and the defendant's character, background, history, mental condition and physical condition.

Prosecution evidence

Even though Michael Jackson's conviction for the first degree murder of Officer Ken Wrede had remained intact, the prosecution introduced the evidence of the fatal shooting in detail. Penal Code section 190.3 allows the introduction at the penalty phase of "…the nature and circumstances of the present offense…" Dr. Lakshmanan Sathyavagiswaran again testified to the autopsy of Officer Wrede that he had performed almost 19 years before. For the past ten years, he had been the Chief Medical Examiner for Los Angeles in charge of the Coroner's Office.

Also in accord with Penal Code section 190.3, prosecutor Darren Levine introduced evidence of the following prior criminal conduct and prior felony convictions for Michael Jackson:

- Robbery with a knife on April 16, 1969, when Jackson was 15 years old
- Sodomy on June 18, 1976, when Jackson was in the United States Army
- A felony conviction for burglary in 1974
- Assault on July 5, 1983, on West Covina Police Officer Gregory Bennallack

The assault on Officer Bennallack took place less than two months before the shooting of Officer Wrede, and in some respects there were similarities in the assaults on both officers. Officer Bennallack testified that he approached Jackson in a fast food store after Jackson was rigid, nervous, and combative and appeared to be under the influence of P.C.P. When the defendant refused the officer's request to come outside and talk, the officer put his hand on Jackson's shoulder and said, "Come on, let's go outside." Jackson forcibly resisted, grabbing the officer with both hands and ripping the police badge from his shirt. After a struggle, Officer Bennallack was able to arrest and handcuff Jackson with the assistance of a second officer.

After the arrest, Officer Bennallack transported Jackson to the jail in his police vehicle. Jackson was placed in the front seat of the vehicle since it had no cage in the back seat. He was handcuffed with his hands behind his back, and he was further restrained by the seat belt. He was sitting next to a shotgun that was mounted on a vertical rack between the driver and passenger seat. The rack was secured by two machine screws into the dash. The police vehicle driven by Officer Bennallack on July 5 had the same interior configuration with regard to the rack and shotgun as the police vehicle used by Officer Wrede on August 31, 1983. (Trial transcript, pages 1430 to 1446.)

During the booking process, Jackson told Officer Bennallack that he was going to rape his wife and kill his children. Officers Bennallack and Kenneth Wrede were good friends. He testified about his reaction when he learned that Michael Anthony Jackson was responsible for Wrede's death.

Q. Did that have an effect on you?

A. Yes, sir.

Q. Why?

A. Because I wished that it was me that was there instead of Ken, because I would have handled it differently. I would have known what to expect. Ken didn't. (Trial transcript, page 1440.)

Officer Terry Lindsay testified that, in a demonstration, he was able to remove the shotgun and shotgun rack from a West Covina police vehicle with one hand while standing outside the vehicle. It took him about eight seconds to rip out the shotgun and the rack in one piece, and it came out fairly easily. (Trial transcript, pages 1450 to 1452.)

The prosecution also introduced victim impact evidence. The United States Supreme Court has ruled that, in imposing sentence, a jury may consider the impact of the crime on society and on the victim's family. Such victim impact evidence assists the jury in assessing "evidence of the specific harm caused by the defendant's crime" by "demonstrating the loss to the victim's family and to society which has resulted from the defendant's homicide." (*Payne v. Tennessee* (1991) 501 U.S. 808.)

Prosecutor Levine called several police officers who had worked with Officer Wrede and described him as a dedicated, hard-working, and compassionate officer who loved his job and helping others. Some described kind and heroic acts that he had performed.

One police officer who testified was Robert (Bob) Smith, who was one of Ken Wrede's best friends. They met when they both worked as non-sworn security officers at Knott's Berry Farm. Smith later became a member of the Los Angeles Sheriff's Department while Wrede joined the West Covina Police Department, but they remained the best of friends. At Smith's wedding, Wrede walked the bride's mother down the aisle. His son was named Andrew Kenneth Smith in honor of Kenneth Wrede. He also wore a memorial wristband that reads "Kenneth Scott Wrede, West Covina Police Department, End of Watch August 31, 1983." Because of Ken's death, he would not allow his children to become part of law enforcement. He expressed dismay that the body of Officer Wrede was allowed to lie in the street for several hours after he was fatally shot.

> *You tell your partner, 'Don't let me die in the gutter, take me away. Take me to the hospital, but don't let me stay there. Let me die with honor.' But Ken died horribly. But to this day I regret not going to that scene and picking up and carrying my friend over to the hospital.* (Trial transcript, pages 1489 to 1490.)

Two of Wrede's sisters, his wife, and both his parents testified. With the assistance of prosecutor Levine, each had selected a series of photographs that were shown to the jury that depicted Kenneth Wrede and their interaction with him. They all described how difficult it was to re-live "Ken's" death through their testimony even though it had occurred 19 years before. They each testified to their love for him and how much they missed him.

Officer Wrede's parents testified that, after their son's death, they had become involved in organizations assisting crime victims and their families. They had formed a group called C.O.P.S. (an acronym for "Concerns of Police Survivors") that helped other police families.

Mrs. Marianne Wrede testified that she remembered when her teenage son would disrupt the family in the evenings by practicing the drums in his bedroom but how proud she was when he played the drums with the high school band in the Rose Parade. She stated that she sometimes drove to Wrede Way, a residential street named in memory of her son. She concluded her testimony as follows:

> *I think I pretty much described the emotional and the physical impact it [the loss of her son] has on you. You don't really feel like a whole person anymore. Someone very special in your life was taken tragically, taken brutally, taken suddenly, and you know that you will never be a whole person again. There will always be a hole in your heart.*
>
> *I begin each day of my life with kissing his picture.* (Trial transcript, page 1653.)

Defense evidence

The defense presented numerous witnesses that fell into three categories, as follows:

1. *Civilian witnesses on August 31, 1983*: James Butler testified that on the morning of August 31, 1983, Jackson smoked a P.C.P.-laced cigarette; Jackson later kicked off his sandals and ran off. Lucinda Ann Smith saw Jackson disoriented on the street, encountered Officer Wrede and told him about the defendant. Officer Wrede told her that he would take care of it.

2. *Family members*: Jackson's mother Lillian Williams testified that Jackson was one of her six children, fathered by three different men. He was born in March 1954. His father was not involved in raising his son, and he did not live with or support him. She would strike her children when she was angry with them, and on one occasion she choked Jackson. Two of Jackson's sisters and one of his brothers corroborated her testimony.

   Defendant's wife, Sabrina Jackson, testified that she married Jackson when he was in his early 20s. She already had a child when they married, and she and Jackson had two children of their own. When he was not taking drugs, he was capable of taking care of himself and his family. They eventually separated because of his drug use.

3. *Mental issues*: Dr. Dale Watson was a psychologist who tested Jackson and determined that his intelligence quotient (IQ) was 79.

An IQ of approximately 70 meant that the subject was mentally retarded. Dr. Watson testified that Jackson's IQ fell in the borderline range, which is "just about retarded." Jackson had a moderate degree of impairment of the brain function and displayed several types of brain impairment.

Dr. Jay Jackman was a forensic psychiatrist. He testified that the beatings inflicted by Jackson's mother severely impaired his development. He had borderline intelligence and brain impairment. Further, the amount of P.C.P. in Jackson's blood after the death of the officer would result in a significant intoxication and impairment.

A "correctional consultant" examined Jackson's prison records and testified that he would not pose a threat to prison inmates or staff if he were sentenced to life in prison without parole.

CLOSING ARGUMENTS

On the morning of July 19, 2002, prosecutor Darren Levine made his closing argument to the jury. Below are some excerpts from his argument. First, he talked about the challenges and dangers of being a peace officer.

And I'll tell you, my belief personally, there is no more honorable job when it's done right, when it's done ethically, when it's done to preserve our way of life. There is no more honorable job than being a peace officer. And as you get dressed, what do you do? You put on a uniform. You put on your badge. But before you put on your shirt, what do you have to do in this world? Officer has to stop and put on a Kevlar vest, a bullet proof vest. Is that a reminder of what your day may be like out there? And then you put on your duty belt. And on your duty belt you have a semi-automatic firearm or a revolver. Back in '83 it was a revolver. And you have extra rounds of ammunition and you have two pairs of handcuffs. And you have mace and you have a spot for your radio. And then you turn to the person you love, whoever that person is, and you say good-bye, let's get a puppy. And you go out and you do your job and you run into people that don't play by the same rules we all play by. You run into predators. And you have sworn, you've given an oath, to protect society. And you go out there with the best training you have. You go out there with good intentions. And you ran into Lucinda Ann Smith who tells you there is a problem, someone is act-ing strangely, and you tell them, "Thank you, Ma'am, I'll take care of that." And you go to a problem. (Trial transcript, pages 2257 to 2258.)

Prosecutor Levine then discussed the circumstances surrounding the death of Officer Kenneth Wrede:

Do you know how horrible this death was? Do you know that he was calling for help and it's not coming? He's getting either grabbed or kicked in the groin to the point where his scrotum has abrasions on it. He's getting punched. He's mostly doing defensive actions except pushing kind of kicks. Four minutes. He could have dumped Jackson, he could have shot and killed Jackson early into this fight. And he didn't. He showed what? Total restraint. Using what? Lowest levels of force. It cost him his life. It cost him what every police officer dreads, every one. No police officer wants to die on the street. You've heard that in testimony. It is a fear: I don't want to die on the street. And on a hot August day, his body is out in that street for four hot hours. This is a circumstance of the crime. I will submit to you right now that the circumstances of this crime are so egregious, are so horrific, are so cruel, are so calloused, are so over the top that the circumstances in this crime are enough in and of itself for a jury to come back with the death penalty. (Trial transcript, page 2265.)

Darren Levine played a video reenactment to the jury of the shooting of Officer Kenneth Wrede. In his commentary to the jury while the tape was being played, he pointed out that when Officer Wrede retreated to the police car after his physical struggle with Jackson, the defendant did not remain where he was or leave the location. Instead, Jackson ran to the pas-senger side of the patrol car to obtain possession of the shotgun. Jackson knew that West Covina patrol cars had a shotgun located in a rack at the front since he had been arrested less than two months before for assaulting Officer Bennallack and placed in a West Covina patrol car that had the same weapon system. After Jackson acquired the shotgun, he faked his surrender and shot the officer.

Levine told the jury that Michael Jackson's criminal history was a factor in aggravation. He argued that the factors in aggravation clearly outweighed the factors in mitigation. Although Jackson had an unstable childhood, his mother loved him and never abandoned him. His siblings loved him. Jackson enjoyed drugs and regularly used them despite efforts by friends and family to get him off drugs. Although defense experts testified that Jackson was under the influence of P.C.P. when he shot Officer Wrede, they said that he knew what he was doing.

JURY VERDICT AND SENTENCING

The case was submitted to the jury late in the afternoon on Friday, July 19, 2002. On Monday, July 22, 2002, after less than one day of deliberation, the jury returned with a verdict of death.

On September 20, 2002, Judge Charles Horan imposed the death sentence on Michael Anthony Jackson. It was over 19 years since the death of Officer Kenneth Wrede.

On February 5, 2009, the California Supreme Court unanimously affirmed the death sentence against Michael Anthony Jackson. In an opinion written by Justice Carlos Moreno, the court rejected all the defense contentions of error. See *People v. Jackson* 45 Cal. 4th 662 (2009). [2]

LESSONS LEARNED

With regard to officer survival, perhaps the most important element for a law enforcement officer is the mental preparation to use deadly force when it is needed. It has been said that a person needs three things to survive in combat – the weapon, the skill, and the will. If a law enforcement officer is not able to fire his weapon when necessary, then the weapon and the skill become meaningless.

Ken Wrede was a typical law enforcement officer in that he was raised

---

2   Justice Joyce Kennard was the only member of the Supreme Court who had participated in the Court's decision in 1989 when it had unanimously affirmed Jackson's first degree murder conviction and original death sentence.

in a stable family environment and starting a family of his own. An officer is not immersed in a world of violence when off the job and surrounded by loving family and friends. However, when on duty, the officer must have a different mind-set and must be prepared to encounter situations involving sudden and deadly violence.

In virtually every case involving the shooting death of a law enforcement officer, it is the suspect that first forms the intent to kill. This puts the officer at a great disadvantage because the officer may not become aware of the suspect's murderous intent until it is too late for the officer to react. It is important for the officer to take measures to maximize his or her safety and recognize the warning signs that might result in a violent confrontation.

The intense scrutiny that an officer receives after an officer-involved shooting should not be a deterrent to firing his weapon. Officer Wrede showed remarkable restraint in his confrontation with Michael Anthony Jackson, and it cost him his life. He would have been perfectly justified in shooting the armed Jackson. Officer Gregory Bennallack was a good friend of Wrede's. He testified that "...I wished that it was me that was there instead of Ken, because I would have handled it differently. I would have known what to expect. Ken didn't." [Trial transcript, page 1440.]

It seems that even experienced police officers underestimate the dangers to officers who exercise restraint when the use of deadly force is appropriate. On November 10, 2015, Los Angeles Chief of Police Charlie Beck announced that the LAPD would award a new medal to officers who showed "commendable restraint" during situations where they otherwise might use deadly force. The Preservation of Life medal would be a department honor on the same level as the prestigious Medal of Valor. The police union issued the following statement in response to the Chief's announcement:

> *This award will prioritize the lives of suspected criminals over the lives of LAPD officers, and goes against the core foundation of an officer's training. What we don't want is to see a flag-draped coffin and the chief speaking at an officer's funeral stating, 'This brave officer will be awarded the Preservation of Life medal.'*

This chapter suggests the following procedures and cautions:

- It is unsafe for an officer to approach a person alone when the officer recognizes the subject to be under the influence of stimulant drugs and/or mentally ill. When such persons act out violently, it takes about six officers to manually control them.
- An officer should call for backup, a supervisor, a TASER, less-lethal munitions, and a rescue ambulance before engaging such a person, if time permits.
- The shotgun rack should be of a type that does not permit jacking a round into the chamber when the device is locked.
- Beware of subjects who give a false impression that they are surrendering. This leads to "relaxing too soon," one of the Ten Deadly Errors from Pierce Brooks's book, "...officer down – code three..."
- When a subject is in proximity to a lethal weapon, an officer should be prepared to immediately use sufficient force until the subject is handcuffed and searched.

Officer Kenneth Scott Wrede

Date of Birth: February 12, 1957

Date Assigned: August 1, 1980

End of Watch: August 31, 1983

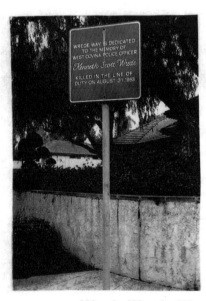

Wrede Way in West Covina, California

Marriage of Ken Wrede to wife Denel in October 1992

The shotgun rack in a West Covina Police vehicle in 1983

The body of Officer Wrede at the left rear of his police vehicle

Left to right: Investigator Joe Vita, Bureau Chief Steve Simonian, Assistant Chief Oreal Cotton, District Attorney Steve Cooley, and Prosecutor Darren Levine. Vita and Levine receive the Sheriff's Exemplary Performance Award for their efforts in achieving the reinstatement of a death sentence against the killer of West Covina Police Officer Ken Wrede.

Deputy District Attorney Darren Levine was a member of CAPOS for over ten years, prosecuting the most violent crimes committed against peace officers. He has obtained four death penalty verdicts, including the verdict against Michael Jackson. He was also the lead prosecutor in the cases in this book involving the murders of officers Richard Phillips and Milton Curtis (Chapter 1), the murder of Deputy David March (Chapter 6), and the murder of Captain Michael Sparkes (Chapter 7).

Mr. Levine is one of the leading experts in the world on the martial art of krav maga, having taught it to thousands of civilians and military officers, both in the United States and abroad.

CHAPTER 4

Detective Thomas Williams

Los Angeles Police Department

"Off-Duty Assassination"

ROBBERY OF GEORGE CARPENTER

In October 1984, 36-year-old George Carpenter was the manager of a movie theater in North Hollywood. On October 14, 1984, at approximately 12:50 a.m., Carpenter and his assistant manager, James Bruceri, drove to the Valley Plaza branch of the Bank of America to make a night deposit of that evening's theater proceeds of approximately $4,600. Carpenter stepped out of the car leaving the money with the assistant manager. A man emerged from a nearby parked car, pointed a gun at him, and demanded that he turn over the money. Carpenter stated that he did not have the money and that the money was in the car. Another man who remained hidden in the parked car yelled at the gunman, "Shoot the mother fucker." The man with the gun then fired a round at Carpenter, which missed. A frightened Carpenter told Bruceri to toss the money bag from the car. The gunmen picked up the bag, and the person in the car stated, "Go ahead. Shoot the mother fucker." The gunman fired another round in the direction of Carpenter, which also missed. The gunman then entered the car, which drove off. James Bruceri noticed that the gunman walked with a noticeable limp.

George Carpenter immediately reported the robbery to the police. He described the suspect vehicle as a light blue Chrysler product with California license plate number 120 CQF. Carpenter had observed the license plate number and memorized it as the vehicle drove off.

California license 120 CQF was for a 1971 Dodge Coronet registered to Haim Gavrieli. He was interviewed and stated that on October 1, 1984, he sold the vehicle to two male blacks for $300 in cash. The actual purchaser of the vehicle did not provide any identification but signed the receipt as "Don Stevens." In subsequent court proceedings, Gavrieli identified Daniel Steven Jenkins as the person who purchased the car and signed the receipt.

The 1971 Dodge license 120 CQF was placed into the police computer system as having been used in an armed robbery committed on October 14, 1984. On October 29, 1984, Daniel Jenkins, while driving the suspect vehicle, was arrested by two patrol officers. The suspect vehicle was impounded after Jenkins' arrest. Jenkins was released on $16,000 bail the following day.

Detective Thomas C. Williams of the Los Angeles Police Department's North Hollywood Detective Bureau was the investigator on the case. After Jenkins' arrest, Detective Williams prepared a photo lineup that included Jenkins' photograph. George Carpenter positively identified the photograph of Daniel Jenkins as that of the robber/shooter. Williams then filed robbery and assault charges against Jenkins with the District Attorney's Office. Jenkins remained free on the $16,000 bail during the pendency of the criminal proceedings in his robbery/assault case.

In April 1985, George Carpenter positively identified defendant Daniel Jenkins at the preliminary hearing, and Jenkins was held to answer to face trial on the charges of robbery and assault with a deadly weapon. Jenkins remained free on bail pending trial on the charges.

ATTEMPTED MURDER OF GEORGE CARPENTER

On July 4, 1985, at 9:00 p.m., George Carpenter was in the Two Guys From Italy restaurant at Bellingham Avenue and Victory Boulevard in North Hollywood on his dinner break from the United Artists movie theater next door.

While he was sitting at the bar drinking a beer, a black adult male entered the restaurant and walked toward the bar. He pulled out a gun and fired six shots at Carpenter, striking him four times. The first shot struck him in the face, entering in the right cheek and exiting behind his left ear. Another shot passed through his abdomen, and two shots entered his right thigh and left thigh. After firing the shots, the gunman put the gun in his pocket and calmly walked out the door.

George Carpenter survived the shooting. He spent three weeks in the hospital under the name of John Smith. The Los Angeles Police Department provided an armed guard during his stay in the hospital. After his release from the hospital, the District Attorney's Office assisted him in relocation. He changed his name and moved out of state.

Prosecutors in Daniel Jenkins' pending robbery case requested that his bail be revoked after the July 4 attack on Carpenter, but Carpenter had stated that Jenkins was not the shooter. Daniel Jenkins remained free on bail.

JURY TRIAL IN ROBBERY CASE

In the parlance of the District Attorney's Office, a "handoff" is a case that is assigned to a prosecutor shortly before it goes to trial. Ideally, a prosecutor should have enough time to become familiar with the facts and properly prepare the case for trial. Courtroom experts believe that proper preparation is a key element in the successful prosecution of a criminal trial. Unfortunately, in some prosecution offices, there may be insufficient time between trials for a prosecutor to properly prepare the next case. However, most prosecutors are resilient and adaptable, and they are able to successfully prosecute their cases despite the handicap of sometimes less than ideal preparation time.

The jury trial against Daniel Jenkins involving the robbery/assault of George Carpenter was originally assigned to Deputy District Attorney Myron Jenkins in the San Fernando Courthouse. However, Myron Jenkins was already engaged in another trial. The case against Daniel Jenkins was given to Deputy District Attorney Maureen Duffy-Lewis, a young prosecutor who had been in the office for only two years. Her lack of experience in the office made her vulnerable to unpopular assignments, such as being given a "handoff" for trial. She was told that jury selection was about to begin and that Detective Tom Williams, the investigator in the case, would be in the courtroom to assist her in the prosecution.

Below is an overview of the jury trial involving the robbery/assault of George Carpenter.

PEOPLE v. DANIEL STEVEN JENKINS
CASE A702427

JUDGE:	Bruce J. Sottile
PROSECUTOR:	Maureen Duffy-Lewis, Deputy District Attorney
DEFENSE ATTORNEY:	Norman Koplof, Deputy Public Defender

CHARGES: Count I — Robbery with Use of a Firearm

                  Count II — Assault with a Deadly Weapon, with

                  Use of a Firearm

LOCATION: Los Angeles Superior Court

                  San Fernando Courthouse, Department B

Testimony in the case began on Monday, October 28, 1985. George Carpenter returned from out of state to testify at Jenkins' trial. Once again, Carpenter positively identified Daniel Jenkins as the man who robbed him and twice shot at him on October 14, 1984. James Bruceri also made an in-court identification of Jenkins as the robber/shooter, and he testified that the suspect walked with a noticeable limp. As the investigating officer, Detective Tom Williams sat at the counsel table next to prosecutor Maureen Duffy-Lewis. At the conclusion of the day's court proceedings, Williams and Duffy-Lewis would walk together to the parking lot and drive their respective vehicles in tandem to the freeway. They both lived in the San Fernando Valley and drove in close proximity on the freeway until Detective Williams exited on the Topanga Canyon off ramp.

The prosecution had a very strong case. In addition to the positive identifications by George Carpenter and James Bruceri, the evidence established that Jenkins' car was the vehicle used during the robbery.

To counter the prosecution case, the defense called Duane Moody and Ruben Moss in an attempt to establish an alibi for Jenkins. They testified that they were at a party with Jenkins at the time of the robbery, although they had trouble remembering who else was at the party or when the party ended. Daniel Jenkins took the stand and denied committing the robbery. He claimed that someone must have "borrowed" the car to commit the robbery since he would leave the car parked near his house with the key in the ignition.

The witness stand is directly across from the prosecutor's seat at the counsel table. While he was on the witness stand, Daniel Jenkins looked straight ahead at Duffy-Lewis and Williams with an icy stare. Duffy-Lewis whispered to Detective Williams if he noticed how the defendant was looking at them. Williams replied, "He would kill us both if he had the chance."

Testimony in the case concluded on Thursday morning, October 31,

1985, when Detective Williams was called as a rebuttal witness for the prosecution. He testified to some routine matters, such as preparing the photo lineup card that he showed to the prosecution witnesses. He also testified that he met Daniel Jenkins on the afternoon of October 31, 1984, when Jenkins came to the North Hollywood police station in an attempt to get his vehicle out of impound. At that time, Detective Williams observed that Jenkins walked with a noticeable limp, and they discussed the injury to his leg.

Prosecutor Maureen Duffy-Lewis concluded her examination of Detective Williams as follows:

> *Question: Did you know Mr. Jenkins before this entire event, this case occurred? Did you personally know him?*
>
> *Answer: No.*
>
> *Question: Do you harbor any ill feelings toward the defendant Jenkins in any way?*
>
> *Answer: No.*
>
> *Question: Are you just here because it's your job to be here?*
>
> *Answer: Yes.*
>
> *Duffy-Lewis: Thank you. Nothing further.* (Trial transcript, page 286.)

The attorneys argued the case to the jury on the afternoon of October 31, 1985. The case went to the jury at around 3:10 p.m., at which time Daniel Jenkins apparently left the San Fernando courthouse.

Later that afternoon, Tom Williams and Maureen Duffy-Lewis walked together for the last time to the courthouse parking lot, where they left in their respective vehicles. Duffy-Lewis drove home to go trick-or-treating with her husband and two small children on this Halloween evening. Tom Williams drove his Datsun pick-up truck to the Faith Baptist Church day care center in Canoga Park to pick up his six-year-old son, Ryan.

DETECTIVE THOMAS C. WILLIAMS

Thomas C. Williams was born on March 14, 1943. He grew up in the San Fernando Valley where he attended military school and college at Cal

State Northridge.

He was described as a man of integrity devoted to his family and to his profession. He joined the Los Angeles Police Department on March 20, 1972, a few days after his twenty-ninth birthday. He worked in the West Valley and Central Divisions before coming to the North Hollywood station, first as a patrol officer and then five years as a detective. In early 1985, he was promoted to Detective II and appeared to have a bright career ahead of him. On October 11, 1985, he was honored as detective of the month for solving a murder at a North Hollywood bar.

Tom Williams' wife was named Norma, and they had two children—seventeen-year-old daughter Susan and six-year-old son Ryan. He owned a pick-up truck with a camper shell and took his family camping. When son Ryan began playing soccer, Williams learned about the game so he could help as an assistant coach and referee soccer games. Williams and his son shared a special moment when Ryan scored his first goal.

DEATH OF TOM WILLIAMS

Halloween was celebrated on October 31, 1985. On that date at approximately 5:30 p.m., the now off-duty Tom Williams arrived at the Faith Baptist Church child care center in Canoga Park to pick up his six-year-old son, Ryan. Williams parked his Datsun pickup truck at the curb in front of the school. He entered the school and returned to the pickup truck with Ryan, who was dressed as a colonial soldier. Williams was intending to take Ryan to a Halloween costume party for his soccer team. Williams placed his son in the passenger side of his pickup truck and walked around to the driver's side when a vehicle approached. Williams saw something and yelled for his son to get down. Numerous shots were fired from the vehicle as it drove alongside Williams' pickup truck. The passing vehicle continued down the street and disappeared from view. Williams sustained several bullet wounds and died at the scene. Ryan Williams followed his father's command to duck down and was not injured.

Various witnesses observed the incident and generally described the vehicle as a gray-colored 1970s model Chevrolet. The driver was observed before the shooting sitting in the vehicle and described as a male white or Hispanic between the ages of 28 and 32. One witness stated that the suspect wore a ski-type mask at the time of the shooting.

Williams' pickup truck had several bullet holes. There were also bullet holes in the outer wall of an adjacent school building. In the street near the pickup truck were several 9-mm shell casings. Although there were costumed children and adults in the area at the time of the shooting, none of them were injured.

The death of Detective Tom Williams made headline news in Los Angeles and was widely reported throughout the United States. Williams' death was unique because it involved the ambush murder of an off-duty police officer based on the performance of his duties. Lt. George Aliano, president of the Los Angeles Police Protective League stated, "We don't expect a 'hit' like that, getting into your own personal life (while) off duty."

Los Angeles Police Chief Daryl Gates prepared a 16-minute videotape that was distributed for showings at roll calls at all 18 LAPD area stations. In the videotape, Chief Gates warned officers to be aware that suspects they arrest can determine their off-duty routines, as was the case with Detective Tom Williams. Chief Gates stated that, "It is a very unfortunate situation, but that's where we are today, and it's very important that we recognize that. So not only should (officers) take care of themselves on duty, but they are going to have to become very much aware of where they are when they're off duty."

Detective Tom Williams was buried at San Fernando Mission Cemetery on November 5, 1985. He was eulogized at Our Lady of the Valley, the Catholic Church in Canoga Park that Williams attended. Nearly 1,600 mourners attended the memorial and graveside services, including over 1,000 officers from police agencies throughout Southern California. With Williams' two children and widow sat his mother, Pauline Williams, in the front row of the church. There was a mile-long funeral procession of 200 motorcycles and numerous vehicles to the San Fernando Mission Cemetery.

At the grave site, a police honor guard fired the traditional gun salute, police helicopters flew above in the "missing-man" formation, and a bag-pipe played "Amazing Grace."

After a bugler sounded "Taps," Chief Daryl Gates presented the American flag that covered the casket to Ryan Williams. The boy was wearing a miniature police badge on the lapel of his blue blazer as he tearfully took possession of the flag.

Ryan Williams turned age seven on November 7, 1985. On November 7, forty North Hollywood detectives gave him a surprise birthday party at his residence in Canoga Park. He blew out the candles on a birthday cake and received numerous presents, including a brand-new bicycle. Young Ryan was able to smile for the first time in over a week.

Ryan's mother, Norma, wanted her son to return to normal activities as soon as possible. With Ryan's acquiescence, he played in a soccer game on Saturday, November 9. After the game, the team went to a pizza parlor to celebrate Ryan's birthday. However, it would be a long time before Ryan could recover from the death of his father. In a religious class that weekend, the students were asked to draw pictures of themselves. Ryan drew a picture of a little boy standing by a grave.

DEPUTY DISTRICT ATTORNEY MAUREEN DUFFY-LEWIS

Maureen Duffy-Lewis had recently moved to a new house in Chatsworth and had not notified the District Attorney's Office of her change of address, although her residential telephone number remained the same. After the murder of Detective Williams, the Los Angeles Police Department and the District Attorney's Office attempted to locate her but were unable to do so. She was not answering her residence telephone, since she was trick or treating with her husband and two small children. The residence where she was believed to be residing was unoccupied. Investigators were concerned that someone may have followed her home from the courthouse and that her life and that of her family might be in jeopardy.

Duffy-Lewis and her family returned to her new home from trick or treating. She answered the telephone, learned of the death of Tom Williams, and disclosed her current location. The police quickly surrounded her new residence and took precautions to ensure that she and her family were not being held hostage inside their home. They carefully exited their home and soon were in the custody of the police. For the next few weeks, Duffy-Lewis and her family lived at her mother-in-law's residence where they received around-the-clock protection from officers of the Los Angeles Police Department and investigators from the District Attorney's Office. She made no further appearances for the prosecution in the robbery/assault case against Daniel Jenkins.[3]

VERDICT IN ROBBERY CASE

The jury in the pending trial of Daniel Jenkins for the robbery and assault of George Carpenter began its deliberations on the late afternoon of October 31, 1985. When the jurors returned on the morning of November 1, they said that they were aware that Detective Williams had been killed the previous evening. Judge Bruce Sottile admonished the jurors to disregard any news accounts that they had heard and to decide the case strictly on the evidence presented in the courtroom. He then told the jury to resume deliberating.

Later that morning the jury reached a verdict, finding Daniel Jenkins guilty of robbery and assault with a deadly weapon. The prosecutor representing the People at the time of the verdict was Deputy District Attorney Michael Knight, who was Duffy-Lewis' immediate supervisor. Daniel Jenkins was in the courtroom free on bail when the jury verdict was announced. He was now facing a maximum sentence of eight years in state prison, and Judge Sottile revoked Jenkins' bail and remanded him to custody. Sentencing was scheduled for November 27, 1985.

On November 27, the sentencing was delayed when Deputy Public Defender Norman Koplof asked to be relieved as Jenkins' lawyer because of a conflict of interest. Koplof declined to explain why he wanted to leave the case. Judge Sottile denied the request, but he granted a delay to allow Koplof time to decide whether to seek a writ from a higher court ordering Judge Sottile to relieve the Public Defender's Office.

In early January 1986, an appellate court overturned Judge Sottile's order requiring Deputy Public Defender Norman Koplof to explain why he wanted to leave the case. Koplof was excused from representing Jenkins, and Judge Sottile appointed veteran defense attorney Howard Price to be his attorney on the case. Price filed a motion to remove Judge Sottile from the case, claiming that the judge was biased against his client.

---

3   On July 8, 1987, Maureen Duffy-Lewis was appointed a judge to the Los Angeles County Municipal Court by Governor George Deukmejian. She later became a judge in the Superior Court.

Judge Sottile filed a written response denying that he was biased against Daniel Jenkins. In a hearing conducted on February 20, 1986, Superior Court Judge Aurelio Muñoz denied the motion to disqualify Judge Sottile, saying there was no reason to believe that he was biased against Jenkins.

Daniel Jenkins was finally sentenced on May 9, 1986. Judge Sottile sentenced him to eight years in state prison for the convictions of robbery and assault with a deadly weapon against George Carpenter. This was the maximum sentence under the law. Deputy District Attorney Kenneth Barshop represented the prosecution at the sentencing hearing.

INVESTIGATION INTO THE DEATH
OF DETECTIVE WILLIAMS

The investigation into the death of Detective Tom Williams was assigned to the LAPD Major Crimes Investigative Section of the Robbery–Homicide Division. This section included the most talented and experienced homicide investigators in the Los Angeles Police Department. Detective Michael Thies, a police officer for 21 years with the past nine years in the Major Crimes Investigative Section, was assigned to head the investigation. Detective Thies went to the crime scene on October 31, 1985, at about 6:30 p.m. and began to coordinate the investigative efforts of the numerous law enforcement officers participating in the investigation.

The District Attorney's Office had a rollout program in which a deputy district attorney would go to the scene where a police officer was murdered or seriously injured. Detective Thies contacted the District Attorney's Command Post and requested that Deputy District Attorney Richard Jenkins, the Deputy-in-Charge of the Crimes Against Peace Officers Section (CAPOS), respond to the crime scene as the rollout deputy. Jenkins then came to the crime scene to assist the LAPD detectives in the investigation. Detective Thies and Deputy District Attorney Richard Jenkins had worked together in the past, and they had an excellent working relationship.

A prime suspect in the murder of Detective Williams was Daniel Jenkins. Williams was the investigating officer in Jenkins' robbery case and had testified in the case on the day of the murder. Police investigators immediately began looking into Jenkins' background and history and identifying his friends and associates.

A BIG BREAK!

On the evening of Friday, November 1, 1985, Aladron Xavier Hunter went to the Los Angeles Police Department's Southwest Division to tell the homicide detectives assigned there what he knew about the murder of Detective Tom Williams. Mr. Hunter was told that the homicide detectives were not in and to contact them on Monday, November 4. Fortunately, Mr. Hunter persisted and called the West Valley Station information operator and was transferred downtown. He eventually contacted Detective Richard Aldahl of the Major Crimes Investigative Section, and at 11:15 p.m. that evening, he was interviewed by Detectives Aldahl and Marlow. A 17-page handwritten statement was taken from Aladron X. Hunter, which is summarized as follows:

On the afternoon of October 23, 1985, he met a friend that he had known for nine years, Voltaire "Jake" Williams. "Jake" agreed to drive Hunter to his grandmother's house. While en route, Jake stated that Hunter could make a lot of money if he would knock off (i.e., kill) some guy. The weapons and stolen cars would be supplied; one car for the kill and drive away and another car to make the getaway to the freeway where Jake would pick him up. Jake said that he would get paid $10,000 for the hit.

Jake told Hunter that he had a friend named "Danny" who wanted to kill a security guard because he did not want the guard to testify against him in court. Hunter told Jake that he was interested because he needed the money.

On the evening of Thursday, October 24, 1985, Jake drove Hunter to the Reseda Skating Rink where they met "Danny". Danny stated that he needed somebody killed so he couldn't testify in court against him. Danny could not do it himself because the police would know that he did it. Jake was afraid and could not do it.

Danny said that it had to be done on Friday and that he would give Hunter the gun, gloves to wear, and provide the cars to use in the crime.

Hunter said that he needed the money and that he would do it.

Danny said that he wanted the security guard killed when he picked up his kid from a day care center in the Valley. The guy normally let his kid in first through the passenger door and then walked around the front of the car and got in the driver's door. Hunter was to drive by and shoot him before he got into the car. Hunter agreed to the plan. Jake drove Hunter home, and stated that he would pick him up on Friday at about one o'clock in the afternoon.

On Friday, October 25, 1985, at 1:00 p.m., Jake picked up Hunter. They went to a residence that Jake said was Danny's house. Jake entered the house and came out carrying a blue shoe box. Hunter looked inside the box and observed a handgun and a pair of driving gloves.

Jake drove to the vicinity of the day care center. Jake showed Hunter the Pontiac that he was to drive during the hit and the Monte Carlo to be used as the second car. Hunter got into the Pontiac with the shoebox containing the gun and gloves and waited while Jake went to use a public telephone. At approximately 5:30 p.m., Jake returned and told Hunter that the guy was on his way and would be driving an orange Datsun pickup truck with a small camper shell in the back.

Hunter parked the Pontiac down the street from the front of the day care center. At about 5:30 p.m., he saw the security guard arrive in the pickup truck and enter the school. Hunter decided that he could not kill anyone. He started the engine of the Pontiac, drove by the pickup truck, and went to the location where Jake was waiting. He got into Jake's car and told him that he could not do it. He gave Jake the shoebox containing the gun and gloves. Jake drove off and dropped Hunter off some distance away.

On the evening of November 1, he learned of the killing of the LAPD detective and decided to contact the police.

Aladron Hunter identified a photograph of Voltaire Williams as "Jake" and also identified a photograph of Daniel Jenkins as "Danny". Hunter also showed detectives the residence of Voltaire Williams.

INVESTIGATION: ARREST OF VOLTAIRE WILLIAMS

Aladron Hunter spoke to police investigators beginning at 11:00 p.m. on November 1, 1985. His statement confirmed that Daniel Jenkins and Voltaire Williams were involved in planning the murder of Detective Tom

Williams. At this time, Jenkins was in custody, having been remanded to custody after his conviction for the robbery of George Carpenter.

Immediately after Hunter's statement, LAPD personnel staked out the residence of Voltaire Williams that Hunter had provided. On November 2, 1985, Williams was arrested as he drove away from his residence. He was taken to the Police Administration Building where he was interviewed by Detectives Frank Garcia and Otis Marlow. After waiving his *Miranda* rights, he gave a lengthy statement, summarized as follows:

> *He was a friend of Danny Jenkins. In mid-October Jenkins told him that some friends had used his car to commit a robbery. The victim got the license number, and Danny was arrested and charged with the crime. He was facing ten years. A security guard was testifying against him in court and he needed the guy dead. Williams agreed to do the killing for $2,000.*
>
> *In the late afternoon, they went to the school, parked at a nearby apartment building and observed the security guard arrive in his pickup truck around 5:30 p.m. and pick up his son. Danny even stole the cars to be used in the shooting and subsequent getaway and provided the gun to be used.*
>
> *The killing of the security officer was to take place the following day. However, that evening, Williams told Danny (Jenkins) that he couldn't go through with it.*
>
> *Voltaire Williams then recruited "Smokey" (Aladron Hunter) to do the hit. Williams introduced "Smokey" to Danny, and the killing of the security guard was scheduled to take place on Friday, October 25. However, Smokey backed out at the last minute from killing the security officer.*

Williams' statement was reduced to a four-page typewritten document that he signed. He also signed a separate document of which he had been advised, and waived, his constitutional rights.

Although Voltaire Williams did not admit to the murder of Detective Tom Williams, at a minimum he implicated himself in a conspiracy to murder the detective since he admitted that he recruited Aladron Hunter to do the hit. Williams' statement was further confirmation that Daniel

Jenkins was responsible for the murder of Detective Tom Williams.

INVESTIGATION: ARREST OF DUANE MOODY; RECOVERY OF MURDER WEAPON

Police investigators were aware that Duane Moody had testified in Daniel Jenkins' jury trial in an attempt to provide an alibi for defendant Jenkins for the night of the George Carpenter robbery. In his testimony, Moody admitted that he was a close friend and associate of Daniel Jenkins.

Duane Moody was arrested on November 2, 1985. He agreed to speak to LAPD detectives. He stated that Daniel Jenkins was obsessed with the idea of killing Detective Williams and believed that he might get caught, so he purchased cyanide pills that he hid in his shoe.

Bungewauna Moody, the wife of Duane Moody, told investigators that on October 30, 1985, she observed Moody personally wrap a MAC 10 automatic rifle and leave their apartment with it.

Duane Moody cooperated with the police in the recovery of the murder weapon. He told the police where he had secreted the weapon, and that it was located at the residence of Ali Woodson. Officers then went to Woodson's apartment and recovered the MAC 10 automatic rifle. Ali Woodson was the lead singer of The Temptations singing group and a close friend of Duane Moody. Woodson told police investigators that Moody dropped off a duffle bag at his Inglewood apartment on Halloween night. He did not look into the bag until several days later when he then discovered that the bag contained the MAC 10 automatic rifle.

Ballistic tests confirmed that this MAC 10 automatic rifle was in fact the murder weapon. It was capable of firing ten rounds per second.

Moody also told the investigators that the vehicle used in the shooting of Detective Williams was a sky-blue Oldsmobile with a white top. He described its current location near the Hollywood Bowl. The automobile was recovered on November 7, 1985, at the location given by Moody. It had been reported stolen on October 22, 1985. The automobile had been parked in a residential area in Canoga Park. A resident noted that the vehicle was parked on the street on the morning of the murder, but when he returned from work at about 5:00 p.m. on October 31, the vehicle was gone. When the vehicle was recovered, the ledge of the driver's door was covered in gunshot residue of the type that the murder weapon emitted profusely. The front part of the vehicle contained nine expended shell casings.

FILING OF CHARGES

After attending the funeral of Detective Tom Williams on the morning of November 5, 1985, Chief of Police Daryl Gates, in an afternoon press conference, announced that four persons were in custody on charges of murder and conspiracy to kill the officer. Daniel Steven Jenkins was in custody awaiting sentencing on his robbery/assault conviction. Duane Moody, Voltaire Alphonse Williams, and Ruben Antonio Moss were each arrested on Saturday, November 2, but Chief Gates delayed the announcement until after the slain officer's funeral.

On Wednesday, November 7, the four suspects appeared in Van Nuys Municipal Court in handcuffs and chains where they were each charged with murder and conspiracy to commit murder involving the death of Detective Tom Williams.

Three special allegations were charged that would make it possible for prosecutors to seek the death penalty if the defendants were convicted of first degree murder. The special allegations were that a police officer was killed in the performance of his duties, the murder was committed in retaliation against a witness in a trial, and the murder was committed by means of lying in wait. All four defendants were ordered held without bail.

DESCRIPTION OF DEFENDANTS

Daniel Steven Jenkins

Jenkins was born in Kansas on August 3, 1955. His family came to Los Angeles about three years after he was born. His father died, and he was raised by his mother. He dropped out of Manual Arts High School his senior year. He once ran a limousine service called Sir Dan's Limousine Service and owned expensive automobiles, including an Excalibur, a Porsche, and a Rolls-Royce.

Jenkins had an extensive criminal record. In May 1978, he was arrested following a routine traffic stop. A search of Jenkins' home after his arrest resulted in the recovery of 59 stolen credit cards, five drivers' licenses, three handguns, a 9-mm automatic handgun, and 90 rounds of ammunition. A police officer testified at Jenkins' preliminary hearing that Jenkins was engaged in the theft of luxury automobiles and keeping personal property from the vehicles. Jenkins entered a guilty plea to two counts of receiving stolen property and received a sentence of five years' probation and a year in county jail.

On Thanksgiving Day in 1978, Jenkins and a co-defendant went to the victim's house and warned him against filing a police report for a pistol-whipping that they had administered on the victim the day before. The victim replied that he had already filed the report earlier in the day. Jenkins and the co-defendant returned to the house armed with shotguns and fired some rounds, striking the victim's father in the shoulder. After a jury was unable to reach a verdict, a mistrial was declared. Jenkins then entered a guilty plea to assault with a deadly weapon and was sentenced to three years' probation with a year in county jail, concurrent with the sentence in the receiving stolen property case.

And, of course, Jenkins was convicted of the October 1984 robbery/assault of George Carpenter for which he eventually received an eight-year prison sentence.

Duane Moody

Moody was age 27. He apparently was a "roller skate addict" who hung around the roller skating rink in Reseda. He had a lengthy criminal record, including arrests for burglaries, grand theft auto, receiving stolen property, and robbery. His only substantial time in custody took place in January 1979 when he was sentenced to the California Youth Authority following convictions for robbery and assault with a deadly weapon.

When arrested on November 2, 1985, Moody was free on $7,500 bail awaiting trial for a burglary committed in January. According to the female victim, Moody drove her to a fast food restaurant, pretended to enter the restaurant while she waited in the car, returned to her apartment on foot and stole money and jewelry.

Voltaire Alphonse Williams

Williams was born on November 25, 1962 in Shreveport, Louisiana, one of six children to Carlton Williams and Ann Reed. He came to Los Angeles when he was nine years old. At the time of his arrest, he was 22 years of age and lived with his brother in Los Angeles. He had not married or fathered any children. He had ambitions of becoming a successful boxer. He was 5 feet 11 inches tall and weighed 175 pounds. He had shown promise as a light heavyweight boxer in his amateur career, compiling a record of 22–5. Williams had two fights as a professional, with one win and one draw. He earned less than $1,000 in each of his professional fights. His last bout was on July 8, 1985, when he fought to a four-round draw in the undercard at The Forum.

Williams had a prior conviction for robbery when he was a juvenile. In 1980, he grabbed a gold necklace from a girl and ran off. He was arrested shortly after the crime and was convicted of robbery. He was sentenced to the California Youth Authority where he spent two years in custody.

Ruben Antonio Moss

Moss was born and raised in Los Angeles. He was age 24 at the time of his arrest. He was 5 feet 10 inches tall, weighed 285 pounds, and played football at Dorsey High School. At one time he was a driver for Daniel Jenkins' limousine service. Moss worked in his father's accounting firm after he left the driving job. He did not have a prior criminal record.

SIGNIFICANT EVENTS BEFORE PRELIMINARY HEARING

Before the preliminary hearing, the following events took place.

1. On December 7, 1985, Daniel Jenkins apparently attempted suicide by suffocation. He was found in his jail cell just before midnight with a plastic bag over his head and a string around the bag. He was still breathing, and deputies rushed him to the jail infirmary. He remained in the jail ward for five days, where he was kept under

observation before being returned to his jail cell. He suffered no permanent injuries.

2. On February 13, 1986, Thomas Williams was one of several officers who received the LAPD's Medal of Valor. In a ceremony attended by about 700 people, the award was accepted posthumously by Williams' daughter Susan. Williams' badge, mounted in a shadow box, was given to his widow Norma.

PRELIMINARY HEARING

Deputy District Attorney Richard Jenkins[4] of CAPOS was assigned to prosecute the case. He filed the charges against the four defendants and was the lead prosecutor for all the judicial proceedings. He was capably assisted in the case by Deputy District Attorney William Gravlin, also assigned to CAPOS. The preliminary hearing began on March 25, 1986, before Judge Brian D. Crahan of the Los Angeles Municipal Court. Below is an overview of the case.

PEOPLE v. DANIEL STEVEN JENKINS, et al.
CASE A811214

JUDGE:	Brian D. Crahan
PROSECUTORS:	Richard Jenkins, Deputy District Attorney
	William Gravlin, Deputy District Attorney
DEFENSE ATTORNEYS:	Howard Price for Daniel Jenkins
	James Epstein for Duane Moody
	David Houchin for Ruben Antonio Moss
	Charles Lloyd for Voltaire Alphonse Williams
CHARGES:	Count I — Murder in the First Degree with Special Circumstances
	Count II — Conspiracy to Commit Murder

---

4   Newspaper articles would occasionally state, tongue in cheek, that prosecutor Jenkins was not related to defendant Daniel Jenkins.

The preliminary hearing concluded on April 23, 1986. The prosecution presented 80 witnesses during the course of the hearing. These included persons who were solicited by one or more of the defendants to murder Detective Williams or who were present when one or more of the defendants discussed plans to murder the officer. These witnesses included some the following individuals:

Aladron Hunter testified to being solicited by Voltaire Williams and Daniel Jenkins to murder Detective Williams. At the last minute, he was not able to go through with the murder.

Tyrone Hicks testified that he was solicited by Ruben Moss and Daniel Jenkins to commit the murder of Detective Williams. A few days before Halloween, Moss drove Hicks to the area of the school and instructed him on how to do the shooting. However, Williams picked up his son before the plan could be carried out. Hicks refused to participate further.

Elihu Broomfield testified that, on October 31, 1985, he met Daniel Jenkins at the courthouse, and they had lunch together. Jenkins told him about the plans to murder Detective Williams.

Michael Canale testified that Duane Moody told him about the plan to murder Detective Williams a few days before the killing occurred.

A resident in the neighborhood of the First Baptist School testified that he was returning home from work on October 25, 1985, when he observed three men in a white car parked in a driveway near the school. He identified Duane Moody and Ruben Moss as two of the men in the vehicle, but he was not sure whether Daniel Jenkins was the third man in the vehicle.

LAPD Detective Alan Pesanti was told by a jail informant named Donald Sutton that Daniel Jenkins tried to hire him to kill George Carpenter.

At the conclusion of the preliminary hearing, Judge Brian Crahan ordered all four defendants to stand trial on the charges of murder and conspiracy. Based on the testimony of Detective Alan Pesanti, the judge ordered that Daniel Jenkins must also stand trial for the attempted murder of George Carpenter.

Judge Crahan stated that, "We have plain and simple murder, with premeditation, of a police officer discharging his official duty... while the perpetrators were lying in wait."

TWO MORE SUSPECTS CHARGED

On March 4, 1986, two more suspects were arrested in the plot to kill Detective Tom Williams. David William Bentley and Reecy Clem Cooper were charged with conspiracy to commit murder in count one and special circumstances murder in count two. The four overt acts alleged in the conspiracy count set forth the theory of the prosecution case against Bentley and Cooper, as follows:

> *Overt Act I: Around mid-June 1985, David William Bentley purchased a KG99 rifle from Edward Denarr.*
>
> *Overt Act II: On or about October 24, 1985, David Bentley, Reecy Cooper, Tyrone Hicks, and Ruben Antonio Moss met with defendant Daniel Steven Jenkins and discussed matters relating to the assassination plot.*
>
> *Overt Act III: On or about October 29, 1985, defendant Ruben Antonio Moss offered a handgun as the murder weapon to David William Bentley, Reecy Cooper, Tyrone Hicks, and defendant Daniel Steven Jenkins.*
>
> *Overt Act IV: On October 29, 1985, Reecy Clem Cooper accompanied Ruben Moss and Tyrone Hicks to Glade Avenue in Canoga Park, California to carry out the murder.*

The key prosecution witness against Bentley and Cooper at their preliminary hearing was Tyrone Hicks, who testified that he was recruited by Bentley and hired by Ruben Moss to drive the car from which Detective Williams would be shot. Cooper would be the gunman. On October 29, Cooper and Hicks lost their chance to kill the detective when he approached the school from an unexpected direction.

Bentley and Cooper were ordered to stand trial as charged after a preliminary hearing that concluded on August 27, 1986.

PRE-TRIAL ACTIVITY

After David Bentley and Reecy Cooper were ordered to stand trial, there were six defendants in two separate cases charged in the plot to murder

Detective Tom Williams. The prosecution moved to consolidate all the defendants together in one case, and the motion was granted.

In August 1986, the prosecution announced that it would be seeking the death penalty against Daniel Jenkins and Ruben Antonio Moss since they were viewed more criminally culpable than the other defendants as they participated in the planning and execution of Detective Williams to a much greater extent.

In early 1987, David Bentley was given immunity to testify as a prosecution witness. The charges against him were dismissed, and he was released from custody.

In March 1987, the prosecution filed a motion to sever Jenkins and Moss from the three remaining defendants (i.e., Duane Moody, Reecy Cooper, and Voltaire Williams), so that the two death penalty defendants and the three non-death penalty defendants could be tried in separate cases. This motion was granted.

JURY TRIAL (DEATH PENALTY CASE)

The first case to go to trial was the case against Daniel Jenkins and Ruben Antonio Moss. It was assigned to Judge Judith Ashmann in the Van Nuys courthouse for jury trial. The following is an overview of the case.

PEOPLE v. DANIEL STEVEN JENKINS AND RUBEN ANTONIO MOSS
CASE A811214

JUDGE:	Judith M. Ashmann
PROSECUTORS:	Richard Jenkins, Deputy District Attorney
	William Gravlin, Deputy District Attorney
DEFENSE ATTORNEYS:	Howard Price and Janet Sherman for Daniel Jenkins
	Michael White and David Houchin for Ruben Antonio Moss
CHARGES:	Count I — Murder in the First Degree with Special Circumstances of Killing a Police Officer, Killing a Witness, and Lying in Wait
	Count II — Conspiracy to Commit Murder

	Count III — Attempted Murder of George
	Carpenter (Jenkins Only)
LOCATION:	Los Angeles Superior Court
	Van Nuys Courthouse, Department E

TRIAL EVIDENCE

During the guilt phase of the trial, each defendant was tried by a separate jury. Most of the witnesses testified before both juries, but occasionally a witness was relevant only for one of the two defendants. On these occasions the witness testified before the jury for which the evidence was relevant, while the other jury was excluded from the courtroom. For example, this occurred when evidence was introduced involving the attempted murder of George Carpenter. Only Daniel Jenkins was charged with this crime, so the jury considering Ruben Moss's case did not hear the evidence relating to this crime.

The evidence introduced at the trial regarding the conspiracy and the murder consisted primarily of the testimony of immunized witnesses Aladron Hunter, Tyrone Hicks, David Bentley, and Jeffrey Bryant. Their testimony was corroborated by witnesses who observed the shooting, persons to whom the defendants made incriminating statements, disposal and recovery of the murder weapon, and telephone records.

The evidence introduced at the trial regarding the attempted murder of George Carpenter consisted primarily of the testimony of immunized witness Jeffrey Bryant. Daniel Jenkins originally hired Jeffrey Bryant and another man to kill Carpenter. Eventually, a man named Anthony Bryant shot Carpenter, while Jenkins and Jeffrey Bryant established an alibi for Jenkins. Jeffrey Bryant disposed of the gun and the vehicle used in the shooting. The testimony of Jeffrey Bryant was corroborated by Jenkins' admissions to witness Elihu Broomfield and by telephone records.

JURY VERDICT

Daniel Jenkins

In July 1988, the jury hearing the case against Daniel Jenkins convicted him of the three counts with which he was charged — the murder of Detective

Tom Williams, the conspiracy to murder Detective Williams, and the attempted murder of George Carpenter. With regard to the murder count, the jury found true the special circumstance allegation that Williams was a peace officer who was killed intentionally in the performance of his duties. This finding made Jenkins eligible for the death penalty. After a penalty hearing, the jury fixed the penalty at death.

A probation report prepared before Jenkins was sentenced stated in its evaluation that, "Defendant has been described as dangerous as much as ten years ago. That he has proven this, is tragically obvious. The callous, unrepentant, cold, brutal, and anti-social lifestyle of this defendant is awesome testimony and justification for the death penalty as recommended by law."

Los Angeles Police Detective Michael Thies told the probation officer that he had spent three years investigating Daniel Jenkins for the murder of Detective Williams. He had uncovered a web of criminal behavior including numerous robbery victims and possibly murder. Jenkins ran a group of robbers, several of whom had been convicted. Jenkins and his band of thieves took hundreds of thousands of dollars during robberies. Detective Thies stated that he had never encountered in his 24 years of police work a more calculated pattern of criminal behavior. He believed that the death penalty for Jenkins was deserved and in the best interest of society.

On October 6, 1988, Judge Judith Ashmann denied Jenkins' motions for a new trial and modification of the verdict and imposed the sentence of death.

Ruben Antonio Moss

In August 1988, the jury hearing the case against Ruben Antonio Moss convicted him of the first degree murder of Detective Tom Williams with the special circumstance allegation found true that Williams was a peace officer who was killed intentionally in the performance of his duties. Moss was also convicted of the conspiracy to murder Detective Williams. After a penalty hearing, the jury recommended life in prison without the possibility of parole.

On December 15, 1988, Moss appeared before Judge Judith Ashmann for sentencing. At the sentencing hearing, Moss's attorney, Michael White, attempted to have the sentence for his client reduced to life imprisonment with the possibility of parole. He submitted a letter signed by seven of the 12 jurors stating their belief that a sentence of life imprisonment without

the possibility of parole was too harsh, and that a sentence of life imprisonment with the possibility of parole was more appropriate, given the degree
of Moss's involvement in the offense. Attorney White also pointed out that
Moss had no known criminal record.

The probation report stated that Moss's efforts to ingratiate himself to
Daniel Jenkins set the stage for him to be exploited and manipulated by
a more sophisticated and criminally oriented companion. A psychiatric
evaluation of Moss described his growing up in a chaotic household domi-
nated by an abusive father. He did not feel successful and attempted to gain
acceptance by helping others. Moss wanted to become Jenkins' best friend,
but Jenkins ultimately exploited him.

Judge Ashmann rejected the defense request to modify the jury verdict.
She sentenced Ruben Antonio Moss to life imprisonment without the possibility of parole.

JURY TRIAL (NON-DEATH PENALTY CASE)

The jury trial of the three defendants for whom the prosecution was not seeking the death penalty began in October 1988. Below is an overview of the case.

PEOPLE v. DUANE MOODY, VOLTAIRE ALPHONSE WILLIAMS,
AND REECY CLEM COOPER
CASE A811214

JUDGE:	Kathryne Ann Stoltz
PROSECUTOR:	Richard Jenkins, Deputy District Attorney
DEFENSE ATTORNEYS:	Michael Adelson and James Epstein for Duane Moody
	Charles Earl Lloyd and Lewis Watnick for Voltaire Alphonse Williams
	Bernard Rosen and David Wesley for Reecy Clem Cooper
CHARGES:	Count I — Murder in the First Degree with Special Circumstances of Killing a Police Officer, Killing a Witness, and Lying in Wait
	Count II — Conspiracy to Commit Murder

LOCATION: Los Angeles Superior Court

Van Nuys Courthouse, Department E

JURY VERDICT

After a ten-week trial, the jury reached verdicts against each of the three defendants, as follows:

Duane Moody

The jury acquitted Moody on the charge of conspiracy to commit murder and were deadlocked 10–2, in favor of acquittal, on the murder charge. Judge Kathryne Ann Stoltz declared a mistrial on the murder charge on March 20, 1989. The prosecution was considering retrying Moody on the murder charge, but on May 1, 1989, Judge Stoltz dismissed the murder charge. She stated that there was "no reasonable likelihood" that a second trial would result in a conviction.

Moody was accused of supplying the weapon that was used to murder Detective Williams. However, Moody claimed that he furnished the gun to Daniel Jenkins "out of fear and intimidation." He claimed that he tried to avoid Jenkins for several days before giving him the gun and even put glue on the safety so it would not be usable. A defense expert testified at the trial that there was glue on the safety.

Reecy Clem Cooper

On March 7, 1989, the jury acquitted Cooper of the first degree murder of Detective Williams. The following day, the jury acquitted Cooper of the conspiracy to commit the murder. Cooper had been in custody for three years since his arrest on March 4, 1986, and he was now a free man after the acquittal.

Voltaire Alphonse Williams

The jury convicted Williams of conspiracy to commit murder in the slaying of Detective Tom Williams.[5] The same jury acquitted Voltaire Williams of first degree murder of the officer.

This jury verdict was consistent with the evidence presented at the jury trial and the jury instructions. Voltaire Williams presented evidence that after Aladron Hunter informed Williams that he was not going to do the killing, Hunter and Williams went to Oakland on Monday, October 28, 1985. They returned to Los Angeles a few days later.

The jury was instructed that if a person withdrew from a conspiracy, the person was not responsible for any crimes committed by co-conspirators after an effective withdrawal. The jury apparently concluded that Voltaire Williams effectively withdrew from the conspiracy when he and Hunter went to Oakland on October 28, 1985. Since the murder of Detective Williams took place on October 31, 1985, Voltaire Williams was not guilty of the murder. However, he was guilty of conspiracy to commit murder for his participation in the conspiracy before October 28.

In a sentencing hearing on April 26, 1989, Judge Stoltz denied Voltaire Williams' motion for a new trial and sentenced him to 25 years to life in prison. He would be eligible for parole in about 17 years.

EPILOGUE – DEPUTY DISTRICT ATTORNEY RICHARD JENKINS

Deputy District Attorney Richard Jenkins was the lead prosecutor for the Los Angeles County District Attorney's Office in the murder of Detective Tom Williams. His involvement in the case began on October 31, 1985, the date of Williams' death, when he responded to the crime scene to assist the LAPD detectives in the initial investigation. He remained on the case as the lead prosecutor throughout all the criminal proceedings. He was the lead prosecutor in the death penalty trial of Daniel Jenkins and Ruben Moss and the sole prosecutor in the non-death penalty case against Duane Moody, Voltaire Williams, and Reecy Clem Cooper. Daniel Jenkins received the death penalty, and Voltaire Williams and Ruben Moss were convicted and received sentences that were commensurate with their

---

5   Some news accounts reported that defendant Williams was not related to Detective Williams.

involvement in the officer's death.

Richard Jenkins had an outstanding career in the District Attorney's Office. He was hired on February 24, 1969, and quickly developed a reputation as an ethical, hard-working, and skilled prosecutor. He was a member of the Organized Crime Division until the summer of 1985 when he took over as the Deputy-in-Charge of the Crimes Against Peace Officers Section. Three months later, he received a call to roll out to the scene of the shooting of Detective Tom Williams.

Jenkins later became the Bureau Director overseeing general criminal prosecutions for downtown Los Angeles. Later he became the Assistant District Attorney overseeing criminal prosecutions for the District Attorney's Office. One of his roles was as Chairman of the Special Circumstances Committee, which decides on which cases the office will seek the death penalty.

Richard Jenkins retired on February 8, 1999, after 30 years of outstanding public service. He and retired Detective Mike Thies remain the best of friends.

EPILOGUE – SUPREME COURT OPINION

On May 4, 2000, the California Supreme Court affirmed the conviction and death sentence of Daniel Steven Jenkins in an opinion that appears in the Official Reports at 22 Cal. 4th 900. In an opinion authored by Chief Justice Ronald George, the Court unanimously rejected Daniel Jenkins' contentions and affirmed his conviction and death sentence.

VOLTAIRE WILLIAMS PAROLE

Of the three persons convicted in the murder of Detective Tom Williams, only Voltaire Williams was eligible for parole consideration. Daniel Jenkins had been sentenced to death, and Ruben Antonio Moss was serving a sentence of life imprisonment without the possibility of parole.

Voltaire Williams had been denied parole on several occasions. However, in October 2016, a two-person panel of parole commissioners found Williams suitable for parole.

The decision to parole Voltaire Williams was strongly criticized by law enforcement officials in California. Governor Jerry Brown sent a letter to the Board of Parole Hearings opposing Williams' release, stating that Williams had not confronted his actions and responsibilities in the detective's killing. Because Williams had been convicted of conspiracy rather than murder, the Governor did not have the authority to reverse the parole decision on his own. Instead, he called for a review by the full panel of parole commissioners. On May 2, 2017, the full panel upheld the ruling to parole Williams. He was released from prison on parole within a few days after spending 27 years in prison.

LESSONS LEARNED

Any murder of a police officer is a tragic event, but the ambush-murder of Detective Tom Williams was especially troubling because he was off-duty when he was killed. He appears to have been the first (and only) peace officer in Los Angeles County murdered when he was off-duty but based on the performance of his duties as a peace officer. There really aren't any "tactical lessons" *per se* for this tragic death. Even as his life was being taken, Detective Williams heroically saved his own child.

This was an outright ambush and assassination of a police officer for his making a case against a violent criminal. Some might say that this was a "one in a million" tragic occurrence and, at that time, it might have been so. But these days, more officers are getting ambushed. The usual advice is to "vary your habits and your driving routes to and from work", but that is easier said than done. Officers should remain alert and aware (and armed) at the gas station, the grocery store, and even picking up one's child from school.

It is disheartening to know that someone could walk into a police station offering information about a cop-killer and be told that the homicide detectives were not available. This is a dereliction of duty. Every police agency should have procedures in place for immediately receiving such critical information.

Law enforcement officers do have several procedures available that can provide separation between their professional and personal lives. These procedures provide for maintaining the confidentiality and non-disclosure of certain public information. Some of these procedures are set forth below.

CHAPTER 4

Telephone number

A police officer's telephone number should be unlisted. Caller ID and call blocking features should be installed on the telephone, and the telephone number should be placed on a "do not call" list.

Checking account

A peace officer should avoid having his or her home address printed on personal checks and should consider changing the address to a post office box or work address.

Department of Motor Vehicle records

In California, Vehicle Code section 1808.4 protects the confidentiality of DMV records upon request of "[a]n active or retired peace officer". In California, DMV records are open to public inspection. However, the DMV provides a procedure whereby designated persons, their spouses, and children may request home address confidentiality on any DMV record for any vehicle, driver's license, or identification card that reflects the designated persons' names.

Property records

Real estate records in California are public records and cannot be made confidential. This problem does not exist if the officer does not own any real estate. If a law enforcement officer does buy property, he or she should consider placing the property in a revocable blind trust in a name other than that of the police officer.

Voter registration

In California, voter registration information is a public record, but access to specific voter information, including home address and telephone number, is restricted. In Los Angeles County, confidential voter registration is available through the Los Angeles Registrar of Voters.

Postal service

When a person moves to a new address and has the mail forwarded, the United States Postal Service gives people the new address and even sells the new address to data vendors. This can be prevented if the person doesn't forward his or her mail but instead contacts each company, magazine, etc., about the change of address. Another option is to fill out the United States Postal Service online form to change an address and indicate that it is a temporary change that provides six months of forwarding that can later be extended for another six months. That information, unlike the changes marked as permanent, is not included in the master list sold to data brokers.

Marriage records

In California, a couple may apply for a confidential marriage license. Once a confidential marriage license has been obtained, only the couple may purchase copies of the marriage license and must present valid picture identification and the required fee to the clerk in order to do so.

Internet use

California Government Code section 6254.21 prohibits the posting of the home address or telephone number of various public officials, including peace officers, without first obtaining the written permission of the individual. However, in this internet age, it can be difficult to maintain complete privacy.

The lesson to be learned from this chapter is that law enforcement officers should follow the procedures outlined herein to separate their private life from their professional careers.

Detective Thomas C. Williams

Date of Birth: March 14, 1943

Date Appointed: March 20, 1972

End of Watch: October 31, 1985

Mike Thies (left) of LAPD's Elite Robbery Homicide Division led the investigation. Deputy DA Dick Jenkins (right) of the District Attorney's Office Crimes Against Peace Officers Unit handled the prosecution.

Los Angeles Police Chief Daryl Gates (far right) comforting family of slain
detective Thomas Williams: daughter Susie and son Ryan

Detective Tom Williams' orange Datsun with camper shell at murder scene; bullet hole in window

Poster at LAPD Robbery Homicide Division

CHAPTER 5

Detective Tommy De La Rosa

Fullerton Police Department

"Undercover Danger"

EVENTS LEADING UP TO JUNE 21, 1990

In June 1990, Detective Tommy De La Rosa was a nine-year veteran of the Fullerton Police Department assigned to its Narcotics Unit. He was fluent in both Spanish and English and could easily assume the identities of drug dealers of many nationalities. As a result, he regularly worked in an undercover capacity posing as a narcotics dealer buying and/or selling narcotics.

An informant named Gilberto Valenzuela (hereafter "the informant") was working with the Fullerton Police Department Narcotics Unit (and specifically with Detective De La Rosa). The informant let it be known that he was working for an individual who had a lot of cocaine to sell and was looking for buyers.

On June 14, 1990, the informant met Luis Benitez at an El Pollo Loco Restaurant in Downey. Benitez told the informant that he knew someone who wanted to buy a large quantity of cocaine and had been told that the informant had a friend who had a lot of cocaine to sell. Benitez then made a phone call. Shortly thereafter, Jose Rodriguez arrived at the El Pollo Loco in a car driven by Jesus Pena. After Benitez introduced the informant, Rodriguez told him that he was interested in buying fifty kilograms of cocaine and asked to be introduced to the person in possession of the large amount of cocaine. Rodriguez and Pena then drove away from the restaurant. Benitez told the informant that Jose Rodriguez had a lot of money to buy cocaine.

On June 15, 1990, Detective De La Rosa went to the El Pollo Loco Restaurant in Downey. In the parking lot was a vehicle containing Jesus Pena, Jose Rodriguez, and Luis Benitez. Rodriguez and Benitez negotiated with De La Rosa and agreed to purchase from him 200 kilos of cocaine at $20,000 per kilo, a total of $4 million. They agreed to complete the transaction within the next two days.

Jose Rodriguez later contacted Detective De La Rosa by phone and stated that he was in possession of the $4 million. They agreed to do the transaction on June 18, 1990.

The Fullerton Police Department had access to 57 kilograms of cocaine that they used to show to potential buyers in "reverse sting" operations when they were involved in the negotiation of sales of large amounts of cocaine to potential customers. Since they had "only" 57 kilograms of cocaine, they packaged flares and boxes of radio parts to resemble additional boxes of cocaine. On the morning of June 18, the informant drove his motorhome to the Fullerton Police Department where 57 kilograms of cocaine were placed in the vehicle.

In the meantime, Detective De La Rosa drove to the El Pollo Loco in Downey. Jesus Pena and Jose Rodriguez arrived about an hour later with Pena, as usual, acting as chauffeur. Rodriguez said that they were ready to do the deal but they wanted first to see the cocaine. Detective De La Rosa then drove by himself to another location where he met the informant and other officers waiting with the motorhome containing the cocaine. The 57 real kilograms of cocaine were transferred from the motorhome to a van which De La Rosa drove back to El Pollo Loco. Rodriguez entered the van and examined the kilos. He then told De La Rosa to wait in the parking lot while he checked about the money. Surveilling officers followed Pena and Rodriguez to some pay telephones. They returned to the parking lot, and Rodriguez told De La Rosa that he wanted to see the entire 200 kilograms of cocaine before doing the deal. Detective De La Rosa drove the van back to the motorhome where the boxes that did not contain cocaine were placed in the van so that it appeared that there were 200 kilograms of cocaine in the vehicle. Detective De La Rosa drove back to the parking lot where Rodriguez looked inside the van and observed the additional boxes. Rodriguez seemed satisfied, and he told De La Rosa that he was going to get the money together and would call him later. Detective De La Rosa left the parking lot in the van. Several hours later, Rodriguez called De La Rosa, told him that the money man was not available, and that the deal would have to be rescheduled.

After a couple of delays, it was arranged for the deal to take place on June 21, 1990.

JUNE 21, 1990

On June 21, 1990, Jose Rodriguez called Detective De La Rosa, and the deal was set for 2:00 p.m. to take place at a McDonald's restaurant in Downey. At 1:00 p.m., De La Rosa briefed the 25 officers assisting in the surveillance, including a helicopter pilot and observer.

At 2:00 p.m., De La Rosa and the informant drove the van containing the 57 kilograms of real cocaine and the additional boxes to resemble cocaine to the McDonald's restaurant. Luis Benitez was already there, and Jose Rodriguez arrived soon thereafter, driven by Jesus Pena. After a brief discussion, Rodriguez and Pena drove to a nearby pay phone. While they were gone, Benitez told Detective De La Rosa that Rodriguez did not want a lot of people involved in the deal and that the informant would have to wait with him while De La Rosa and Rodriguez went to complete the transaction. Shortly after Rodriguez and Pena returned to the McDonald's restaurant, Rodriguez got into the van with De La Rosa and told Benitez and the informant to remain at the restaurant and that he would be back in an hour or an hour and a half.

De La Rosa was wearing a loose blue shirt hanging outside his pants, and he had a .38 caliber five-shot revolver concealed in his waistband. He was also in possession of a pager which had a concealed voice transmitter that could be monitored by surveilling officers. Should De La Rosa be in danger, he would summon back-up officers for assistance by saying, "Help. Help. Put the gun away." Rodriguez was overweight and wearing a tight shirt tucked into his clothing, and he did not appear in possession of a weapon.

Jesus Pena left the McDonald's first, driving slowly, watching the van driven by De La Rosa with Rodriguez as the passenger. Pena then drove ahead, parked, and watched through bushes as the van drove by. Pena then got back in the car and followed, keeping a watch on the van. Pena continued surveillance of the van and again went ahead, stopping at a pay phone along the route, where he waited. This time as the van drove by he realized that the plan was working. De La Rosa was apparently transporting $4 million of cocaine, had been separated from the surveilling officers, and was alone with Rodriguez. It appeared to Pena that everything was in place for a robbery to be completed as planned. Pena returned to his car while thrusting his fist in the air in a victory gesture.

In the meantime, Rodriguez directed De La Rosa onto the freeway, and they eventually took an off-ramp in the city of Downey. De La Rosa stopped the van at a pay phone, which Rodriguez used on and off, for about thirty minutes. At about 3:15 p.m., Rodriguez directed De La Rosa to a one-block residential street that ended in a cul-de-sac. After the van entered the cul-de-sac, De La Rosa was out of range and monitoring officers were not receiving any transmissions from De La Rosa's transmitter. The helicopter observer broadcast to surveilling units that the van had entered a cul-de-sac and that they should hold back. De La Rosa parked the van in the driveway at 8937 Arrington Avenue. The location consisted of a front house and a back house (actually a converted garage) with a patio covering obscuring the area between the two houses. The helicopter observer saw De La Rosa and Rodriguez exit the van, walk up the driveway, and disappear from his view. The helicopter was circling in a wide orbit so persons on the ground would not be aware of its presence.

About sixty seconds later, the helicopter observer saw something "blue" in front on the van. At the time, the helicopter observer was not aware what the blue thing was. In fact, it was the body of Detective De La Rosa who had run out of the rear house, collapsed, and died in the driveway. His now-empty .38 caliber five-shot revolver was next to his body. (An autopsy determined that De La Rosa had been shot five times, three times in the back, with one of the bullets perforating his heart.)

Shortly after seeing the blue, the helicopter observer saw two persons running from the front house to the back of the property. He radioed to the officers on the ground what he had seen, and these officers quickly converged upon the property.

In the meantime, several residents near 8937 Arrington Avenue heard numerous gunshots over a period of about 20 to 30 seconds. A tenant in the apartment complex and a maintenance man near the swimming pool heard the shots and saw a man wearing a jacket running out between the two buildings. Police officers later found a .380 automatic in a trash dumpster where the man was running. This man was Raul Meza who was arrested in the apartment complex by the wave of officers converging at the location. Meza rented and lived in the rear house at 8937 Arrington Avenue.

A witness named Enrique Alvarado lived two houses away from 8937 Arrington Avenue. He knew Raul Meza and had even gone with him on the morning of June 21 to the Downey courthouse to help him take care of some traffic tickets. He also knew that Jose Yuriar lived with Raul Meza at 8937 Arrington Avenue and that Jesus Araclio was a friend of theirs. Alvarado heard numerous shots — first a short volley of four to six shots and then a second volley with many more shots. He saw two men running from the front house where the shots came from. A few moments later, Jose Yuriar and Jose Araclio burst into his house carrying weapons. They hid a .12 gauge shotgun and a .38 automatic under the mattress. In an attempt to avoid police detection, the two men washed and cleaned up and Araclio changed his shirt. They then pretended to play cards. By now there were police officers all over the place. Officers knocked on the door, entered, asked a few questions, discovered evidence, and arrested Yuriar and Araclio. The officers recovered the .12 gauge shotgun and the .38 automatic from under the mattress.

Jose Rodriguez was found dead in the rear house at 8937 Arrington Avenue. He had been shot three times. Two wounds in Rodriguez' chest and stomach were from rounds fired from De La Rosa's gun. The third wound was to Rodriguez' arm from a .380 bullet fired from Raul Meza's gun. A 9-mm automatic was found lying beside Rodriguez' right hand.

As the fatally wounded Tommy De La Rosa fled from the rear house to the driveway where he collapsed, he passed the door of the front house where Jose Yuriar and Jesus Araclio were located. From behind a screen door in the front house, Yuriar fired once at De La Rosa with the sawed-off .12 gauge shotgun, and Araclio fired four times with the .38 caliber revolver. The five shots all missed their target. (Ballistics tests showed that a .12 gauge casing and four .38 caliber casings found in the front house matched the two weapons that Yuriar and Araclio hid under the mattress in Enrique Alvarado's house.) De La Rosa fired the last bullet from his .38 caliber five-shot revolver at the front house. It completely missed the screen door from where Yuriar and Araclio were shooting and struck a side window.

No money was found at the crime scene. However, there was a suitcase in the rear house next to the television set. The suitcase contained two bricks, a pillow, and a heavy jacket. The bricks gave the suitcase weight, and the other articles took up space so the bricks would not rattle around. The presence of the heavy suitcase would give the appearance of a container filled with money.

RECONSTRUCTION OF CRIME

Both Tommy De La Rosa and Jose Rodriguez were shot in the rear house. The helicopter observer was broadcasting his observations to the officers on the ground, and these communications were taped. The time sequence of what occurred was provided by the tape of the communications from the helicopter. Just over 60 seconds elapsed from the time that Tommy De La Rosa and Jose Rodriguez got out of the van until the time that De La Rosa collapsed in the driveway.

Detectives measured the distances and determined that the distance from the van to the rear house was approximately 75 feet and that the distance from the rear house to where De La Rosa collapsed on the driveway was approximately 55 feet. The detectives conducted time and distance studies to determine the length of time it would take to traverse these distances. They concluded that it took about 20 seconds to walk from the van's location on the driveway to the rear house, and about seven seconds to jog from the rear house to the location on the driveway where De La Rosa collapsed. That left slightly more than 30 seconds that De La Rosa was at the rear house where the shootout occurred. During the 30-second period, a total of 15 shots were fired from the three guns in the rear house.

When De La Rosa entered the rear house, he was expecting to meet the money man, and Raul Meza was there to play the role. The windows of the rear house were covered with sheets, and it took De La Rosa a few seconds for his eyes to adjust to the dark interior.

With all five weapons used in the gun battle having been recovered, firearms experts were able to reach some conclusions and form opinions based on the physical evidence at the crime scene and the recovery of bullets and shell casings.

1. In the rear house, fifteen shots were fired: nine shots from Rodriguez' 9-mm automatic; two shots from Raul Meza's .380 automatic; and four rounds from De La Rosa's .38 caliber five-shot revolver. De La Rosa received five gunshot wounds while in the rear house—three

to his back, one to his leg, and one to his hand.

2. When De La Rosa entered the rear house, both Jose Rodriguez and Raul Meza produced guns. De La Rosa struggled with Rodriguez in an attempt to prevent Rodriguez from firing his weapon. During the struggle, De La Rosa's gold chain with a cross was torn from his neck. (The gold chain was later found on the floor of the rear house.)

3. While De La Rosa was struggling with Rodriguez, Meza fired two shots into De La Rosa's back with his .380 automatic. Both shots resulted in through-and-through wounds, completely passing through De La Rosa's body. One of the two .380 automatic bullets ended in the wall. The other bullet was recovered from Rodriguez' elbow, indicating that Rodriguez and De La Rosa were in close proximity when this shot was fired.

4. De La Rosa received a gunshot wound to his right hand that entered the thumbnail, exited the other side of the thumb, ripped the thumb pad, and struck the forearm. The wound caused massive damage to his right hand, rendering it incapable of holding a firearm. There were traces of lead under the handgrips of De La Rosa's gun, indicating that he was holding the gun in his right hand when he received this injury. He probably dropped his gun after he was struck in the hand. After De La Rosa dropped his gun, he bent over to pick it up.

5. The bullet that was the immediate cause of death resulted in a through-and-through wound that entered the middle of De La Rosa's back, went through part of his lungs, going through the heart, and exiting in the center of his chest. Once the bullet blew out part of his heart, Tommy De La Rosa was essentially dead. He had only 10 to 15 seconds of consciousness left because his heart had ceased to function. Somehow De La Rosa managed to stagger back to the driveway in this condition before collapsing to the ground. The fatal shot was probably fired by Raul Meza.

6. The gun battle in the rear house ended when De La Rosa shot and killed Jose Rodriguez. Rodriguez had a gunshot wound to his right armpit area and a second gunshot wound that entered the center of his abdomen and exited just below his waistband. A bullet from De

La Rosa's gun was laying on top of Rodriguez' belt buckle, just an inch or so from the exit wound.

7. As previously indicated, Jose Yuriar and Jesus Araclio hid silently in the front house. As the mortally wounded De La Rosa was staggering back to the driveway, Jose Yuriar fired at De La Rosa with a 12 gauge sawed-off shotgun, and Jose Araclio fired four shots from a .38 automatic. All the shots missed. De La Rosa fired a wild shot with the last round from his .38 caliber five-shot revolver before reaching the driveway and collapsing.

One of the first officers to arrive at the scene tried to give CPR to De La Rosa, but he wasn't breathing or responding. Blood and air were escaping from a bullet hole in his left side. De La Rosa was carried to the helicopter, and CPR was given on the way to the USC Medical Center. He was wheeled to the trauma unit, and his chest was opened. A few minutes later, Tommy De La Rosa was pronounced dead.

All persons involved in the negotiations to purchase cocaine and with the subsequent shooting at 8937 Arrington Avenue were arrested on the day of the murder.

Raul Meza, Jose Yuriar, and Jesus Araclio were arrested at the scene of the shooting of Detective De La Rosa.

Luis Benitez was arrested at the parking lot where he was waiting with the informant for De La Rosa to return after completing the narcotics transaction.

Jesus Pena was arrested at the residence of Jose Rodriguez. He was the 22-year-old nephew of Rodriguez who was acting as Rodriguez' "chauffeur" to help create the illusion that Rodriguez was a big narcotics dealer.

INITIAL CRIMINAL PROCEEDINGS

The jury trial into the murder of Detective Tommy De La Rosa did not commence until the summer of 1992. The trial was delayed because of the large number of defendants that were initially charged with the murder and because of some difficult legal issues of criminal culpability for murder involving co-conspirators and aiders-and-abettors. Following is a summary of the criminal proceedings in the case.

On June 25, 1990, a four-count criminal complaint was filed against the eight persons who were arrested on the date of De La Rosa's murder. Count One charged all eight arrestees with the murder of De La Rosa on the theory that murder was a natural and probable consequence of a $4 million, 200 kilogram cocaine deal. Count Two charged attempted robbery against Jesus Araclio, Raul Meza, Jose Yuriar, and Jesus Pena. Count Three alleged a conspiracy to commit the crime of the purchase for sale of cocaine against all eight defendants. Count Four charged a conspiracy to commit the crime of attempted robbery against Araclio, Meza, Yuriar, and Pena.

Deputy District Attorney William Gravlin of the Crimes Against Peace Officers Section (CAPOS) was assigned as the lead prosecutor in the case. Because the case involved issues of narcotics tactics and procedures, Deputy District Attorney Ellen Berk of the Major Narcotics Division was assigned as the second chair in the case. Berk had prosecuted cases involving the Fullerton Police Department as the arresting agency.

The preliminary hearing began on January 16, 1991, before Judge Jack Massey in the Downey Municipal Court and concluded after ten days of testimony. All eight defendants were held to answer as charged, including the murder count alleged in Count One against all defendants. The defendants were later arraigned in the Norwalk Superior Court.

All the defendants made a motion to dismiss the charges pursuant to Penal Code section 995, which allows defendants to challenge the sufficiency and admissibility of evidence presented at the preliminary hearing. The prosecution filed a written opposition to the defense motion. The hearing on the defendants' motion to dismiss was assigned to Judge John Torribio of the Norwalk Superior Court, who presided in a court that normally heard only civil cases. Although the record is unclear, Judge Torribio apparently was concerned that the informant was not called as a witness at the preliminary hearing despite a request by the defense that the informant be made available for examination. The judge dismissed all the charges against all eight defendants on April 8, 1991.

The case was immediately refiled on the same day of the dismissal, so the defendants remained in custody. Rather than have another lengthy preliminary hearing, the prosecution scheduled a hearing before the Los Angeles County Grand Jury.

On April 30, May 1, and May 2, 1991, prosecutors William Gravlin and Ellen Berk presented the evidence involving the murder of Tommy De La Rosa and the negotiations to purchase cocaine to the Los Angeles County Grand Jury. On the afternoon of May 2, the Grand Jury returned an indictment against the eight defendants. In Count One, the indictment charged all eight defendants with the murder of Tommy De La Rosa. Special allegations of killing the victim during a robbery and while lying in wait were made against defendants Jesus Araclio, Raul Meza, Jose Yuriar and Jesus Pena, making them eligible for the death penalty. Count Two charged Araclio, Meza, Yuriar, and Pena with the crime of attempted robbery. Count Three charged all the defendants with the crime of conspiracy to purchase for sale cocaine. Count Four charged Araclio, Meza, Yuriar, and Pena with conspiracy to commit robbery. And Count Five charged all the defendants with the crime of attempted purchase for sale of cocaine.

After the indictment, the case was reviewed by the District Attorney's Special Circumstances Committee to determine the appropriate punishment for the defendants against whom special circumstances in the murder count were alleged. On August 20, 1991, the Chairperson of the Committee announced that death was the appropriate penalty for defendants Jesus Araclio, Raul Meza, and Jose Yuriar.

After the grand jury indictment, the case remained in the Criminal Courts Building in downtown Los Angeles. In September 1991, the prosecution formally moved to sever the case into two separate trials. On September 12, 1991, Judge Curtis Rappe granted the People's motion to sever, resulting in two separate cases for trial purposes. Pursuant to Judge Rappe's ruling, the three defendants facing the death penalty were to be tried separately from the remaining five defendants. Judge Rappe also granted a prosecution request that both cases be transferred for trial to the Norwalk Superior Court.

In late September 1991, all the parties appeared before Judge Robert Armstrong, the presiding judge of the Norwalk Superior Court. Judge Armstrong announced that the case involving the five non-death penalty defendants would be tried immediately. However, the defense attorney representing Frederico Marriott was not ready for trial, so his case would be tried later with the three death penalty defendants. The prosecution was given ten days to prepare before the commencement of the trial of the four remaining defendants (Jesus Pena, Miguel Escobar, Ydalvys Escobar, and Luis Benitez).

When the prosecutors returned for trial in early October 1991, Judge Armstrong announced that he was transferring the case to Judge John Torribio. He was the judge who had previously granted the defense motion under Penal Code section 995 and dismissed the original filing against all the defendants. Judge Torribio had ruled that there was insufficient evidence to support the murder charges against the non-death penalty defendants. For these reasons, the prosecution filed an affidavit of prejudice pursuant to section 170.6 of the California Code of Civil Procedure to disqualify Judge Torribio from hearing the case. This section gives each side *one* challenge in a case to disqualify a judge. The case was then assigned to Judge Charles Frisco, and the four defendants proceeded to jury trial in Judge Frisco's court. The case was prosecuted by William Gravlin and Ellen Berk. The jury found the defendants not guilty of the murder charges but convicted them of conspiracy to buy cocaine and the attempted purchase of cocaine with the intent to sell. Prosecutor Berk told the press that she was not surprised of the acquittal on the murder charges but was gratified that the defendants were convicted of the drug counts.

In a sentencing hearing for Jesus Pena and Miguel Escobar on June 12, 1992, Judge Frisco heard statements from Detective Dan Hughes and from Doyle Anthony, who was De La Rosa's father-in-law. Anthony told the court that the actions of the defendants not only led to the death of Tommy De La Rosa but also destroyed the lives of the family and robbed a little girl of her father. Anthony was trembling as he spoke to the court and stopped occasionally to regain his composure. He stated that, "There are no words to describe the pain and devastation I felt and what the family felt on the day that Tommy was murdered." He asked Judge Frisco to impose the maximum sentence.

Detective Dan Hughes, who was De La Rosa's partner, told the court, "If this case does not fit the standard for imposing the maximum sentence possible, then our partner, Detective Tommy De La Rosa, clearly died in vain, and those of us who continue to risk our lives for a drug-free society will have been betrayed and forgotten by the judicial system."

Judge Frisco sentenced Jesus Pena and Miguel Escobar each to the near-maximum of 18 years in prison. In a subsequent sentencing hearing, the judge sentenced Luis Benitez to 18 years in prison and gave Ydalvys Escobar a three-year prison sentence.

PRE-TRIAL PROCEEDINGS: DEATH PENALTY CASE

The trial for the remaining four defendants (three of whom were eligible for the death penalty) remained in the court of Norwalk Presiding Judge Robert Armstrong. In mid-March 1992, Judge Armstrong assigned the case to Judge J. Kimble Walker for trial.

Judge Walker had been a Superior Court judge since 1980 and had sat in a civil assignment. He had never presided over a capital murder case. Prosecutors believed that he was too unfamiliar with criminal law and too defense-oriented to properly preside over such a serious case with complex legal issues. The prosecution filed a second affidavit of prejudice pursuant to section 170.6 of the Code of Civil Procedure against Judge Walker, on the theory that since the case had been severed into two separate cases, the People were entitled to exercise two affidavits instead of the normal one. However, Judge Armstrong ruled that the prosecution had used the one challenge to which they were entitled (against Judge Torribio), and he denied the prosecution's challenge to remove Judge Walker from hearing the case.

In a June 5, 1992, letter, Fullerton Police Chief Phil Goehring wrote of his concerns about Judge Walker's qualifications to Robert Parkin, the presiding judge of Norwalk Superior Court. Chief Goehring's concern was that Walker's lack of experience in criminal law could allow the killers of Detective Tommy De La Rosa to be freed on a legal technicality. Judge Walker remained on the case. The trial was set before Judge Walker to commence on August 10, 1992. The remaining four defendants remained in custody with no bail.

In April 1992, Deputy District Attorney Daniel Lenhart replaced William Gravlin as the lead prosecutor on the case. Lenhart was a former marshal for Los Angeles County from 1966 to 1970. He joined the District Attorney's Office as an investigator in 1972, went to law school at night, and passed the State Bar. He became a Deputy District Attorney in 1980 and eventually was assigned as the Deputy-in-Charge of CAPOS, prosecuting cases in which police officers were the victims of murder and/or violent assaults. Deputy District Attorney Ellen Berk remained on the case to assist Daniel Lenhart.

Below are the major participants and the charges in the case when the jury trial began on August 10, 1992, before Judge J. Kimball Walker.

PEOPLE v. JESUS ARACLIO, RAUL MEZA, JOSE YURIAR, AND FREDERICO MARRIOTT
CASE BA038224

JUDGE:	J. Kimball Walker
PROSECUTORS:	Daniel Lenhart, Deputy District Attorney
	Ellen Berk, Deputy District Attorney
DEFENSE ATTORNEYS:	Richard A. La Pan and Pat Patterson for Jesus Araclio
	Carole Telfer, Deputy Public Defender for Raul Meza
	Javier Ramirez and Michael Meza for Jose Yuriar
	Andrew Stein for Frederico Marriott
CHARGES:	Count I — Murder with Special Circumstances of Robbery and Lying in Wait
	Count II — Attempted Robbery
	Count III — Conspiracy to Purchase Cocaine for Sale
	Count IV — Conspiracy to Commit Robbery
	Count V — Attempted Purchase for Sale of Cocaine
MISCELLANEOUS:	Defendants Araclio, Meza, and Yuriar eligible for the death penalty, if the Special Circumstances are found true.

JURY TRIAL

The trial in the case began on August 10, 1992. A jury was selected, and on Friday, August 21, the attorneys made their opening statements. The prosecution began its presentation of evidence on August 24, 1992. The prosecution case was straightforward, relying primarily on the testimony of police officers involved in the surveillance on June 21, 1990, the arrest of the defendants, the recovery of the guns involved, the examination of the crime scene, and expert testimony.

During the trial, Judge J. Kimball Walker made a series of rulings and comments that frustrated the prosecutors and the Fullerton police officers watching the trial involving the death of their fallen comrade. Some examples:

1. Before any witnesses were called, Judge Walker ordered the prosecution to divulge the home address and phone number of retired Los Angeles Police Detective Brian Murphy. "I'm going to order you to give us his last home residence and phone number... Clearly he'll not be permitted to testify during the course of your case in chief if this information is not available beforehand." (Trial transcript, pages 1406 and 1407.)

    At one point Judge Walker stated that, "I don't think you have a privilege of setting up a meeting and then having him say I don't want to show up." The judge may have been confusing the deposition procedure that applies in civil cases where attorneys can depose the parties on the other side.

    There is no similar procedure in criminal cases; defense attorneys and defense investigators can seek interviews with prosecution witnesses, but these witnesses are not required to speak to the defense. In fact, law enforcement officers routinely decline to be interviewed by the defense. The defense attorneys are already familiar with the case based on the mandatory discovery that they receive and the evidence introduced at the grand jury or preliminary hearing.

2. The People's first witness was Fullerton Police Officer Craig Brower. Prosecutor Ellen Berk marked for identification seven photographs on a poster board showing the cocaine as it appeared in Detective De La Rosa's van. The defense did not object, probably because this was a routine procedure in criminal cases. However, Judge Walker, on his own motion, instructed Berk to remove the photos from the easel on which they were placed, "...I think that it's inappropriate to display them in the presence of the jury until they come into evidence." (Trial transcript, page 1556.)

    The defense was never ordered to refrain from showing to the jury an item marked for identification.

3. At times, Judge Walker expressed frustration at the slow pace of the proceedings. On September 3, 1992, the judge told Deputy District Attorney Dan Lenhart that he was sick of this case and that the prosecutors better start moving things along. September 3 was only the seventh day of trial, and one day had been lost due to the illness of one of the defense attorneys. The slow pace in the presentation of the evidence was due in large part to the number of defendants on the case.

    Every prosecution witness was subject to cross-examination by four defense attorneys, and this resulted in some witnesses testifying for a full day or more.

4. Judge Walker often used Evidence Code section 352 to limit or exclude evidence that the prosecution wanted to introduce. Section 352 states as follows:

> *The court, in its discretion, may exclude evidence if its probative value is substantially outweighed by the <u>probability that its admission will (a) necessitate undue consumption of time</u> or (b) create substantial danger of undue prejudice, of confusing the issues, or of misleading the jury.* (Emphasis added.)

Below are some examples of Judge Walker using Evidence Code section 352 to exclude evidence that the prosecutors tried to introduce.

4–a. On cross-examination, Detective Thomas Basham admitted to kicking one of the defendants (Raul Meza) while Meza was on the ground while being taken into custody. The defense attorney then asked the officer if he was given immunity for that action, and he stated that he had not. On redirect examination, prosecutor Ellen Berk attempted to rehabilitate the officer by asking him why he struck Meza. The judge sustained a defense objection to the question, and Berk asked for a sidebar conference. At the conference outside the presence of the jury, Judge Walker stated that, "...the prejudicial effect and the waste of time, including this time prior is far outweighed by the unnecessary response." (Trial transcript, pages 1981 to 1983).

Judge Walker never told the defense attorneys that they were wasting time by asking for a conference outside the presence of the jury.

4–b. During the examination of the criminalist who performed a trajectory analysis of the bullets fired, the following dialogue took place among the court, prosecutor Dan Lenhart and Meza's attorney, Carole Telfer:

> Ms. Telfer: I'm going to object. We already have evidence that they are bullet impacts.
>
> The Court: I think this is getting beyond the probative value in relationship to the time it's taken.
>
> Mr. Lenhart: All right, your honor.
>
> The Court: That is an objection under 352 of the Evidence Code, ma'am?
>
> Ms. Telfer: Yes
>
> The Court: Thank you. Sustained. (Trial transcript, page 3235.)

Here the court invited the defense attorney to make the objections under Evidence Code 352, which he then sustained.

4–c. Prosecutor Dan Lenhart was introducing evidence that ammunition matching the .38 automatic and the 12-gauge shotgun used by defendants Jesus Araclio and Jose Yuriar was found in the rear home where defendant Raul Meza was living. This evidence was highly relevant since it tended to show that Meza supplied the guns to Araclio and Yuriar. When the defense finally objected, Judge Walker excluded any further testimony on this issue, stating that, "I think its probative value is exceeded by its unnecessary waste of time and extremely prejudicial under Evidence Code 352..." (Trial transcript, pages 3406 to 3407.)

4–d. On September 10, 1992, a prosecution witness was identifying drug paraphernalia from the crime scene. Suddenly the judge yelled that one of the baggies contained cocaine and that he wanted it out of his courtroom. Prosecutor Lenhart explained that the baggies contained a cutting agent and not cocaine. When Judge Walker asked, "Who's going to tell me that?" Lenhart replied, "Well, obviously he's [the witness] not because the court won't let him." (Trial transcript, pages 3430 to 3433.)

In a subsequent conference in Judge Walker's chambers outside the jury's presence, the judge stated that going through each piece of evidence was a waste of time. Prosecutor Lenhart argued that the jury was entitled to see the actual physical evidence, drawing the following response:

> *The Court: The jury is entitled to see what I choose to let them see and think we are wasting a lot of time. Frankly, counsel, I think you are stalling.*
>
> *Mr. Lenhart: I don't know what advantage I gain by doing that, your honor.*
>
> *The Court: I don't either unless you're just not prepared to put on your case.* (Trial transcript, pages 3432 to 3433.)

5. On September 11, 1992, Judge Walker disallowed the chemist's testimony that the 57 kilo packages in the van driven by Detective De La Rosa on June 21, 1990, contained cocaine. In a conference in chambers the judge asked, "What does this [the van with cocaine] have to do with these people?" Mr. Lenhart replied, "Your honor, if the court has been listening to all the testimony." After a lengthy discussion, Judge Walker ordered the chemist excused as a witness and stated, "We'll deal with him later." (Trial transcript, pages 3515 to 3526.)

6. September 14, 1992, the defense attorneys argued that evidence of conspiracy to commit robbery was totally lacking and that these conspiracy charges should be dismissed. In his comments from

the bench, outside the jury's presence, Judge Walker suggested that maybe Officer De La Rosa was the robber rather than the defendants:

> *Now, I don't think that it's all that clear and this is a tragic situation, whether or not Mr. De La Rosa, the victim of the criminal indictment in this case, is the victim or the perpetrator of a robbery is another inference; that he's trying to rob someone of $4 million, just as likely...*
>
> *I'm not going to say that because the guy is a cop acting undercover that his cover gives him any more right to steal money from drug dealers than he has the right to steal... they have the right to steal from him.* (Trial transcript, pages 3677 to 3678.)

After hearing Judge Walker's comments, Leslie De La Rosa left the courtroom in tears. She told the media that she was outraged that Judge Walker described her husband, a decorated police officer, as "on the same level, if not lower, as those who killed him."

Judge Walker eventually ruled that he would give the prosecution the opportunity to prove the existence of the conspiracy.

WITNESS DANNY HUGHES

The most dramatic testimony in the trial came from Detective Danny Hughes of the Fullerton Police Department who was called as a witness on September 21, 1992. At the time that he testified, he had been a police officer with the Fullerton Police Department for the previous seven years and had been in the Major Narcotics Unit since September 1989. When Detective Hughes joined the Major Narcotics Unit, it consisted of five officers, including Detective Tommy De La Rosa. De La Rosa became Hughes's friend, partner, and training officer. Hughes participated in over 25 investigations in which Detective De La Rosa worked in an undercover capacity. On almost every occasion, Hughes would monitor the wire that De La Rosa wore as an undercover officer.

Hughes covered a wide number of topics in his testimony. He described a previous undercover operation in which Detective De La Rosa went alone into a house. He discussed Gilberto Valenzuela, a paid informant for whom De La Rosa was the case agent. Valenzuela was considered a tested and reliable informant who received $46,500 in 1989 for services and information that he provided in various narcotics investigations.

Hughes testified to the events that began on June 11, 1990, that eventually led to the purported sale of 200 kilograms of cocaine on June 21, 1990. He testified that he attended a briefing on the early afternoon of June 21 that was conducted by Detective De La Rosa. Over 20 officers from five police agencies attended the briefing in which the game plan for the operation was discussed.

The undercover operation involved a reverse sting in which 200 kilograms of cocaine would be proffered for $4 million. The game plan was to surveil Detective De La Rosa to the McDonald's in Downey where he would meet someone. De La Rosa and the informant would then be followed by surveillance officers to a residence where the transaction was to take place. De La Rosa would give a visual arrest signal and/or a verbal arrest signal over his transmitter, and the surveilling officers would make entry at the residence. The visual arrest signal was Detective De La Rosa putting his hands through his hair, and the verbal signal would be him saying he was going to like this. Over 20 law enforcement officers were participating in the surveillance, including a helicopter unit.

Detective Hughes resumed the witness stand on September 23, 1992. He began his testimony on this date with his observations on the afternoon of June 21, 1990, during surveillance of the McDonald's in Downey where Detective De La Rosa, Jesus Pena, Jose Rodriguez, the informant and Luis Benitez had congregated. His testimony included his observation of the victory gesture given by Pena when De La Rosa drove off with only Jose Rodriguez in the van.

Prosecutors Daniel Lenhart and Ellen Berk wanted to introduce into evidence a statement by Detective De La Rosa at the briefing on June 21, 1990. At the briefing, De La Rosa stated that he intended to go with the informant to the location where only one person would be who had the money. He intended to look at the money, leave the location, and give the arrest signal. This was important evidence since the fact that De La Rosa went alone with Rodriguez to the residence indicated that the defendants wanted to isolate De La Rosa so he would be more vulnerable to a robbery of the cocaine and that they never intended to purchase the cocaine.

Judge Walker had been erratic and unpredictable in his evidentiary rulings, and he had often limited the evidence that the prosecutors wanted to present to the jury. Prosecutors Lenhart and Berk believed that De La Rosa's statement at the briefing was admissible because the California Supreme Court had ruled in the *Alcalde* case that a declaration of present intent to do a future act was not hearsay. However, Judge Walker was not familiar with the *Alcalde* case. At a heated conference in chambers, the prosecutors told the judge about the *Alcalde* decision but he declined to change his ruling. When the prosecutors expressed their incredulity at his decision, Judge Walker stated the following:

> *The Court: That's why I'm sitting up here and you are sitting down there. I have to make the decisions which sometimes distress counsel, and I'm going to do it in this case.* (Trial transcript, pages 4726 to 4727.)

Detective Hughes continued his testimony and discussed going to 8937 Arrington Avenue. Prosecutor Ellen Berk asked him, "And where was Detective De La Rosa when you saw him?" The defense attorneys objected to Hughes responding to the question and the following colloquy took place:

> *The Court: I'll allow you to object as it's not part of the direct, and we'll deal with that later.*
>
> *Det. Hughes: Deal with being fair in the case, your honor, being a little better.*
>
> *Ms. Telfer: I'm going to object.*
>
> *The Court: Mr. Hughes, the determination of what is fair is going to be determined by the court and by this jury, and your comments are out of order. If you wish to apologize to the jury, I'll give you this opportunity.*
>
> *Det. Hughes: I apologize to the jury that I think you're not being told the truth in this matter.*
>
> *Ms. Telfer: Objection, your honor.*
>
> *The Court: Mr. Hughes, I'm going to cite you for contempt.* (Trial transcript, pages 4733 to 4734.)

Both Judge Walker and Detective Hughes spoke in a quiet and low-key manner. Neither acted angrily during this exchange that served the basis for the contempt. Judge Walker later scheduled a contempt hearing to take place after the conclusion of the trial.

Detective Hughes continued his testimony without further incident. He identified the court order that he obtained for the release of kilos of cocaine to be used in the reverse sting operation. He testified that he hand-cuffed defendants Jesus Araclio and Jose Yuriar after they were removed from the Alvarado residence and escorted them to the curb. It was at this time that he learned of the death of his friend and partner Tommy De La Rosa. He began to cry and saw Araclio and Yuriar laughing while looking in his direction.

EXPERT TESTIMONY: DEAL OR NO DEAL?

The prosecution called Brian Murphy as an expert witness. Murphy had recently retired after 28 years with the Los Angeles Police Department. He spent the last 21 years in the Major Violators Section of the Narcotics Division investigating major violators involved in trafficking large quantities of narcotics. In his career he had been involved in the seizure of over 40,000 pounds of cocaine and over $30 million in United States currency. For many years, he was a supervisor in the Major Violators Section overseeing numerous narcotics investigations, with many involving undercover operations. For the past 15 years, he had been teaching all over the United States on the method of operations of major narcotics traffickers with his primary subject being undercover operations, undercover officer survival, and supervisory responsibility. He was familiar with the method of operation of major narcotics traffickers, specifically in the area of cocaine transactions.

In his testimony, Murphy identified various factors that would indicate that a legitimate narcotics transaction was taking place. First, and probably of the greatest importance, are both parties capable of handling the amount of narcotics or money involved in consummation of the narcotics transaction? Second, a major purchaser or distributor of narcotics has to establish his credibility or bona fides; often this is accomplished by transactions involving smaller amounts of narcotics before a major transaction takes place. Third is a security factor so that the exchange takes place at a neutral site or public place. Sometimes the parties will have additional people to witness the exchange to reduce the vulnerability of acting alone.

Detective Murphy also pointed out that the greater the amount of cocaine involved in the transaction, the more likely that the cocaine will be given to the buyer on consignment. The buyer normally does not have a large amount of money readily available, especially when the transaction involves millions of dollars. A consignment deal normally takes place when the parties have had prior dealings and established their credentials.

None of the defense attorneys cross-examined Brian Murphy. His testimony was important since it allowed the prosecutors to argue to the jury that what started off as a legitimate narcotics transaction became a robbery or rip-off when Jose Rodriguez entered the picture. Suddenly the factors indicating a legitimate transaction no longer existed as the amount of cocaine to be purchased quickly increased to 200 kilograms, and the buyers were able to isolate Detective De La Rosa.

DEFENSE CASE: RAUL MEZA

On September 29, 1992, the defense began the presentation of its evidence. After some preliminary witnesses, defense attorney Carole Telfer called her client, defendant Raul Meza, as a witness. He testified as follows:

He was 51 years of age. He was the owner of the Mazatlan Bar on East Rosecrans Boulevard in the city of Compton. In 1980 or '81, he met co-defendant Jesus Araclio at the bar, and they became good friends.

Meza occasionally saw a person named Efrain Costello at the bar, and he believed Efrain was dealing narcotics. In 1980 or '81, he saw Jose Rodriguez and Efrain together at the bar. Meza was afraid of Efrain because he believed Efrain had killed his (Meza's) brother in 1985. In fact, he stopped going to the Mazatlan Bar after his brother's death, and someone else ran the bar when he was not there.

In January 1990, he and co-defendant Jose Yuriar moved into the rear house at 8937 Arrington Avenue where they lived until their arrest on June 21, 1990. After the tenant in the front house moved out, they would sometimes sleep overnight in the vacant residence. Meza was a user of cocaine, and he put curtains on the windows of the rear house so he would not be seen using or packaging cocaine.

In late April or early May 1990, Meza learned that Efrain was trying to contact him. Meza met Efrain and gave him the Arrington address and his telephone number. In early June, Efrain came to the Arrington address with a suitcase that he left at the residence.

In mid-June 1990, Efrain came to the Arrington address with Jose Rodriguez and told Meza that he wanted to rent the houses to do a dope deal. Meza agreed and Efrain and Rodriguez left the location. According to Meza, Efrain returned by himself to the Arrington address and placed in the rear house a black plastic bag filled with money.

On the morning of June 21, 1990, Meza went with his neighbor Enrique Alvarez to the Huntington Park court to take care of some outstanding traffic tickets. After returning to the Arrington address, Meza received three phone calls in rapid succession from Efrain. In the third phone call, a highly agitated Efrain stated that he would be over in ten or fifteen minutes. Jesus Araclio and Jose Yuriar were at the residence during the phone calls, and Meza told them to go to the front house and to give him some help if it was needed. Yuriar was armed with a 12-gauge shotgun that belonged to Meza.

In the meantime, Meza took possession of a .380 automatic in the rear house and placed it in his waistband and put on a jacket. He remained by himself in the rear house. A few moments later a van arrived, and Jose Rodriguez exited the passenger side and the driver also exited. They walked to the rear house and entered. The driver of the van asked, where was the gentleman with the money? Meza responded that there was no man with the money there. The driver of the van got angry, and he and Rodriguez began fighting. The driver was reaching for a gun from his waist area, while Rodriguez was attempting to retrieve a weapon from his crotch area. Meza then pulled out his gun and fired two shots in the direction of the two combatants. He saw blood on the left rear shoulder area of the driver. Meza ran out the door and heard four or five shots. He jumped over the fence that separated the house from the adjoining apartment buildings and heard more shots. He threw the gun in a trash bin and took off the jacket that he was wearing. A few moments later he was arrested by police officers converging on the area.

When asked by his attorney why he shot the gun, he responded as follows:

Q. Why did you shoot the gun?

A. To run. I was afraid.

Q. And why did you need to shoot the gun in order to run?

A. I don't know why. When they tried to take out their weapons, I took mine out as well.

Q. What was going through your mind at that time? What were you thinking?

A. That they were going to fight with me to kill me.

Q. And why did you think that, if you know?

A. Because I had seen the weapon on the man before getting to the house. He had it like this. And the shirt was tight and you could plainly see the weapon. (Trial transcript, page 5471.)

[Authors' commentary: Raul Meza's testimony hurt the defense more than it helped. His testimony corroborated the prosecutor's reconstruction of the events at the time of the shooting and who fired the shots from which weapon. Meza even admitted firing two shots at Tommy De La Rosa, and his testimony did not establish a legal defense, such as self-defense.]

DEFENSE CASE: JOSE YURIAR

On October 13, 1992, defense attorney Javier Ramirez called his client Jose Yuriar to testify in his own behalf. He testified to the events of June 21, 1990, as follows:

On June 21, 1990, he was living at 8937 Arrington Avenue with Raul Meza. In the early morning, Meza left with Enrique Alvarado to go to court. Later that morning, he walked to the store with Jesus Araclio, who had slept at the front house the night before.

Meza returned from court with Enrique Alvarado. Shortly after returning, Meza received three phone calls in rapid succession that Meza stated were from Efrain. After the third phone call, Meza was visibly upset and stated that Efrain was coming over and may start a fight. Meza asked for a pistol, and Yuriar gave him a .380 automatic that was in a dresser drawer in the rear house. Meza told Yuriar to go to the front house and help if Efrain was going to start a fight.

Yuriar went to the front house armed with a shotgun. He did not re-member whether Meza gave him the shotgun or told him that it was in the front house. Araclio was also in the front house armed with a pistol.

A few minutes after entering the front house, Yuriar heard the sound of a car door closing, and then saw two persons walking along the driveway toward the rear house. The two persons entered the rear house and disap-peared from view. Then he heard a yell or screams and shots fired. He then saw Raul Meza run from the house and then heard some more shots. He saw a second person come out of the rear house and point a gun in his direction. He picked up the shotgun that was next to him, pumped a shot in it, and fired a shot through the open door. When he fired the shot, the man who pointed the gun was no longer there. Araclio fired some shots from his pistol, but Yuriar didn't know if he fired before Araclio.

After firing their weapons, Yuriar and Araclio ran out the back door of the front house. They went to Enrique Alvarado's house carrying their weapons. He knocked on the front door which was opened by Mrs. Alvarado. Enrique Alvarado was also inside the house. Mrs. Alvarado placed the guns beneath the mattress in the bedroom. A few minutes later he heard the screeching of cars stopping and someone knocked on the door. Enrique Alvarado opened the door, and police officers entered the residence and placed him and Araclio under arrest.

Yuriar admitted lying to the police when he was interrogated after his arrest, but he claimed that he was beaten by the police before he made any statements.

DEFENSE CASE: FREDERICO MARRIOTT

Defendant Frederico Marriott also testified at the trial. He was charged with murder as well as conspiracy to purchase cocaine for sale. He was not involved in the killing of Tommy De La Rosa other than helping broker a narcotics transaction between De La Rosa and Jose Rodriguez. The prose-cution theory for the murder charges against Marriott was that he was part of a conspiracy involving the purchase of 200 kilograms of cocaine for $4 million and that a murder was a reasonable and foreseeable consequence of such a conspiracy.

In his testimony, Marriott did his best to distance himself from the murder charge. He testified that he was involved in introducing De La Rosa to Jose Rodriguez, but he was not involved in the negotiations between them. He was hoping to receive a $500 brokerage fee for helping to set up the transaction.

He testified that he did not know the three co-defendants in the case — Jesus Araclio, Raul Meza and Jose Yuriar.

Marriott's defense strategy was to admit his participation in the cocaine conspiracy and to deny any knowledge or involvement in a plan to rob or murder the person in possession of a large amount of cocaine. The strategy worked, since Judge Walker dismissed the murder charges against Marriott for insufficiency of the evidence before the case was submitted to the jury.

CONCLUSION OF TRIAL, INSTRUCTIONS

Jesus Araclio was the only defendant who did not testify. Both sides rested on October 26, 1992. On the morning of October 27, the attorneys met with Judge Walker to discuss the instructions to be given to the jury.

On October 27, before instructing the jury, Judge Walker dismissed the murder charges against Frederico Marriott, stating that, "The Court is just unable in any logic to state that in a conspiracy to purchase cocaine a robbery is a reasonable and natural consequence to follow in any such event, and I decline to do so." (Trial transcript, page 7988.)

Judge Walker read the instructions to the jury, concluding with two special instructions directed at Detective Danny Hughes and prosecutor Daniel Lenhart. First, the instruction involving Detective Hughes:

During the course of the trial, Officer Dan Hughes from the Fullerton Police Department, when testifying, referred to the murder of Officer De La Rosa after he was ordered by the Court not to do so. He also intimated that the truth of the case was being withheld from the jury.

Whether or not a killing amounts to murder is a question of fact and law for the jury to decide. Witnesses cannot testify as to legal conclusions. The court has the responsibility of deciding what evidence is relevant to the issues in this case, what evidence is trustworthy and reliable, and what evidence should be admitted.

Officer Hughes's conduct in this regard was an attempt to prejudice this jury, and you should not use his remarks in evaluating the guilt or innocence of any defendant in this case. However, you may consider his conduct in evaluating the motive, bias and interest of this officer as it relates to his credibility in this case.

The special instruction read to the jury regarding prosecutor Daniel Lenhart was the following:

When questioning defendant Raul Meza, Deputy District Attorney Lenhart asked Mr. Meza if he had been arrested for the possession of drugs for sale on August 31st, 1978. At that time, this Court sustained an objection and advised you that arrests had no relevance. At this time, I am advising you there is no evidence of any such arrest and the prosecutor's questioning amounted to an attempt to prejudice you against the defendant. Therefore, you must disregard that improper question and disregard any insinuations to be made therefrom in deciding the issues in this case.

This special instruction was given just before Lenhart's argument to the jury. Judge Walker must have known that such an instruction could lower Lenhart's stature in the eyes of the jury and reduce his effectiveness and credibility in his argument to the jury.

ARGUMENTS AND VERDICT

The attorneys presented their closing arguments to the jury on October 28 and 29, 1992. Daniel Lenhart gave the People's opening argument to the jury on the morning of October 28. Since the prosecution has the burden of proof, Lenhart gave the final argument to the jury on the afternoon of October 29. In this argument, he gave his opinion as to who fired the shot that killed Tommy De La Rosa:

But you will have this bullet to look at and to make that evaluation whether or not that would cause a hole the same size or just slightly larger than the entrance hole on the neck. And I think that you are going to have to come to the conclusion that was not this 9-mm round that did it or any hollow point 9-mm round that would do that. It was in fact a 380 round, the 380 round that was fired by Raul Meza that blew out Tommy De La Rosa's heart and ended his life. Tommy was shot. He was shot in the back, and he was shot in the back by Raul Meza. (Trial transcript, page 8446.)

In other words, Jose Rodriguez was firing a 9-mm automatic with hollow point bullets that would have caused a massive exit wound. Since the exit wound was the same size or slightly larger than the entrance wound, the fatal shot came from Meza's 380 automatic.

The jury began its deliberation on the morning of Friday, October 30. On the afternoon of November 3, 1992, on its third day of deliberations, the jury reached a verdict.

The jury convicted defendants Jesus Araclio, Jose Yuriar, and Raul Meza of first degree murder as charged in count one and of attempted robbery as charged in count two. The special circumstance allegations that the murder was committed during an attempted robbery was found true.

Defendant Frederico Marriott was found guilty of conspiracy to purchase cocaine for sale as charged in count three with a special allegation that the amount of cocaine exceeded 100 pounds found true.

Since defendants Araclio, Yuriar, and Meza were convicted of first degree murder with special circumstances, they could receive a death sentence or a sentence of life in prison without the possibility of parole. Judge Walker ordered the jury to return on Friday, November 6, 1992, for the penalty phase of the case.

Defendant Marriott's sentencing was set for November 17, 1992.

PENALTY PHASE

Under the California death penalty statute, the prosecution at the penalty phase can introduce (a) prior criminal activity of the defendant, and (b) victim impact testimony.

The penalty phase for defendants Jesus Araclio, Raul Meza, and Jose Yuriar began on November 6, 1992, before Judge Walker. The same jury that convicted these defendants would decide whether they would receive a penalty of death or of life in prison without the possibility of parole.

The prosecution called one witness at the penalty phase. Sergeant Joseph Klein was a police sergeant for the Fullerton Police Department. He had been a police officer for the City of Fullerton. Prior to Detective De La Rosa's death, he had known him for ten years. De La Rosa joined the Fullerton Police Department in 1980 and worked assignments in uniform patrol, uniform crime scene investigator, S.W.A.T. team, and the Narcotics Bureau. The witness ran the S.W.A.T. team and De La Rosa was his team leader and entry person. The witness was later in charge of the Narcotics Bureau and brought De La Rosa into the Bureau in 1986. De La Rosa was the primary undercover officer, respected nationwide for his undercover skills.

At the time of his death, the 43-year-old Tommy De La Rosa was married to his wife, Leslie, for seven years. They had a baby girl who was a year and a half in age at the time of his death. He had two children from a previous marriage — a 19-year-old daughter, Tracy, and a 17-year-old daughter, Nicole. Both daughters had babies under one year of age at the time of De La Rosa's death. De La Rosa was survived by his mother and father, and he had three sisters and two brothers.

In 1983, after being a police officer for only three years, he was nominated as outstanding employee of the year for the City of Fullerton by the Chief of Police. In 1984, he was selected by his peers as the outstanding police officer of the year. In 1989, he was selected as the outstanding Latino police officer of the year. In 1990, he was honored posthumously as the outstanding narcotic officer of the year and the outstanding police officer of the year in the Fullerton Police Department. He was awarded in 1990 as the narcotics officer of the year by the California Narcotic Officers' Association.

The jury was not told about Tommy De La Rosa's military service. He had a distinguished military career, having served two combat tours in Vietnam as a United States Marine. He received a Purple Heart for being wounded during combat.

The attorneys for the three defendants called family members, friends, and other associates to give positive testimony about their clients. On the morning of November 12, 1992, the jury was instructed on the law and retired to deliberate the penalty for the defendants.

At 3:00 p.m. on November 12, 1992, the jury, after just three hours of deliberation, returned a verdict of life imprisonment without the possibility of parole for defendants Jesus Araclio, Raul Meza, and Jose Yuriar.

The date for sentencing was set for January 4, 1993.

SENTENCING

On January 27, 1993, the three defendants convicted of first degree murder with special circumstances appeared before Judge J. Kimball Walker to make motions for a new trial and for sentencing.

Judge Walker denied the defense requests for a new trial and sentenced Jesus Araclio, Raul Meza, and Jose Yuriar to life imprisonment without the possibility of parole.

During the sentencing hearing, Judge Walker used unusually harsh and critical language in blasting the prosecution and the police. The judge said that the police lied and prosecutors withheld evidence and used a paid informant in their "zeal" to obtain a conviction in the case. Judge Walker blasted his critics for what he termed their "intimidation tactics". He stated, "They were trying to intimidate me into ruling in favor of the prosecution. It's just shocking in the worst, worst way." The judge stated that the trial amounted to a "sophisticated lynching".

In rejecting the defense motions for a new trial, Judge Walker stated that, "It gets close to a sham, and a sham ought to produce a new trial, but I don't think it's there." He stated that there was sufficient evidence to support the conviction in the case.

Outside the courtroom, Detective Danny Hughes stated that Judge Walker's tirade showed that he was biased and against the police. He also stated that the prosecutors were correct in trying to remove him from the case. During the trial, Detective Hughes had been cited in contempt by Judge Walker, but the contempt action was dismissed when Hughes later apologized to the court.

During the sentencing hearing, Judge Walker sentenced Frederico Marriott to a six-year prison term, rejecting a 15-year sentence recommended by the prosecutors.

EPILOGUE

Detective Dan Hughes remained with the Fullerton Police Department and rose through the ranks to become the Acting Chief of the Fullerton

Police Department in January 2012. In January 2013, he became the full-time Chief of the Fullerton Police Department.

Deputy District Attorney Daniel Lenhart continued in the District Attorney's Office in several supervisory positions until his retirement from that office in 2000 to become the second in command of the Long Beach City Prosecutor's Office. He permanently retired in 2006 after more than 40 years of public service.

Chief Hughes has taken action so that Tommy De La Rosa's sacrifice and service to his country and community will not be forgotten. In 2013, one of the Fullerton Police Department police cars, Unit 811, was dedicated to the memory of Detective De La Rosa. A banner honoring De La Rosa has been on display down the street from the Fullerton Police Department. His name is on a "Wall of Honor" in the Fullerton Police Department, and the interchange of the 5 and 91 Freeways has been designated the "Fullerton Police Detective Tommy De La Rosa Memorial Interchange."

LESSONS LEARNED

Narcotics offenses comprise a large percentage of the cases in the criminal justice system. Many large police agencies have officers assigned specifically to process the routine narcotics cases generated by their departments. These officers act as court liaison officers for their departments by handling the paperwork created by the arrests, submitting the cases for filing to the appropriate prosecuting agency, and arranging for officers/witnesses to be available for proceedings in court.

The two major law enforcement entities in Los Angeles County — the Los Angeles Police Department and the Los Angeles County Sheriff's Department — each have a large contingent of officers assigned exclusively to the investigations of major narcotics offenses. Some mid-size police departments in Los Angeles County also contain narcotics units that investigate major narcotics cases. Some smaller departments assign officers to multi-agency task forces that investigate major narcotics.

Narcotics officers must become proficient in certain procedures and techniques that are common in narcotics investigations. These include the preparation and service of search warrants; obtaining wiretap orders and monitoring the conversations over phones pursuant to the wiretap orders;

using and handling informants; the surveillance of narcotics suspects; and conducting undercover operations in which a police officer poses as a buyer or seller of narcotics.

Detective Tommy De La Rosa was murdered during an undercover narcotics operation. Precautions were taken to provide security and protection for Detective De La Rosa. At 1:00 p.m. on June 21, 1990, De La Rosa conducted a briefing to the approximately 25 officers from various agencies who would provide surveillance and monitor his movements for the transaction that was scheduled to take place later that afternoon.

When Detective De La Rosa and Jose Rodriguez left the McDonald's parking lot on the afternoon of June 21, 1990, to consummate the narcotics transaction, several elements were in play to provide security and protection for Detective De La Rosa. He had on his person a concealed voice transmitter that was being monitored by surveilling officers. He had a handgun concealed in his waistband. Unmarked police vehicles were following his movements. A police helicopter containing a pilot and an observer were monitoring Detective De La Rosa and communicating his movements to the ground units.

The monitoring of Detective De La Rosa became ineffective when he entered the cul-de-sac in his van with Jose Rodriguez and became separated from the surveillance and monitoring units. He had become isolated and walked into an ambush. Perhaps Detective De La Rosa continued on with the undercover operation and took some risks since he knew he was covered by over 20 officers providing for his security and protection.

The lesson to be learned is that many activities performed by law enforcement officers can be very dangerous. An undercover operation can be a dangerous activity for the undercover officer, especially when a large amount of money and/or narcotics is involved. It is not possible to eliminate all the risks and dangers in the activities performed by police officers; sometimes a tragedy results, including the death of an officer. The training that officers receive involving officer safety and awareness increase the officer's chances of survival; it does not eliminate the risk and dangers to officers that could result in a death in the line of duty.

FULLERTON
POLICE DEPARTMENT

End of watch June 21, 1990

SENIOR OFFICER TOMMY DE LA ROSA

Date of Birth: May 13, 1947
Date Appointed: September 26, 1980
End of Watch: June 21, 1990

Tommy De La Rosa with daughter Ashley

Fullerton Police Chief Dan Hughes with Tommy De La Rosa's
daughter Ashley and wife Leslie in June 2015 commemorating
the memory of Tommy De La Rosa 25 years after his death.

Aerial view of 8937
Arrington Avenue,
Downey

Note the silver Chevy
van in driveway

**Patio area separating front and rear houses
at 8937 Arrington Avenue**

Body of Jose Rodriguez in rear house

- 1 and 2 are empty .380 shells
- 3 are blood stains
- 5 is an empty 9mm shell

CHAPTER 6

Deputy David March

Los Angeles County Sheriff's Department

"Changing the Law to Get a Killer"

INTRODUCTION (COMMENTARY OF STEVE COOLEY)

On April 29, 2002, I was notified that a Los Angeles County Deputy Sheriff had been shot and killed in the city of Irwindale. Shortly thereafter, I learned that it was David March, an individual I had met about a year earlier, as he had attended a fundraiser in support of my candidacy for District Attorney. His brother-in-law, James "Kimo" Hildreth, was a District Attorney investigator who had brought him to that event.

I felt that it was important to go to the scene of the murder and did so later that afternoon. A modest but moving memorial consisting of flowers, candles, etc., was in place near the blood stains on the street.

A few days later, I attended the funeral for Deputy David March. I learned that he was born in March 1969 and that he was 32 years of age when he died. He was raised in the Santa Clarita Valley where he lived with his wife and daughter. After he graduated from Canyon High School, he worked security at Magic Mountain and worked briefly at his father's business. He had always wanted to be a peace officer, but his initial application to the Sheriff's Department was rejected. The mayor of Santa Clarita was Bob Kellar, a retired LAPD officer, and he took David March under his wing and tutored him for his second application to the Sheriff's Department. This time he was accepted by the Sheriff's Department and did well at the Sheriff's Academy. He worked in the County Jail for four-and-a-half years and then was assigned to the Temple Station where he was a patrol officer until his death.

The procession after the funeral to the grave site was several miles long. I was moved by the sheer number of people along the procession route holding flags and signs of support. At the funeral, I stood next to his father, John March, who later became a dear friend. I promised him that we would not forgive, we would not forget, we would not give up.

John March later told me that at the funeral he observed a young male

Hispanic standing next to the coffin weeping. John wanted to talk to him but was unable to because of the crowd. Six years later, John was at the yearly memorial at the site of the killing and was handed a cell phone by a deputy. The person on the phone said, "You don't know me, but I was at Dave's funeral. Dave arrested me eight years ago, he was at my trial, he visited me in jail, and he was there when I got out. He told me that I needed to straighten out my life, and he helped me do that. Now I am a youth pastor helping kids stay away from drugs and gangs." John thanked him and broke into tears of pride as he told his wife what the call was about.

JORGE ARROYO-GARCIA — EARLY YEARS AND CRIMINAL HISTORY

Jorge Arroyo-Garcia was born on November 3, 1976, in the Morelia, Michoacan area of Mexico. He entered the United States illegally in 1990. His last known school education was the seventh grade at McKinley Intermediate School in Redwood City, California.

Garcia was arrested as a juvenile on February 25, 1994, by the Drug Enforcement Administration. He attempted to exchange three pounds of methamphetamine for ten pounds of hydriotic acid, used to manufacture methamphetamine. He was convicted and committed to the California Youth Authority (CYA). At the time of his commitment to CYA, he identified his older brother, Hector Garcia-Arroyo, as his legal guardian and also named several aunts and uncles in the United States.

In the mid-1990s, Garcia lived with his brother, Hector Garcia-Arroyo, in Redwood City, California. In 1996, Garcia went to Baldwin Park in Los Angeles County, where he moved in with a friend. He remained in the Los Angeles area until April 30, 2002, when he fled to Mexico after the shooting death of Los Angeles County Deputy Sheriff David March. While in Los Angeles, Jorge Arroyo-Garcia was involved in the following criminal activity:

June 4, 2000, Arrest for Weapon Possession

On June 4, 2000, at approximately 1:20 a.m., Officer Batres of the El Monte Police Department was on patrol duty at the Valley Mall. He observed about ten to fifteen males standing near several vehicles from where he could hear loud music. Several males got into a white Chevy two-door pickup truck, which drove away from the mall. Officer Batres could hear loud music coming from the vehicle, which was in violation of the California Vehicle Code. He followed the vehicle and noticed that the truck's windows were tinted, which was also a California Vehicle Code violation.

Using his siren and loudspeaker, Officer Batres initiated a traffic stop. As he was making the traffic stop, he observed several of the occupants moving about inside the truck. Since he was working a one-man patrol car and since the detained vehicle contained multiple occupants, Officer Batres requested over the police radio for backup officers to respond to the location.

There were five male Hispanic young adults in the truck, with three occupants in the front cab of the truck and two seated in the rear passenger area. After backup officers arrived, Officer Batres approached the driver of the vehicle and asked the driver in both Spanish and English for permission to search the truck. The driver consented to a search, and the vehicle was searched pursuant to the consent. One of the backup officers found a Tech 9 assault-type weapon and a magazine containing 19 rounds wrapped in a T-shirt under the middle portion of the rear seat. Jorge Garcia-Arroyo was seated in the back seat directly above the area where the weapon was located. He told the officers that his name was Daniel Garcia.

Since the officers could not ascertain who was in possession of the gun, all five occupants of the truck were arrested and transported to the El Monte Police Department. At the station, each arrestee was interviewed. Jorge Arroyo-Garcia (whom the officers still believed was named Daniel Garcia) stated that he was the person who had purchased the weapon for $20 since it looked good, was cheap, and he didn't know if it was stolen. He further stated that the gun was wrapped in a T-shirt, and he placed it in the rear area of the truck.

By June 6, 2000, two days after his arrest, Jorge Arroyo-Garcia's true name had been determined. On that date, the El Monte Area Office of the District Attorney's Office charged him with one felony count of possessing a concealed weapon in a vehicle and one misdemeanor count of falsely representing himself to an officer. The 23-year-old Garcia was represented by the Public Defender's Office and remained in custody on $25,000 bail.

On June 23, 2000, before Judge Peters Meeks, Jorge Arroyo-Garcia entered a plea of *nolo contendere*, or no contest, to count one of possessing a concealed firearm in a vehicle. A plea of *nolo contendere* means that the defendant is not contesting the charges and, for purposes of the criminal case, is basically the same as a plea of guilty to the charge. Many defendants prefer a plea of *nolo contendere* because then they don't have to admit that they committed the offense. Judge Meeks sentenced Garcia to formal probation for three years with various fines and conditions including spending 364 days in county jail. The count two misdemeanor charge was dismissed.

With credits reducing his custody time, Garcia was released from county jail well before completing the full 364 days. However, he remained on formal probation, which required that he report to his probation officer. The Probation Department reported to the court that Garcia had deserted probation and, on March 21, 2001, his probation was revoked and a no-bail bench warrant was issued for his arrest.

Garcia was never arrested on the bench warrant. Apparently, he did not like being in custody, since he told several persons that he would kill a police officer rather than go to jail again.

November 18, 2001, Assault with Firearm

In 2001, Jorge Arroyo-Garcia was involved in a relationship with Maricruz Contreras Sanchez, and he moved into the home at 14344 Olive Street in Baldwin Park, California that she shared with her mother, sister, and brother-in-law. The relationship came to an end, and Garcia was forced to move out of the house. On November 18, 2001, Garcia telephoned Maricruz at her home and threatened her. She hung up the phone, and Garcia called back. This time Maricruz's brother, Refugio Contreras Sanchez, answered the telephone. Refugio told Garcia that Maricruz had nothing to say to him and hung up the phone. Garcia called again and told Refugio that he was coming over.

At approximately 7:52 p.m. on November 18, 2001, Refugio was walking in front of 14344 Olive Street when Garcia drove by the residence. Garcia was alone in a white Nissan Sentra and fired multiple shots at Refugio with a blue steel handgun. Garcia then drove off. Refugio was not injured in the shooting.

February 16, 2002, Assault with Firearm

On February 16, 2002, at approximately 8:07 p.m., Refugio Contreras Sanchez was driving through the Olive Square Market parking lot adjacent to his sister's residence at 14344 Olive Street. A black Nissan Maxima pulled slowly alongside Refugio Sanchez's vehicle. Jorge Arroyo-Garcia was driving the black Nissan, and he fired numerous shots from a blue steel handgun at Sanchez and his vehicle. Bullets struck his car, but Sanchez was not injured.

Refugio Sanchez reported both shooting incidents from November 18, 2001, and February 16, 2002, to the Baldwin Park Police Department. Detectives took photographs of Sanchez's bullet-stricken car from the February 16 incident.

As of April 28, 2002, Jorge Arroyo-Garcia had not been arrested or charged with the shootings at Refugio Contreras Sanchez, as the matter was still under investigation.

It is unknown whether Jorge Arroyo-Garcia knew that he was being investigated for shooting at Refugio Sanchez. However, he routinely carried a 9-mm semi-automatic handgun. Garcia also told several friends and associates that he would kill a policeman, if necessary, to avoid going to jail. This could be a deadly scenario for any law enforcement officer who might come in contact with Garcia.

THE SHOOTING DEATH OF DEPUTY DAVID MARCH

April 29, 2002 – Early Morning

During 2002, Jorge Arroyo-Garcia frequently drove the 1989 black Nissan Maxima bearing California license number 4BCZ512. The vehicle was registered to Martina Murillo, who was the wife of Jose Bustos Cabrera. Both Garcia and Cabrera were born and raised in the Morelia, Michoacan region of Mexico, and they were the best of friends. Garcia often slept in a white van at the rear of Jose Cabrera's residence.

On the evening of April 28, 2002, a male named Juan Gabriel Vasquez saw Garcia driving the black Nissan Maxima. He also observed that Garcia was carrying a black semi-automatic pistol in his waistband.

On the morning of April 29, 2002, at about 5:45 a.m., Jorge Arroyo-Garcia drove Carolina Rocha to work in the black Nissan. Approximately 90 minutes later, Garcia sat with Alfonso Castanon in the black Nissan for about 20 minutes in front of the Grand Home Inn on Valley Boulevard in El Monte. During this time Castanon observed a 9-mm handgun in Garcia's waistband. Garcia drove away from the Grand Home Inn at approximately 8:30 a.m. Between 9:00 a.m. and 10:30 a.m., he had breakfast at Cabrera's Family Restaurant, located at 625 East Live Oak Avenue in Arcadia. He was served breakfast by an acquaintance, Juan Gabriel Vasquez. At approximately 10:30 a.m., Garcia left the restaurant alone, driving the black Nissan.

Shooting Death of Deputy David March

On the morning of April 29, 2002, David William March was a peace officer working as an on-duty, uniformed patrol deputy for the Los Angeles County Sheriff's Department, assigned to patrol the Temple Station area in a one-man marked patrol car. Shortly after 10:30 a.m., Deputy March conducted a traffic stop of Garcia driving the black Nissan. This traffic stop occurred at the south curb of the eastbound traffic lanes at 242 East Live Oak Avenue in Irwindale. This location was just about a mile east of Cabrera's Family Restaurant at 625 East Live Oak Avenue in Arcadia.

At 10:38 a.m., as he was initiating the traffic stop, Deputy March entered the license plate number "4BCZ512" on the mobile display terminal (MDT) in his patrol car. Deputy March then approached the black Nissan on foot.

Jorge Arroyo-Garcia emerged from the black Nissan and fired five times at Deputy March with his 9-mm semi-automatic handgun. Deputy March was fatally wounded. Garcia immediately fled in the black Nissan.

Several civilians observed the shooting of Deputy March and the suspect leave in a black Nissan. Some civilians came to the assistance of Deputy March. One civilian, at 10:39 a.m., activated the emergency button on the MDT in Deputy March's patrol car.

Jorge Garcia – Flight to Mexico

After fleeing the scene of the murder of Deputy David March, Jorge Garcia abandoned the black Nissan on the street in front of 14143 Chilcot Street in Baldwin Park. This was on a cul-de-sac approximately 2.5 miles from the location of the traffic stop and murder of Deputy March. Witness Sonia Martinez lived directly across the street from where the black Nissan was abandoned. She observed Garcia, who was alone, park and then exit the vehicle. Garcia then walked to Baldwin Park Boulevard and out of her sight. When interviewed by investigators, she positively identified a photograph of Jorge Garcia as depicting the person she saw exit the black Nissan.

At approximately 11:00 a.m., Garcia arrived on foot at the Buenos Aires Store at 14354 Olive Street in Baldwin Park. This store was situated in a strip mall approximately half a mile from the location where Garcia had abandoned the black Nissan. *(Garcia had been a frequent customer of this store when he lived with Maricruz Contreras Sanchez, their house being a short distance from the Buenos Aires Store.)*

Garcia made a telephone call from the Buenos Aires Store to Jose Bustos Cabrera, who was the co-owner of the black Nissan with his wife Martina Murillo. According to Cabrera, Garcia called him at home and said that the black Nissan had broken down and that he needed a ride. Alberto Reyes was at Cabrera's home when Garcia made the telephone call. Cabrera and Reyes drove to the strip mall in Cabrera's green Infiniti and picked up Garcia there. Garcia was shaken, crying, and perspiring. They drove him to the residence of Cabrera's cousin, Homero Mora Cabrera. During the drive, Garcia told Jose Cabrera and Alberto Reyes that he had shot and killed a policeman. Garcia stated that he had been stopped by the police because of the broken front lights of the Nissan Maxima. Garcia had exited the car when the officer approached him. The officer asked for a driver's license, but Garcia did not have one. When the officer began to search him, Garcia used his left arm to push the officer away and used his right arm to pull his gun from his waistband. He shot the officer several times and shot him again after he fell to the ground. He then fled in the car and abandoned it in a cul-de-sac street in Baldwin Park. Cabrera and Reyes observed that Garcia was still carrying his black 9-mm gun in his waistband.

Garcia asked Cabrera if he had any money. Because Garcia was armed and acting emotionally, Cabrera gave him his wallet. Garcia took $500 from the wallet and returned it to him. Garcia was dropped off at the residence of Homero Mora Cabrera, and Jose Cabrera and Alberto Reyes drove away from the location.

Garcia remained at the home of Homero Mora Cabrera for several hours. Arrangements were made for taxi transportation of Garcia to Tijuana, Mexico for $200. A taxi driver picked up Garcia in front of Homero Cabrera's residence at approximately 9:40 p.m. on April 29, 2002. Garcia was driven to the international border where he was dropped off at a taxi stand on the Mexican side of the border.

INVESTIGATION OF THE MURDER
OF DEPUTY DAVID MARCH

Sergeants Kenneth Gallatin and Steven Katz of the Homicide Bureau of the Los Angeles County Sheriff's Department were the officers in charge of the investigation of the murder of Deputy David March. At approximately 11:30 a.m. on April 29, 2002, they arrived at the scene of the shooting at 242 East Live Oak Street in Irwindale to take command of the investigation. Numerous law enforcement officers participated in the investigation that was overseen by Sergeants Gallatin and Katz. What follows is a general overview of the investigation that was conducted:

Deputy David March's black and white patrol car was at the crime scene. In the street by the patrol car there were five spent 9-mm shell casings. Also on the street was the front panel to the ballistic vest that was bloodstained. This vest had been removed by responding deputy sheriffs and paramedics at the scene to treat Deputy March for the wounds that he had received.

Deputy March's patrol car was equipped with a mobile digital terminal (MDT). This device is a computer that allows a user to access different data bases to check registration information on vehicle license plate numbers of stolen or wanted cars, driver's license status, warrants, and stolen property or guns. The MDT is also used to dispatch calls, i.e., to direct deputy sheriffs to specific locations where citizens have requested their assistance.

The last entry made in the MDT of Deputy March's patrol car was to check the status of California license plate number 4BCZ512. This license plate was for a 1989 four-door Nissan Maxima registered to Martina Murillo at 918 Huntington Drive, Apartment K, City of Duarte, County of Los Angeles.

Officers went to the Huntington Drive location and learned that Martina Murillo had moved to 5019 Heleo Street, Temple City. Officers then went to the Heleo Street location. At this time in the investigation, any person with access to the Nissan Maxima was a possible suspect or person of interest in the shooting death of Deputy March.

Investigators located Martina Murillo and spoke to her on the evening of April 29, 2002. She stated that on the evening of April 28, 2002, her husband, Jose Bustos Cabrera, had loaned their Nissan Maxima to Jorge Arroyo-Garcia. The following day Garcia told her husband that he had shot and killed a police officer while driving their car.

The Nissan Maxima had been parked in front of 14143 Chilcot Street in Baldwin Park. On the afternoon of April 29, 2002, a Parking Enforcement Officer had cited the vehicle for illegal parking during street sweeping hours. When the officer heard that investigators were looking for the Nissan Maxima, she remembered the citation and the vehicle and told the investigators. The Nissan Maxima was located and impounded on May 1, 2002. It was examined by forensic experts who removed a drop of blood from its left rear tire. Laboratory analysis determined that the blood on the left rear tire of the Nissan Maxima was the blood of Deputy David March.

A detective from the Baldwin Park Police Department recognized that the Nissan Maxima had been identified as the vehicle involved in the attempted murder of Refugio Contreras Sanchez on February 16, 2002. Sanchez had identified Jorge Arroyo-Garcia as the shooter on February 16, 2002, as well as another shooting incident on November 18, 2001, in which Garcia had previously shot at him.

Within a few days after the death of Deputy David March, the investigation had clearly established that Jorge Arroyo-Garcia was responsible for the murder. However, the investigation had also established that Garcia had fled to Mexico. As long as Garcia remained in Mexico, he would not be tried or punished for the cold-blooded murder of Deputy David William March.

EXTRADITION

With Jorge Arroyo-Garcia having fled to Mexico, the Los Angeles County District Attorney's Office initiated the process of returning him to Los Angeles County to be prosecuted for the murder of Deputy David March.

The extradition of criminal suspects from one country to another is governed by the Extradition Treaty between the two countries on this subject. The United States – Mexico Extradition Treaty went into effect in 1980. It provided that neither country was bound to deliver its nationals for extradition, but this provision did not create a problem in most cases. The Treaty further provided that where the offense for which extradition is sought is punishable by death, a country may refuse to extradite unless the country seeking extradition assures that it will not impose the death penalty. Under the Treaty, the death penalty is the only punishment for which such assurances may be required. For many years, Mexico had extradited many suspects to California and other states without serious problems.

In October 2001, the Mexico Supreme Court ruled that the goal of penal law in Mexico was "rehabilitation" and that "a life sentence violates the Mexico Constitution." Mexico then extended this interpretation to the Extradition Treaty, deciding that it would no longer extradite a fugitive who is subject to life imprisonment with or without the possibility of parole unless assurances are given that guarantees a sentence of a determinate number of years. Under this interpretation, Jorge Arroyo-Garcia could remain in Mexico and avoid being prosecuted in the United States for the murder of Deputy David March.

EFFORTS TO CHANGE MEXICAN EXTRADITION POLICY (COMMENTARY OF STEVE COOLEY)

Even before the death of Deputy David March, the District Attorney's Office had been frustrated in its attempts to extradite some murderers who had fled to Mexico. One particularly aggravated case was the brutal murder in June 1999 of two young girls as they walked to school. The murderer, Juan Manual Casillas, had fled to Mexico; and the District Attorney's Office was seeking his extradition. However, Mexico refused to extradite based on the decision by the Mexico Supreme Court.

Jan Maurizi, my Director of the Bureau of Branch and Area Operations Region II, was an expert in extradition law. In the latter part of April 2002, just days prior to the murder of Deputy March, she went to San Antonio, Texas, to attend the U.S. Attorney General's United States/Mexico Conference on Extradition. She assumed that the Mexican authorities would announce a change in their extradition policy, but they refused to do so. Lt. Joe Hartshorne of the Los Angeles County Sheriff's Department also attended the conference. During the conference, on April 29, 2002, Lt. Hartshorne received a telephone call and stepped out of the room. He returned and told Ms. Maurizi with a heavy heart, "We just lost another deputy." He didn't have a name or any details – just that a deputy had been shot and killed by an unknown suspect who had fled. Ms. Maurizi felt a wave of panic because she had a son who was a deputy sheriff working patrol at the time.

Even before the death of Deputy March, I had employed a multi-faceted approach to compel Mexico to extradite violent felons facing life sentences. But the brutal murder of David March gave that effort a new impetus.

I had appointed Jan Maurizi to coordinate many of the efforts in the extradition fight. She began a multi-year effort to change Mexico's policy on the extradition of violent criminals. She contacted the Office of International Affairs, the State Department, and met with members of the Senate and House of Representatives. She met with and briefed White House Counsel, and she gave presentations to law enforcement and victims' rights groups. Ms. Maurizi and I actively spoke on this issue on talk shows in an effort to raise public support and awareness for our cause. Popular local radio talk show hosts John Kobylt and Ken Chiampou were particularly supportive of this issue and keeping it alive.

One of the major elected officials who joined the effort was United States Senator Dianne Feinstein. In July 2003, she sent a five-page letter to Mexican President Vicente Fox urging him to act to resolve the problem. The letter included the following language:

> *In California, for example, over 40 different crimes are punishable by possible life sentences and neither a judge nor a prosecutor can give assurances of a determinate term for these crimes. As a result, Mexico's policy encourages people committing serious crimes in California to flee to Mexico and escape just punishment. Indeed, individuals in the United States with a criminal history have a pervasive incentive to kill an arresting police officer and head for Mexico rather than face possible prosecution and imprisonment in the United States.*

In 2004, the District Attorney's Office, under the direction of Ms. Maurizi, launched the website "Escaping Justice.com." This website featured tragic stories of Los Angeles County crime victims and their relatives who were being denied justice because the suspects in their cases had fled to Mexico. Among the persons lending support to this effort were the parents and widow of Deputy David March. The website also sought the public's help in locating fugitive suspects, and it also served as a clearinghouse for information about the Mexican court decision.

Also, the District Attorney's Office sponsored and successfully lobbied for the passage of Assembly Bill 1432, which allowed re-prosecution of any fugitive who re-entered the United States after conviction or acquittal in a foreign jurisdiction. The bill was signed into law by California Governor Arnold Schwarzenegger in 2004.

Additionally, in August 2005, the District Attorney's Office helped congressional representatives draft a federal law that would have imposed sanctions for noncompliance with an extradition treaty. That legislation was enacted into law in October 2005. A month later, on November 29, 2005, the Mexico Supreme Court reversed its 2001 ruling. As a result, the extradition of suspects from Mexico reverted to its prior status. Mexico would now extradite its citizens to the United States upon receiving assurances from the requesting state that it would not seek the death penalty.

"COMPROMISE" EFFORTS
(COMMENTARY OF STEVE COOLEY)

The change in Mexico's policy was a successful conclusion to the heroic efforts of many persons to achieve justice in the murder of Deputy David March. Now Jorge Arroyo-Garcia could be returned to the United States for trial and face a sentence of life in prison for his crime. This result was achieved despite the "compromise" efforts by persons one would expect to strongly support the District Attorney's position.

John and Barbara March, the parents of David March, remained strongly committed. They contacted government officials and often appeared on talk shows and on television to lobby for a change in the law. Terry March, the widow of David March, initially supported these efforts, but she eventually went on talk shows criticizing me for not giving in to Mexico's demands to have the trial and sentence handled in Mexico.

David Dreier, one of the most powerful congressmen in the House of Representatives, drafted a bill with the support of Sheriff Lee Baca. The bill proposed a federal law that provided for a maximum sentence of 22 years for killing a federal or law enforcement officer and then fleeing the country. Once a person was convicted under this federal law, state authorities would have been prevented from prosecuting that individual for the murder of the law enforcement officer. This proposed law was strongly supported by Sheriff Baca, who wanted closure to this long-standing and unresolved issue. If implemented, this law would provide a great incentive for cop-killers to flee the United States. Neither Congressman Dreier nor Sheriff Baca had discussed this proposed law with me or my office. I learned about it when they announced it at a press conference. When I heard about it, I exploded and issued a harsh public statement condemning it. Sheriff Baca criticized my comments, but I believe that my reaction helped scuttle this ill-advised proposal.

In 2004, California Senator Barbara Boxer was running for re-election to the United States Senate. In a debate with her opponent, she was asked about the extradition issue. She was caught flat-footed and looked, at a minimum, uninformed on the issue. She called me the following day and wanted to know why she had not been informed on the subject. The next day Jan Maurizi sent the Senator a thick packet of letters, memoranda, etc., that had been sent by the District Attorney's Office to Senator Boxer's office over a couple of years, none of which had been responded to. Senator Boxer's non-involvement was in sharp contrast to California's other U.S. Senator, Dianne Feinstein, who played a supportive role in the return of Garcia to the United States for trial.

During my one and only conversation with Senator Boxer, I would have to describe her as functionally uninformed, rude, abusive, and boorish. In my view, she was one of the worst and most ineffective United States senators in California history. Her non-involvement in a matter as important as extraditing murderers from Mexico was just a stark example of her complete ineptitude.

WITNESS MARTINA MURILLO

On the late evening of April 29, 2002, the day of the murder of Deputy David March, Sheriff's investigators interviewed Martina Murillo. She knew Jorge Arroyo-Garcia as Armando Garcia. She stated that her husband, Jose Bustos Cabrera, and Garcia were born and raised in Morelia, Michoacan, Mexico. They were friends, and Garcia would occasionally stay with her and her husband because he was sometimes homeless. She and her husband owned a black Nissan Maxima that Garcia would occasionally borrow. On the evening of April 28, 2002, her husband loaned their black Nissan Maxima to Garcia. The following day, her husband told her that Garcia had told him that he had killed a police officer while driving the black Nissan Maxima.

On May 27, 2003, Detective Mark Lillienfeld of the Los Angeles County Sheriff's Department conducted another interview with Martina Murillo. She stated that a little over a year after the murder of Deputy David March, she and her husband Jose Bustos Cabrera were visiting her husband's relatives in Morelia, Michoacan, Mexico. There she met and spoke with Garcia. He told her that he was driving her Nissan Maxima when he was pulled over by a police car. Deputy March approached him as he sat in the driver's seat and asked him for his driver's license. Garcia told the deputy that he didn't have a license. Deputy March ordered him out of the Nissan and went with him to the patrol car. There he pulled out a gun and shot the deputy who fell to the ground. He shot him several more times in the neck area. Deputy March was shaking as he lay on the ground after being shot and was trying to reach for his own gun, so Garcia shot him in the head. Garcia then ran to the Nissan Maxima and drove off. He eventually made his way to Tijuana, Mexico and ultimately to Morelia, Michoacan, Mexico.

This statement by Martina Murillo to Detective Lillienfeld on May 27, 2003, gave Sheriff's investigators and the District Attorney's Office information from a credible witness that Garcia was, in fact, hiding in Mexico. This would be crucial information in any subsequent extradition application to Mexico that Garcia was in Mexico to avoid appropriate prosecution and punishment under California law.

ARREST AND EXTRADITION OF
JORGE ARROYO-GARCIA

Approximately three months after the Mexico Supreme Court reversed its ruling of October 2001, Jorge Arroyo Garcia was arrested by Mexican authorities on February 23, 2006, in a small town outside Guadalajara,

Mexico. He was now subject to extradition to the United States if assurances were given that the Los Angeles County District Attorney's Office would not seek or impose the death penalty.

The actual request for extradition would be handled by the Office of International Affairs in the United States Department of Justice. It was up to the Los Angeles County District Attorney's Office to provide the Office of International Affairs with the proper documentation for the extradition request. Under the United States – Mexico Extradition Treaty, the United States Government had 60 days after Garcia's arrest to send to Mexico a formal request for extradition.

Bureau Director Janice Maurizi of the District Attorney's Office prepared a Prosecutor Affidavit of 19 pages that was sworn and signed on April 5, 2006, before California Superior Court Judge Steven R. Van Sicklen. Her affidavit and supporting documents included the following information as required by the extradition treaty between the United States and Mexico:

- Facts and personal information of the person sought that will permit his identification.
- Description of the offense and statement of the facts of the case.
- Text of the applicable legal principles of the requesting party on the disposition of the case regarding the essential elements of the offense, the punishment of the offense and the statute of limitations.
- Certified copy of the arrest warrant.
- Evidence that the laws of the requested party would provide for the apprehension and commitment for trial of the person sought if the offense had been committed within its jurisdiction.
- Assurances that the death penalty will not be imposed.

This Prosecutor's Affidavit contained eleven supporting documents that were attached to and incorporated into the affidavits as Exhibits A through K. These Exhibits included certified copies of the complaint and arrest warrant, a description of the relevant statutes, certified copies of Garcia's 2000 conviction, and the affidavits of Detective Mark Lillienfeld, Juan Gabriel Vasquez, Jose Bustos Cabrera, Martina Murillo, Sonia Martinez, Detective Johnny Patino, and Refugio Contreras Sanchez.

The Prosecutor's Affidavit was accompanied by a letter dated April 5,

2006, under my name as District Attorney to the Office of International Affairs in the United States Department of Justice. The letter provided assurances that the Los Angeles County District Attorney's Office would not seek the death penalty nor would a penalty of death be imposed in the case charging Jorge Arroyo-Garcia with the murder of Los Angeles County Deputy Sheriff David March on April 29, 2002, and other charges.

The Request for Extradition, including supporting documents, was transmitted through diplomatic channels, with the appropriate seals and ribbons, and translated into Spanish. After their delivery to the Secretariat of Foreign Affairs through the United States Embassy in Mexico, the "package" was sent to the Office of the Attorney General who sent the documents to the district judge in the Mexican jurisdiction where Jorge Arroyo-Garcia was being held.

After Jorge Arroyo-Garcia's arrest by Mexican authorities on February 23, 2006, he remained in custody until his Mexican appeals were exhausted and then extradited to the United States in early January 2007.

On January 9, 2007, a SWAT unit from Mexico took Garcia by airplane from Mexico City to Tijuana. In Tijuana, local and federal authorities took him into the United States. One of the peace officers who took custody of Garcia at the United States/Mexico border was Detective Mark Lillienfeld of the Los Angeles Sheriff's Department. Detective Lillienfeld had received Deputy March's handcuffs from his family, and he used the handcuffs in transporting Garcia to the Orange County Men's Central Jail. It was a symbolic act that the use of these handcuffs represented that Deputy David March had participated in the arrest of the man who had murdered him.

On January 11, 2007, Garcia was transported to the Pomona Superior Court where he was arraigned on the charges against him. Deputy District Attorney Darren Levine represented the prosecution, and Deputy Public Defender Grady Russell was appointed to represent Garcia.

GUILTY PLEA

On January 25, 2007, Detectives Mark Lillienfeld and Steven Katz transported Jorge Arroyo-Garcia from the San Bernardino West Valley Detention Center, where he was being housed, to Department M of the Pomona Superior Court for a court appearance before Judge Charles Horan. On the return trip to the Detention Center, Garcia made several spontaneous statements to Detectives Lillienfeld and Katz regarding the following:

Garcia discussed the possibility of pleading guilty to the charges against him. He specifically asked where he would be housed if he pled guilty to the charges, whether he would be able to marry his common law wife, and whether he would be able to receive visits from her while in state prison custody. Garcia asked whether he could use Detective Katz's cell phone to call family members in Mexico to discuss the possibility of pleading guilty to the pending charges. Detective Katz allowed Garcia to use his cell phone, but Garcia was unable to reach his relatives.

Detectives Lillienfeld and Katz reported Garcia's statements to prosecutor Darren Levine. Levine in turn contacted Garcia's defense attorney, Grady Russell, to advise him of Garcia's statements. Arrangements were later made for Garcia to phone and talk to his family members while in the presence of his attorney.

On March 2, 2007, Jorge Arroyo-Garcia was prepared to plead guilty to the charge against him involving the murder of Deputy David March. On that date, he appeared before Judge Charles Horan in Department M of the Pomona Superior Court. Below is a summary of the principals in the case and the charge to which he entered a guilty plea:

PEOPLE v. JORGE ARROYO-GARCIA
CASE KA056968

JUDGE: Charles Horan

PROSECUTOR: Darren Levine, Deputy District Attorney
Crimes Against Peace Officers Section

DEFENSE ATTORNEY: Grady Russell, Deputy Public Defender

COUNT AND SPECIAL ALLEGATIONS TO WHICH GARCIA PLED GUILTY:

— Count I (Penal Code section 187, Murder in the Second Degree)

— Penal Code section 190(c) (1) (Special Allegation of Killing a Peace Officer in the Lawful Performance of His Duties)

— Penal Code section 190(c) (4) (Special Allegation

	of Personal Use of a Firearm in the Commission of
	the Murder)
NOTE:	The special allegations in Penal Code section 190 (c)
	with a plea to second degree murder provided for a
	sentence of life imprisonment without the possibility
	of parole.

As part of the guilty plea, Jorge Arroyo Garcia signed a five-page "Written Advisement and Waivers" and initialed 23 paragraphs contained in the document. Paragraph 19, initialed by Garcia, provided a factual basis for the plea, as follows:

19. [initials] I offer to the court the following as the basis for my plea of guilty: On April 29, 2002, within the County of Los Angeles, I intentionally killed a peace officer, Los Angeles County Sheriff's Deputy David March, while personally using a nine millimeter semi-automatic pistol.

Further, I knew Deputy David March was a peace officer in the lawful performance of his duties when I shot and killed him.

Judge Charles Horan carefully questioned Garcia on each of the terms that he initialed in the "Written Advisement and Waivers" which was in effect a plea agreement. Garcia read the language in Paragraph 19 that he shot and killed Deputy David March to the court. Judge Horan then accepted Garcia's guilty plea to murder in the second degree with the special allegations.

After entering his guilty plea, Garcia made a lengthy statement in Spanish in which he asked for forgiveness by friends and family of the man he killed.

Judge Horan then sentenced Jorge Arroyo Garcia to life imprisonment without the possibility of parole pursuant to Penal Code section 190 (c). Two counts involving the attempted murder of Refugio Contreras Sanchez were dismissed.

In my role as District Attorney, I attended the court proceedings along with Sheriff Lee Baca. After the proceedings I made the following statement:

Justice was done today. The man who gunned down Deputy David March nearly five years ago and left him to die on a street in Irwindale will be locked away forever. It is the same sentence he would have received had he gone to trial. Had it not been for the persistence and joint efforts of local, state, federal, and Mexican officials, this day would not have come, and Jorge Arroyo Garcia would still be a free man in Mexico. These criminals are being sought and will be caught. They will be returned to the United States—as Garcia was two months ago. They will be prosecuted. Justice will be served. Garcia is the first of several being returned from Mexico who will be sentenced to life in prison for his crimes. His guilty plea brings hope to hundreds of next of kin, victims, and survivors of crimes in which the perpetrator fled to Mexico to avoid prosecution.

EPILOGUE – CALIFORNIA STATE PRISON AT CALIPATRIA

The Written Advisement and Waivers signed by Jorge Arroyo-Garcia was also signed by Deputy District Attorney Darren Levine and Deputy Public Defender Grady Russell. It stated in Paragraphs 5 and 6 that efforts would be made to have Garcia serve his sentence at the California State Prison at Calipatria and that authorities would not oppose legal visits by his family members. This prison facility is located in Imperial County near the Mexican border, and Garcia's incarceration there would facilitate prison visits by his family. This was a minor benefit for Garcia that helped insure his guilty plea and a quick and appropriate resolution to the case.

In a letter dated February 20, 2007, to the California Department of Corrections, Captain Raymond H. Peavy of the Los Angeles County Sheriff's Homicide Bureau requested that Jorge Arroyo-Garcia be housed at the Calipatria State Prison in Imperial County, California.

Jorge Arroyo-Garcia is presently serving his sentence of life imprisonment without the possibility of parole at the California State Prison in Calipatria.

EPILOGUE – CONCLUSION

On October 2, 2001, the Mexico Supreme Court issued its ruling that Mexican nationals subject to a sentence of life imprisonment could not be extradited to a requesting country. Almost immediately, the Los Angeles County District Attorney's Office took measures to overturn the effects of the Court's decision.

Sometimes it takes a dramatic or tragic event to provide a human face to a problem. The murder of Los Angeles County Sheriff's Deputy David March took place on April 29, 2002, which was approximately seven months after the Mexico Supreme Court decision. Suddenly, there was a real life event that made the court decision more than just a theoretical possibility.

The murder of Deputy March provided much of the impetus for efforts to have the Mexico Supreme Court reverse its 2001 ruling. The eventual sentence of Jorge Arroyo-Garcia to life in prison without the possibility of parole was the result of the efforts of many individuals, but a major rallying point for those efforts was the murder of Deputy David March.

EPILOGUE – DAVID MARCH CREDO

A few weeks before his death, Deputy David March underwent a department review of his performance. As part of the review, he was told to write his personal goals. He wrote the following:

> *My goals in life are simple. I will always be painfully honest, work as hard as I can, learn as much as I can, and hopefully make a difference in people's lives.*

After the death of Deputy David March, this became the official credo of the Los Angeles Sheriff's Department.

LESSONS LEARNED

This chapter has two lessons to be learned.

1. *Traffic stop*: Deputy David March was working a one-man police

car when he conducted a fatal traffic stop. Deputy March detained Jorge Arroyo-Garcia for a traffic violation in a black Nissan. Several witnesses observed the shooting of Deputy March and stated that as he approached the driver's side of the Nissan on foot, Garcia emerged from the Nissan and fired several shots at Deputy March, fatally wounding him. In describing the incident to Jose Cabrera, Garcia stated that when Deputy March began to search him, he used his left arm to push the officer away and used his right arm to pull his gun from his waistband and shoot the officer.

Under either scenario, Deputy March was vulnerable because he was working a one-man police car and made a traffic stop of a wanted person who was armed and dangerous and did not want to be arrested. Garcia made up his mind to shoot David March, and there was nothing the deputy could do to stop it.

2. *"We will not give up"*: The theme of the first chapter of this book was "we will not forget" the murder of a law enforcement officer. In that case, the 1957 murder of two El Segundo police officers was finally solved over 40 years later after the murders were committed.

The theme of this last chapter is that "we will not give up" in efforts to bring to justice the killer of a police officer. In every chapter in this book, the perpetrator was captured and convicted of the murder of the officer based on the coordinated efforts of law enforcement and the District Attorney's Office. The most challenging aspect in bringing to trial the suspect involved in the murder of Deputy David March was when the killer sought refuge in Mexico. It appeared that he might avoid arrest and prosecution for this brutal murder under statutory law and judicial fiat in existence in Mexico at that time. However, the Los Angeles County District Attorney's Office and local officials enlisted the assistance of the federal government. Pressure was put on Mexican officials who ultimately relented and allowed the return of the suspect to the United States where he was convicted of the murder of Deputy March. This case is the classic example of "we will not give up."

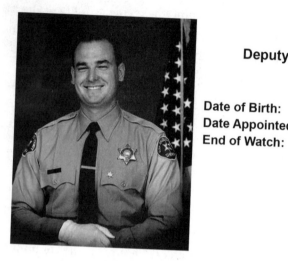

Deputy David March

Date of Birth:	March 29, 1969
Date Appointed:	July 19, 1995
End of Watch:	April 29, 2002

David March Memorial

District Attorney Steve Cooley and other dignitaries attend the funeral of Deputy David March

Jorge Arroyo Garcia is returned to the United States from Mexico

FOR LAW ENFORCEMENT USE ONLY!

Special Bulletin

WANTED FOR MURDER
SUSPECT ARMED AND DANGEROUS

GARCIA, Armando MH/25
DOB: 11-03-76, 5-7 to 5-9, 195 to 230, short black hair combed back, dark complexion, mustache and chin whiskers

AKA: Daniel Garcia & "CHATO"; TT's: Back Shoulder "Garcia"

5019 Heleo St., Temple City; 1832 Park Rose Ave., Duarte

CII #A10279529 & A22177424

Suspect GARCIA is wanted for the murder of Deputy David March on April 29, 2002, at 242 E. Live Oak Avenue in Irwindale. Suspect Garcia is also wanted by the Baldwin Park Police Department in connection with two attempted murders that occurred in their city on or about November 18, 2001 and February 16, 2002. Suspect Garcia is also wanted by the El Monte Police Department for weapons charges under No Bail Warrant Number XEAKA04875501.

Attention: SERGEANT K. GALLATIN or SERGEANT S. KATZ
File Number 002-00051-3199-011   Phone (323) 890-5500 Fax (323) 887-1160
L.A.S.D. Homicide Bureau, 5747 Rickenbacker Road, Commerce 90040

Created April 30, 2002 (pjv)   Verify information before taking action

Escaping Justice.com

Carlos & Anabella Vara | Kenny Caldera | Deputy David March | Steven Morales | Tiffany Rios | Jessica Zavalla & Olivia Munguia

D.A. Steve Cooley Opposes Proposed Legislation that Gives Cop-Killers a Break

What Do These People Have In Common?

They and hundreds of others like them have been victims of senseless, brutal, cold-blooded murders in Los Angeles County by fugitives who have escaped justice for the price of a bus ticket across the border.

Are You a Victim?

Countless fugitives have found safe haven in Mexico because the laws of Mexico protect them from prosecution here in the United States where the crimes were committed.

District Attorney website created by Director Jan Maurizi (left) of the District Attorney's Office to tell the stories of crime victims who were denied justice when fugitive suspects found safe haven in Mexico.

John March and Steve Cooley with Deputy David March's hand-cuffs. The handcuffs were placed on Armando Garcia upon his arrival to the United States after his extradition from Mexico.

CHAPTER 7

Captain Michael Sparkes

Los Angeles County Police Department

"Know Where You Are"

MICHAEL LAWRENCE SPARKES

In early August 2004, Michael Sparkes was living a wonderful life. He was enjoying a successful career in the Los Angeles County Police Department where he had risen through the ranks and was a captain in charge of security services at Harbor-UCLA General Hospital. He was a popular and effective leader.

He was a happily married man, having married Deloris Shields in March 1996 at age 46. In 1997, the son that he had always wanted—Michael Lawrence Sparkes, Jr.—was born. He was a loving and doting father.

Captain Sparkes was a religious man and was a faithful member of the Greater Bethany Community Church. He became a minister and worked in the Ontario community where he diligently tried to keep young men from getting into gangs.

It had been a long journey for Captain Michael Sparkes. He was born in Chicago on January 10, 1951. He graduated from high school in 1969 and enlisted in the United States Navy. He served on the U.S.S. McDonough until his honorable discharge from the Navy in 1972. For the next three years, he was a member of the Charleston, South Carolina, Police Department. In 1975, he moved to Los Angeles and joined the Los Angeles County Police Department where he remained for the next 29 years until his untimely death on August 10, 2004.

AUGUST 10, 2004

In early August 2004, Captain Michael Sparkes was on an exercise program to lose weight. He regularly rode his bicycle near his home in south central Los Angeles before going to work. In the early morning of August 10, 2004, he was riding his bicycle in the vicinity of Avalon Boulevard and Redondo Beach Boulevard in the city of Compton. He was wearing a sweatshirt with his name stenciled across his chest. He was also wearing a large fanny pack around his waist that contained his police badge and police identification, his cellular phone, and his 16-shot 9 mm Beretta handgun.

At approximately 5:30 a.m., Miguel Magallon and Orvis Anthony were traveling eastbound on Redondo Beach Boulevard in Anthony's dark gray Nissan Maxima. Anthony was driving the car, and Magallon was in the front passenger seat. They were in possession of an AK-47 style assault rifle. They observed Captain Sparkes riding his bicycle near the intersection of Avalon and Redondo Beach Boulevards. Magallon told Anthony to stop the car so they could rob Captain Sparkes. Anthony stopped the car in an alley ahead of Sparkes, and Magallon exited the vehicle armed with the AK-47. Magallon moved toward Captain Sparkes and out of Anthony's sight. Magallon confronted Captain Sparkes on a dirt sidewalk just east of the intersection of Avalon Boulevard and Redondo Beach Boulevard. Captain Sparkes was able to remove his handgun from his fanny pack, and he and Magallon exchanged gunfire. Crime scene evidence indicated that Magallon fired his rifle at least six times at Captain Sparkes, who sustained at least one serious wound during this initial exchange of gunfire. Magallon was not injured at this time.

Magallon then ran back to the waiting Nissan Maxima, got into the front passenger seat, and told Anthony to circle the block and return to the location. In the meantime, the seriously wounded Captain Sparkes took cover behind a large traffic signal control box in front of a business located at 15300 South Avalon Boulevard. He used his cellular phone to call 911, and he told the 911 operator that he was a police officer and that he had been shot. He stated that he was at Avalon and Artesia, which was the wrong location since he was actually a short distance away.

When Anthony and Magallon returned to Captain Sparkes's location, Magallon fired an additional six to seven shots from the passenger side of the Nissan Maxima. Some of Magallon's shots penetrated the traffic box that Captain Sparkes was using for cover. Captain Sparkes managed to fire about five shots at the Nissan Maxima, one which penetrated the door striking Magallon in the abdomen. Anthony and Magallon then fled the location in the Nissan Maxima.

The 911 call by Captain Sparkes was recorded and lasted over ten minutes. During the recorded 911 call, Captain Sparkes was moaning and pleading for the ambulance to arrive. The sounds of gunfire were heard by the 911 operator and recorded on the tape of the 911 call. Below is a partial transcript of the 911 call.

Michael Sparkes: Oh, help me Jesus. Help me Jesus.

911 Operator: 911, what are you reporting?

Michael Sparkes: Officer down now. I'm at Avalon and, a, shit, Artesia. I been shot. God damn.

911 Operator: Avalon-

Michael Sparkes: God damn.

911 Operator: -And Artesia?

Michael Sparkes: Yeah.

911 Operator: Who got shot? [Sound of gun fire]

Michael Sparkes: Come on man, they had, they killed me.

911 Operator: Did he get away?

Michael Sparkes: They had got away man. Come on, I-I was out, I'm laying in the street bleeding to death, come on, man.

911 Operator: Okay. We'll get –

Michael Sparkes: Somebody down here, shit.

911 Operator: I just heard more shots fired. Are they still around?

Michael Sparkes: Yeah, they're still around, sit, sittin' in the alley, man.

911 Operator: Okay.

Michael Sparkes: Come on.

911 Operator: Okay. Where are they at?

Michael Sparkes: Ah man.

911 Operator: What are they driving?

Michael Sparkes: I can't tell you that. I can't tell you that.

911 Operator: Okay.

Michael Sparkes: Yeah, oh, shit, man.

911 Operator: Okay. Are you on the corner of Avalon and Artesia. Stay on the phone. Don't hang up.

From the tape of the recorded 911 call, it was evident that Captain Sparkes was in severe pain and was aware that he was bleeding to death.

Deputies from the Los Angeles County Sheriff's Department arrived at the crime scene and observed Captain Sparkes lying in the dirt next to the traffic signal control box. He was still conscious and identified himself as a police officer and stated that he was seriously wounded. The responding deputies observed that he had sustained multiple gunshot wounds and was bleeding heavily. His badge was observed open on the ground next to him. Captain Sparkes had his semi-automatic pistol in his hand. His weapon was in the slide lock position, indicating that he had fired all the rounds in the magazine.

Captain Sparkes was transported by ambulance to Harbor-UCLA General Hospital, the hospital at which he was in charge of security. He was pronounced dead at approximately 7:45 a.m. An autopsy performed on the body of Captain Sparkes ascribed the cause of death to multiple gunshot wounds. There were three gunshot wounds to his abdomen, two to his left leg, and four to his right leg and foot. The autopsy surgeon recovered six bullets or bullet fragments from the body of Captain Sparkes.

ARREST OF ORVIS ANTHONY

Immediately after the shooting of Captain Sparkes, Orvis Anthony drove his Nissan Maxima to his residence at 15817 South Lorella Avenue, Gardena. Miguel Magallon was in the front passenger seat bleeding heavily from a serious gunshot wound to his abdomen. Anthony placed the assault rifle in the trunk of a 1986 Mazda 626 that was parked in front of his residence. This was a "stash car" used by gang members to store weapons and other contraband. Anthony then drove the Nissan Maxima to Memorial Hospital in Gardena where he dropped off Magallon for treatment for his gunshot wound.

After dropping Magallon off at the hospital, Anthony was speeding back to his residence. At approximately 5:45 a.m., a Los Angeles Police Department motorcycle officer, Deshon Horton, observed a gray Nissan Maxima travel eastbound through a red light on Redondo Beach Boulevard at an intersection near the 110 Freeway. Officer Horton effected a traffic stop of the vehicle which contained the driver and sole occupant,

Orvis Anthony, Jr. Officer Horton determined that Anthony was driving under the influence of alcohol and placed him under arrest. He obtained Anthony's home telephone number and called Anthony's father, telling him that his son had been arrested for drunk driving and to come pick up the car. A short time later Orvis Anthony, Sr. and his wife arrived at the location.

Before releasing the Nissan Maxima to Anthony's father, Officer Horton was informed of the shooting incident by a passing deputy. Officer Horton examined the Nissan Maxima more carefully and observed multiple bullet holes in the front passenger door of the car. He notified his department of this information and was told to remain at the scene with the vehicle and Orvis Anthony, Jr.

The Homicide Bureau of the Los Angeles County Sheriff's Department was assigned to investigate the murder of Captain Sparkes. Investigator Robert Harris from the Homicide Bureau responded from the office and was the first member of the Bureau to arrive on scene. After inspecting the crime scene, Investigator Harris drove to Redondo Beach Boulevard and Figueroa Street, where Orvis Anthony, Jr. was being detained. LAPD motor officer Horton briefed Investigator Harris of the arrest of Anthony. Investigator Harris examined the Nissan Maxima and observed five bullet holes on the front passenger door. At least one projectile appeared to have passed through the door into the passenger area of the vehicle. There was a white pillow in the back seat, which appeared to have blood on it.

Investigator Harris spoke to Anthony's father, who had responded to the location to pick up his Nissan Maxima since his son had been arrested for drunk driving. He stated that his son had been at the house early in the morning with his friend and next door neighbor, Miguel, and that there were no bullet holes in the car when he had seen it the previous day.

The Nissan Maxima was impounded, and Orvis Anthony was transported to the Century Regional Detention Facility.

CONFESSION OF ORVIS ANTHONY

Detectives Scott Fines and John Corina of the Sheriff's Homicide Bureau were the lead detectives in charge of investigating the murder of Captain Michael Sparkes. On August 10, 2004, at approximately 10:30 p.m., they interviewed Orvis Camillo Anthony at the Lennox Sheriff's Station. The interview was both audiotaped and videotaped.

In preliminary questioning, Anthony stated that he lived with his parents at 15817 South Lorella Avenue, Gardena. His father was an African-American and his mother was of Guatemalan descent. He stated that he resided in the "T Zone Crip" area but claimed that he was no longer involved with any gang.

Anthony was advised of his constitutional rights, which he waived and agreed to talk to investigators without an attorney. Initially, he discussed his arrest for drunk driving and taking his friend Miguel to the hospital for a gunshot wound. Anthony then gave the following statement regarding the shooting death of Captain Sparkes:

He stated that he and Miguel had spent the evening and early morning drinking and visiting with girls. They decided to rob a convenience store or gas station. He was driving his Nissan Maxima, and Miguel was the front seat passenger. Miguel had an AK-47 in the front seat with him. As they approached the intersection of Avalon Boulevard and Redondo Beach Boulevard, they observed Captain Sparkes near the utility box. Miguel said something to the effect of "Stop. Stop. Let's rob him."

Anthony turned into the first alley east of Avalon Boulevard and stopped the car. Miguel exited the car armed with the AK-47. He turned the corner out of Anthony's view. Miguel returned to the car and entered the front passenger seat still armed with the AK-47. Miguel told Anthony to drive around the corner and to return to the location

Anthony drove the Nissan Maxima down the alley, made two right turns, and returned to the location where Captain Sparkes was located. Miguel leaned out the open passenger-side window and fired approximately six or seven rounds in the direction of the victim. As they passed a utility box near where the victim had been standing, Anthony observed several muzzle flashes coming from the area of the victim. He only saw muzzle flashes and did not hear gunshots from the victim's gun because the AK-47 was much louder.

Anthony continued driving eastbound on Redondo Beach Boulevard, and Miguel told him that he had been wounded. Anthony then drove to his residence on Lorella Avenue where he placed the AK-47 in the trunk of an older model blue Honda or Toyota car parked on the street near his residence. The car was an abandoned car that was normally parked on the street and unlocked. He then drove Miguel to Gardena Memorial Hospital and dropped him off.

After he dropped Miguel off at the hospital, Anthony drove eastbound on Redondo Beach Boulevard where he was stopped by a motorcycle officer and arrested for drunk driving.

Anthony stated that he received the AK-47 rifle from a man known to him as "Monster" a few days ago, and that Monster asked him to hold it.

RECOVERY OF MURDER WEAPON

After the interview was completed, Anthony agreed to show the investigators where he stashed the AK-47. Anthony was transported to the area of his residence at 15731 Lorella Avenue, Gardena. A faded blue Mazda 626 was parked in front of 15731 Lorella Avenue, and Anthony stated that this was the car where he stashed the AK-47.

The Mazda was impounded as evidence and towed to Kruger's Tow. Investigator Robert Harris prepared and obtained a search warrant for the vehicle. The search of the vehicle resulted in the seizure of an AK-47 rifle from the trunk area of the Mazda vehicle. Ballistics tests later confirmed that this AK-47 rifle was the weapon that was used to murder Captain Sparkes.

ADDITIONAL INTERVIEWS WITH ORVIS ANTHONY

After showing the investigators the Mazda containing the AK-47, Orvis Anthony agreed to return to the crime scene and conduct a walk-through at the location. It was approximately 2:30 a.m. on the early morning of August 11, 2004, when Anthony took investigators on a walk-through of what occurred when Captain Sparkes was murdered. The walk-through and the statements provided by Anthony during the walk-through were videotaped.

On August 11, 2004, at approximately 3:50 a.m., investigators returned to the Lennox Sheriff's Station where another interview was conducted with Orvis Anthony. He was again informed of his *Miranda* rights, which he waived, and agreed to speak to investigators. This interview was also audiotaped and videotaped. In each of his statements to investigators, Orvis Anthony was consistent in describing the events concerning the death of Captain Sparkes.

After the last statement, Orvis Anthony was transported to the Inmate Reception Center and booked for murder.

MIGUEL MAGALLON

On the afternoon of August 10, 2004, Investigators Scott Fines and John Corina went to Gardena Memorial Hospital to check on the status of Miguel Magallon. Dr. Arthur Fox told the detectives that Miguel Magallon was his patient. Magallon had sustained a gunshot wound to the abdomen area, and there was a projectile inside his body. However, Magallon refused to consent to allow Dr. Fox to remove the projectile from his body. Since Magallon was a suspect in the murder of Captain Sparkes, a deputy was posted by his bedside pending further investigation.

On August 12, 2004, Investigators Fines and Corina returned to Gardena Memorial Hospital when they were informed by Dr. Fox that Magallon was alert and suitable for an interview. On that date at approximately 6:50 p.m., the investigators interviewed Magallon at the hospital. He was advised of his *Miranda* rights, which he waived, and agreed to speak to the investigators. He admitted that he was the front seat passenger in a Nissan Maxima driven by his friend Orvis Anthony. He stated that he was very drunk and had little recollection of the events of that night. The interview terminated when Magallon stated that he wanted a lawyer.

FILING OF CHARGES

On August 16, 2004, a felony complaint was filed against Orvis Camillo Anthony and Miguel Angel Magallon under case number TA075921. The complaint charged both defendants with the murder of Captain Michael Sparkes in Count One and the attempted robbery of Captain Michael Sparkes in Count Two. Count One alleged special circumstances that Captain Sparkes was a peace officer murdered while in the performance of his duties; that the murder was committed during the attempted commission of a robbery; and that the murder was committed by means of discharging a firearm from a motor vehicle. The proof of a special circumstance made the defendants eligible for the death penalty.

Deputy District Attorney Darren Levine of the Crimes Against Police

Officers Section (CAPOS) was assigned to prosecute the case.

AGREEMENT WITH ORVIS ANTHONY

The prosecution against the two defendants was delayed as Miguel Magallon recovered from his gunshot wound and the attorneys prepared for the preliminary hearing. Attorney Earl Evans was representing Orvis Anthony, and he was aware that the prosecution had an air-tight case against his client, highlighted by several taped confessions and the recovery of the murder weapon. Attorney Evans and prosecutor Darren Levine discussed a case settlement for Anthony. They reached an agreement that in exchange for a sentence of 50 years to life, Anthony would testify truthfully at the preliminary hearing and at the trial. This proposed settlement was approved by members of the District Attorney's Executive Staff.

In November 2005, Orvis Anthony, attorney Earl Evans and prosecutor Darren Levine signed an "agreement of leniency" that formalized the case settlement. The document stated that Anthony would plead guilty to one count of first degree murder and one count of attempted robbery of Captain Michael Sparkes, admit some special allegations, and receive a sentence of 50 years to life in state prison. In exchange for this plea, Anthony had to testify truthfully and completely under oath at all court proceedings in the case. If he failed to comply with the agreement, the agreed-upon disposition would become void, and Anthony would be subject to prosecution to the full extent allowed by law.

PRELIMINARY HEARING

On January 9, 2006, Orvis Anthony pled guilty before Judge John Cheroske to one count of first degree murder and one count of attempted second degree robbery with an admission that a principal personally and intentionally discharged a firearm causing death and an admission that the offense was committed for the benefit of a street gang. Pursuant to the agreement of leniency, Anthony would receive a sentence of 50 years to life in state prison. His sentencing was scheduled to take place on September 26, 2006.

The preliminary hearing began on January 10, 2006, before Judge Steven Suzukawa in the Compton courthouse. It was exactly 20 months since the murder of Captain Michael Sparkes on August 10, 2004. Deputy District Attorney Darren Levine of CAPOS was the prosecutor, and William Sadler was the court-appointed defense attorney for Miguel Magallon.

On January 11, 2006, Orvis Anthony testified at the preliminary hearing and provided testimony consistent with the statements that he had previously given to the law enforcement investigators. Cross-examination of Anthony by defense attorney William Sadler covered over 100 pages of preliminary hearing transcript.

The preliminary hearing took four days and concluded on January 13, 2006. Miguel Magallon was bound over for trial as charged by Judge Suzukawa.

POST-PRELIMINARY HEARING PROCEEDINGS

After the preliminary hearing, Miguel Magallon was arraigned in the Superior Court on January 25, 2006. However, it would be almost three-and-a-half years before the case would go to trial. Between the preliminary hearing and the trial, the following significant events occurred in the case.

Change of Attorneys

Deputy District Attorney Phillip Stirling of CAPOS was assigned to assist Darren Levine in the prosecution of the case against Miguel Magallon.

Defense attorneys Victor Salerno and Robert Longoria were appointed by the court to represent Miguel Magallon.

Determination of Penalty

The Los Angeles County District Attorney's Office has a Special Circumstances Committee that determines whether the death penalty will be sought in a murder case where special circumstances are alleged. Deputy District Attorneys Darren Levine and Phillip Stirling submitted a 15-page memorandum dated September 28, 2006, to Assistant District Attorney Curtis Hazell, the Chairman of the Special Circumstances Committee. The memorandum discussed the facts of the crime, the available evidence (including Anthony's testimony), the defendant's criminal background, and other factors involving the appropriateness of the death penalty. The

Special Circumstances Committee determined that death would be sought as the appropriate penalty for Miguel Magallon.

Assignment of Trial Judge

The Magallon case was transferred to the Clara Shortridge Foltz Criminal Justice Center in downtown Los Angeles. The ninth floor contains high security courtrooms with experienced judges presiding over the most serious and complex cases. The case was assigned to Judge Kathleen Kennedy's courtroom on that floor.

JUDGE KATHLEEN KENNEDY

Kathleen Kennedy was born and raised in Los Angeles. She graduated magna cum laude with an economics degree from Loyola Marymount University in 1974 and graduated from Loyola Law School with a law degree in 1977. She passed the bar and worked three years doing civil litigation in the law offices of her father, Brian J. Kennedy.

She joined the District Attorney's Office in 1980, where she worked as a prosecutor until her appointment to the Los Angeles County Municipal Court by Governor George Deukmejian in 1988. She was elevated by court unification to the Los Angeles Superior Court in January 2000.

Judge Kennedy came to the public eye when she presided over the preliminary hearing of O. J. Simpson in July 1994. In 2004, she was assigned to Department 109 on the Ninth Floor of the Clara Shortridge Foltz Criminal Justice Center. She has been the trial judge in numerous murder cases, including the trial of the "Grim Sleeper" serial killer, Lonnie David Franklin, Jr., in 2016.

Despite her background as a prosecutor, she has developed a reputation as a capable, fair, and hardworking judge who favors neither the prosecution nor the defense.

ORVIS ANTHONY REFUSAL TO TESTIFY AT TRIAL

To protect Orvis Anthony while he was in custody, jail authorities placed him in special modules which segregated certain county inmates from the general jail population. Despite these precautions, Anthony was attacked by another inmate on August 9, 2007, who slashed him with a knife on the right side of his nose and in his left hand.

On or about May 13, 2009, Orvis Anthony stated, through his attorney Earl Evans, that he would not testify at Magallon's trial. As a result, on May 18, 2009, Deputy District Attorneys Darren Levine and Phillip Stirling, Detective Scott Fines, and Earl Evans met Anthony at the Los Angeles County Jail. They all encouraged Anthony to testify truthfully at Magallon's upcoming jury trial in accordance with his leniency agreement with the prosecution. Anthony repeatedly stated that he did not want to testify based on religious grounds and because he was concerned for his safety and the safety of his family.

On May 26, 2009, Deputy District Attorneys Levine and Stirling and attorney Evans had another meeting with Orvis Anthony. Again they attempted to convince Anthony to testify. Anthony remained insistent that he would not testify at the trial.

On June 4, 2009, Orvis Anthony appeared in the courtroom of Judge John Cheroske. Anthony had entered a guilty plea before Judge Cheroske on January 9, 2006. Anthony's sentencing had been continued several times since it was to be imposed after he testified at Magallon's trial. Attorney Evans and prosecutor Levine informed the judge that Anthony was refusing to testify at Magallon's trial based on religious grounds and fear for his safety and that of his family. Judge Cheroske questioned Orvis Anthony, and Anthony confirmed to the judge that he would refuse to testify at Magallon's trial. Judge Cheroske then granted the People's motion to set aside Anthony's guilty plea and reinstated criminal proceedings against him.

PROSECUTION CASE WITHOUT ANTHONY'S TESTIMONY

Orvis Anthony had been the centerpiece of the prosecution case against Miguel Magallon. Aside from the defendant Magallon, Anthony was the only witness to the murder of Captain Michael Sparkes. He provided direct evidence that Magallon was the moving force behind the murder and fired the fatal shot against Captain Sparkes in an execution-style slaying. The loss of Anthony's testimony would greatly weaken the prosecution's case.

Without Anthony's testimony, the evidence against Miguel Magallon consisted of the following:

Gunshot Residue

Both Magallon and Anthony were examined for evidence of gunshot residue shortly after their arrests. It was determined that Magallon's hands had five unique particles of gunshot residue, while Anthony had only one particle which was consistent with gunshot residue. This evidence indicated that Magallon had recently fired a weapon.

Firearms Evidence

The Sheriff's Crime Lab's Firearms Section determined that the five bullets recovered from the body of Captain Sparkes and the 7.62 casings found at the crime scene were all fired from the recovered AK-47 style assault rifle. It was also determined that the bullets recovered from Anthony's Nissan Maxima were fired from Captain Sparkes's semi-automatic firearm.

DNA Evidence

Magallon's DNA was recovered from the blood found on the pillow recovered near the front passenger seat of Anthony's Nissan Maxima.

Magallon's Letters from Jail

While Magallon was in custody awaiting trial, he wrote a letter to a fellow gang member and attempted to send the letter through the United States Mail system. The letter was intercepted by Sheriff's deputies assigned to the County Jail. In the letter, Magallon made statements revealing his hatred of law enforcement and his lack of remorse concerning the murder. The letter included the following language:

I've been siten in this hell dog just writen reading waiten for mail tryen to use the phone but fuck these muthafuckaz be acten like bitchez like as if they knew the pig that got smoked-yeah I said it pig pig pig fuck them bitches one less you got to worry about beaten the shit out of innocent people or killen a kid talken bout we thought he had a weapon or shooten somebody in tha back...

Witness Eliel Garcia

On August 10, 2004, at approximately 5:30 a.m., Eliel Garcia was working at a business on the southeast corner of Avalon Boulevard and Redondo Beach Boulevard. He heard six to seven gunshots, climbed atop a flatbed pickup truck, and observed the injured Captain Sparkes and the vehicle used in the crime. However, he was unable to provide any information about the person or persons involved in the crime.

Without the testimony of Orvis Anthony, Magallon's defense attorney could argue to the jury that Anthony, and not Magallon, was the driving force in the murder of Captain Sparkes. After all, Anthony was at the scene of the murder, and he owned the Nissan Maxima and had control of the AK-47 that was used in the crime.

FORMER TESTIMONY EXCEPTION TO HEARSAY RULE

Orvis Anthony testified at the preliminary hearing, and prosecutors Darren Levine and Phillip Stirling wanted to use that testimony at the trial of Miguel Magallon. However, Anthony's testimony at the preliminary hearing was hearsay, which made it inadmissible at Magallon's trial unless it came under an exception to the hearsay rule. Levine and Stirling hoped that they could introduce Anthony's preliminary hearing testimony under Evidence Code section 1291, the former testimony exception to the hearsay rule.

Evidence Code section 1291 provides in part the following:

(a) Evidence of former testimony is not made inadmissible by the hearsay rule if the declarant is unavailable as a witness and...

(2) The party against whom the former testimony is offered was a party to the action or proceeding in which the testimony was given and had the right and opportunity to cross-examine the declarant

with an interest and motive similar to that which he has at the hearing.

Evidence Code section 1291 has a requirement that the "declarant" [i.e., Orvis Anthony] must be "unavailable as a witness." However, Evidence Code section 240 lists "privilege" as a grounds upon which a witness becomes unavailable to testify.

Prosecutor Darren Levine prepared a trial brief for the trial judge in which he argued that Orvis Anthony's preliminary hearing testimony was admissible at Magallon's jury trial pursuant to Evidence Code section 1291. Since Anthony was asserting his privilege against self-incrimination in refusing to testify, the "unavailability" requirement was satisfied.

In his brief, Levine cited the 2008 California Supreme Court decision in *People v. Williams* (2008) 43 Cal 4th 584. In the *Williams* case, the court ruled that the preliminary hearing testimony of the defendant's accomplice in a capital case was admissible when the accomplice invoked his right against self-incrimination during the trial. This was entirely consistent with the prosecution position in the Magallon trial.

It appeared that Anthony's preliminary hearing testimony might be presented to the jury after all.

OVERVIEW OF JURY TRIAL

Jury selection in the trial of Miguel Magallon began on June 11, 2009. Below is an overview of the case.

PEOPLE v. MIGUEL ANGEL MAGALLON
CASE TA075921

JUDGE:	Kathleen Kennedy
PROSECUTORS:	Darren Levine, Deputy District Attorney (CAPOS)
	Phillip Stirling, Deputy District Attorney (CAPOS)
DEFENSE ATTORNEYS:	Victor Salerno, Attorney At Law, Bar Panel
	Roberto Longoria, Attorney At Law, Bar Panel

CHARGES: Count I — First Degree Murder, with Special
                                    Circumstances
                                    Count II — Attempted Robbery
LOCATION: Los Angeles Superior Court
                                    Clara Shortridge Foltz Criminal Justice Center,
                                    Department 109

PRETRIAL HEARING REGARDING ORVIS ANTHONY

On June 18, 2009, Judge Kathleen Kennedy and the attorneys took a break from jury selection to handle some pretrial motions. One defense motion was a hearing to examine Orvis Anthony to determine his claim of privilege against self-incrimination and his availability as a witness. Anthony was called as a witness and testified holding a piece of paper and with his attorney Earl Evans standing next to him at the witness stand. Anthony was examined by prosecutor Darren Levine and gave the following testimony:

Q. *Will you answer any of my questions in this case?*

A. *As in testifying?*

Q. *Yes. Are you going to testify in this case?*

A. *No.*

Q. *Do you have a statement that you want to read?*

A. *Yes. I refuse to testify in this case on my Fifth Amendment Privilege Against Self-incrimination because any testimony I may—I give may tend to incriminate me.*

Q. *If I were to ask you further questions, would that be your response to every one of my questions?*

A. *Yes, sir.*

Q. *I have no further questions.* (Trial transcript, page 348.)

Both defense attorneys Victor Salerno and Roberto Longoria attempted to cross-examine Anthony but without success. Anthony was excused as a witness.

Judge Kennedy was aware that criminal proceedings against Orvis Anthony had been reinstated and that he was facing a preliminary hearing in the case. She made the following findings:

All right. The witness has left the courtroom. The witness has clearly asserted his Fifth Amendment right in this matter. The court finds that he does have a valid Fifth Amendment privilege. The court further finds that he's unavailable to testify at the trial. (Trial transcript, page 350.)

Judge Kennedy noted that Miguel Magallon's defense attorneys had the opportunity to cross-examine Orvis Anthony at the preliminary hearing. She ruled that Anthony's preliminary hearing testimony could be presented to the jury at Magallon's trial.

JURY SELECTION AND OPENING STATEMENT

As previously indicated, jury selection began on June 14, 2009, interrupted occasionally as the attorneys litigated pre-trial motions before Judge Kathleen Kennedy. If the jury eventually found Miguel Magallon guilty of first degree murder with special circumstances, that would also determine whether he should receive the death penalty. As a result, the jury had to be "death qualified" to determine whether each juror hearing the case could impose the death penalty in an appropriate case.

Jury selection was completed on the week of June 20, 2009.

On June 25 and 26, Deputy District Attorney Darren Levine gave the opening statement for the prosecution. He used a PowerPoint presentation to introduce the jury to the facts of the prosecution's case, told the jury about the testimony of Orvis Anthony, and played parts of the 911 call made by Captain Sparkes.

In his opening statement, defense attorney Victor Salerno conceded that Magallon had shot Captain Sparkes, but he told the jury that his client was too drunk to form the specific intent for first degree murder. He also stated that Magallon was not a gangster, and that he didn't know that Captain Sparkes was a cop.

PEOPLE'S CASE-IN-CHIEF

The prosecution began the presentation of its case-in-chief on Monday, June 29, 2009. The centerpiece of the prosecution case was the preliminary hearing testimony of Orvis Anthony that would be read to the jury. Prosecutors Darren Levine and Phillip Stirling wanted to set the stage for this testimony so the jury would know enough about the case to place the testimony in proper context. Their first witness was Deloris Sparkes, the widow of Captain Michael Sparkes. She testified that her husband typically would get up at 5:00 a.m. and ride his mountain bike in the area for exercise. He would wear gym clothes and carry a fanny pack with his gun, badge, music headset, and cell phone. Over the next few days, witnesses testified to the circumstances of the crime, the arrest of Orvis Anthony, and statements by Miguel Magallon at the hospital that he was shot in the abdomen by unknown assailants and refused to have the bullet removed.

On July 2, 2009, Judge Kennedy told the jury that she had made a determination that Orvis Anthony, the next witness, was unavailable for the purposes of actually testifying at the trial and that the transcript of the preliminary hearing where Anthony testified was going to be read to them. Over the next two court days, Anthony's preliminary hearing testimony was read to the jury.

The rest of the prosecutors' case-in-chief progressed quickly. This included the recovery of the murder weapon, ballistics evidence, gunshot residue evidence, DNA evidence, the 911 tape, and contradictory statements made by the defendant. None of this evidence directly connected Miguel Magallon as the actual shooter of Captain Sparkes, although it did establish his involvement in the crime. However, this evidence tended to corroborate the testimony of Orvis Anthony that Magallon was the shooter.

The prosecution rested on the morning of Monday, July 13, 2009.

DEFENSE CASE-IN-CHIEF

Orvis Anthony had testified that he and Miguel Magallon began drinking in the late afternoon of August 9, 2004. At approximately 6:00 p.m., they each drank a 40 ounce bottle of malt liquor. They then split another 40 ounce bottle of malt liquor. Later that evening, they drove to a 7–11 market and stole a 12-pack of beer. They consumed beer from the 12-pack and some additional beer at a friend's house. They stopped drinking around midnight when they took a short nap at the friend's house. Anthony estimated that Magallon drank 12 to 14 cans of beer. When asked to describe Magallon's state of sobriety, Anthony testified that he was alright, talkative, not falling down drunk, and not confused.

The defense attempted to pursue the strategy that Magallon may have been intoxicated by calling two female witnesses who observed Magallon and Anthony while they were drinking. They testified that Magallon appeared to be under the influence. Dr. Gordon Plotkin, an expert witness called by the defense, estimated that Magallon consumed 41 to 43 beers. He testified that, in his opinion, Magallon's state of sobriety rendered him unable to form the requisite intent for first degree murder.

Miguel Magallon did not testify in his defense.

Both sides rested on Thursday, July 16, 2009.

CLOSING ARGUMENTS

Closing arguments in the case began on July 17, 2009. Deputy District Attorney Phillip Stirling gave the prosecution's opening argument to the jury. He provided an appropriate discussion of the charges, the applicable law, and the evidence against the defendant.

Defense attorney Victor Salerno tried to mitigate the defendant's involvement in the murder of Captain Sparkes. He pointed out that Orvis Anthony had provided the car and the weapon and had initially suggested committing a robbery. He argued that, "We wouldn't be here without Anthony." He further argued that Magallon was too intoxicated to form the necessary intent for first degree murder and told the jury to convict his client of second degree murder.

Deputy District Attorney Darren Levine gave the final argument to the jury. He strongly refuted the defense argument that Magallon's culpability should be mitigated because of the use of alcohol. He pointed out that, although Anthony suggested the commission of a robbery, it was Magallon who stated that he wanted to do the robbery. And it was also Magallon who told Anthony to drive back to the crime scene, obviously with the intent to murder Captain Sparkes. Prosecutor Levine concluded his argument as follows:

> *At some point yesterday, defense counsel said to you, I have not done this in so many years, or it is not often that I do this where I come up and say convict my guy on second degree murder. He used the "C" word. It is in there. He used it. I sound like a prosecutor. Convict my guy of second degree murder.*
>
> *To convict him -- I mean, you are not -- you collectively are brilliant, the jury. Does he not get that? I sound like a prosecutor. Convict my guy of second degree murder.*
>
> *He came, in his argument, to negotiate with you. He came to make a deal with you. He put -- he used bait. You know what the bait was? The second degree murder. He hopes you will bite on the bait. "A second degree murder in this case is repugnant. Repulsive. Ridiculous. It would be an affront to justice; it would be an affront to the system. It is not the truth.*
>
> *Please, I ask you, only do justice. Do the right thing and convict him of every charge, every allegation and every special circumstance because Miguel Magallon deserves no less.*
>
> *Thank you.*

These were the last words that the jury heard from an attorney during the guilt phase of the case. Judge Kennedy then instructed the jury, and they retired to deliberate.

JURY VERDICT

On the morning of Friday, July 24, 2009, the jury announced its verdict in the trial. Miguel Angel Magallon was convicted of the first degree murder and second degree robbery of Captain Michael Sparkes. The conviction included a finding of two special circumstances – murder during an attempted robbery and murder during a drive-by shooting.

The jury also found true multiple special allegations, including murder to enhance a street gang and personal use of a firearm.

The jury could not agree on the special circumstance that the victim was a peace officer killed in the performance of his duties. However, the fact that the jury found true two other special circumstances made Miguel

Magallon eligible for the death penalty.

The jury and the attorneys on the case were ordered to return to the courtroom on Monday morning to begin the penalty phase.

PENALTY PHASE

The California death penalty statute states in part as follows:

In the proceedings on the question of penalty, evidence may be presented by both the people and the defendant as to any matter relevant to aggravation, mitigation, and sentence including, but not limited to, the nature and circumstances of the present offense, any prior felony conviction or convictions whether or not such conviction or convictions involved a crime of violence, the presence or absence of other criminal activity by the defendant which involved the use or attempted use of force or violence or which involved the express or implied threat to use force or violence, and the defendant's character, background, history, mental condition and physical condition. Penal Code section 190.3

The prosecution at the penalty phase introduced the evidence of criminal activity by Miguel Magallon:

1999 Attempted Murder

On July 16, 1999, at the age of 16, Magallon was a "South Los" gang member who fired approximately six shots at a vehicle containing rival gang members. One of the shots struck the driver in the back of the head. The victim sustained a serious injury that left him seriously impaired.

Criminal Conduct While In Custody

Magallon was in continuous custody in the Los Angeles County Jail from his arrest on August 10, 2004, until the conclusion of his trial. While in custody, he was involved in the following criminal activity:

- On July 5, 2005, Magallon threatened a jail deputy by yelling, "Fuck you, you lame motherfucker, I will fuck you up. I am an Aztec Warrior."
- Later on July 5, 2005, Magallon threatened another jail deputy by yelling that he would throw the contents of his colostomy bag at him.
- On December 22, 2005, a search of Magallon's cell resulted in the recovery of numerous letters containing lyrics referencing gang violence and wanting to get a pig.
- On April 27, 2007, Magallon and an inmate held another inmate who was slashed in the arm by an inmate with a loose razor blade.
- On May 28, 2007, Magallon leaned through his cell bars and slashed inmate Lockwood with a loose razor blade, causing a laceration from his left ear to the center of his chin.
- On June 8, 2007, a six-inch plastic shank was recovered in a vacant cell next to Magallon's cell. Magallon was heard to state, "I've been caught", in Spanish.
- On June 30, 2007, Magallon used and then returned a razor blade that had been altered in which the actual blades were removed and replaced with tin foil. This and other blades were recovered from an adjoining cell.
- On January 22, 2008, Magallon struck another inmate in the face as the inmate was being escorted in front of Magallon's cell.
- On July 27, 2009, a jail deputy pulled inmate Henry Cota from the bars of Magallon's cell as Cota was being held and stabbed by Magallon and another inmate. The razor was flushed down the toilet before it could be recovered. [This incident took place two days before opening statements in Magallon's trial and caused Judge Kennedy to have one of his legs shackled as a security risk].

In addition to evidence of prior criminal activity, the prosecution can also introduce victim impact evidence that describes the victim and the effect that the victim's death had on other persons. Prosecutors Levine and Stirling called numerous witnesses who established that Michael Sparkes was born in Chicago in 1951 and was abused as a child. He had a horrible family life and joined the Navy to get away. After his Navy service, he became a police officer for the Charleston Police Department in South Carolina. He moved to Los Angeles in 1975 and joined the Los Angeles County Police Department. He worked hard, received a series of promotions, and eventually became a Captain in charge of security at Harbor-UCLA General Hospital. He was very much involved in his church and attempted to keep young men from getting into gangs. He was working on becoming an elder and an ordained minister in the church. He was making Captain's pay and could easily have moved to a different neighborhood, but he remained where he was because he wanted to continue to help his community.

After a previous failed marriage, he found the right relationship and had the son that he always wanted. Michael, Jr. was seven years old at the time of his father's death.

The defense called friends and family as witnesses in an effort to convince the jury to spare the life of Miguel Magallon. They established that he was 21 years old when he murdered Captain Sparkes. He grew up in a tough neighborhood raised by a loving mother. He was a good artist and musician and received a Catholic education where he learned right from wrong. He got his high school diploma, married in 2001, and had a son the following year. Members of his family asked the jury to spare his life.

In a surprise move, Miguel Magallon took the witness stand during the penalty phase. He claimed that he had drunk heavily prior to the murder and only had a partial recollection of the events. However, he admitted being armed with an AK-47 and intending to rob the victim. He claimed that the intended robbery victim shot first and that he then fired his weapon. He denied leaving the location and returning to finish the job. He was shot in the abdomen and was driven to the hospital by Orvis Anthony. He stated that the bullet was still in his body. He denied the various acts of criminal activity that had been introduced by the prosecution during the penalty phase, with one notable exception. When asked about the slashing of Albert Lockwood in May 2007 by prosecutor Phillip Stirling, he testified as follows:

Q. Did you slash the face, the left neck of Albert Lockwood?

A. Yes, I did.

Q. Why?

A. He disrespected me.

Q. How so?

A. He called me a punk bitch.

Q. And so you did what exactly, sir?

A. Cut him in the neck.

Q. With what?

A. With a razor.

Q. In your hand?

A. Yes.

Q. Was it attached to anything?

A. No.

Q. What did you do with the razor?

A. I threw it away.

Q. How?

A. I flushed it.

Q. Did... he called you a quote, punk bitch?

A. Right.

Q. So in response, you slashed his neck?

A. Right. (Trial transcript, pages 4944 to 4945.)

On cross-examination Miguel Magallon admitted being a member of the Street Knights gang. In fact, on August 1, 2009, the day before he testified, he personally tattooed "Street" on his right hand and "Knight" on the left hand. He had numerous other gang tattoos on his body, including an Aztec Calendar on his back and the letters "S" and "K" on his chest. Magallon denied any knowledge or connection to the Mexican Mafia prison gang.

Closing arguments in the penalty phase began on the morning of August 5, 2009. Deputy District Attorney Darren Levine was the first attorney to argue. At the conclusion of his nearly two-hour closing argument, Levine played a photo and video montage depicting the life of Captain Sparkes, beginning when he was a boy with his puppy and a tricycle, then as a uniformed officer, and finally as a father teaching his son to swim and ride a bike. The video was dramatically interrupted by the noise of shots from an AK-47 and excerpts from the 911 call made by the dying Captain Sparkes. Some members of the jury and some spectators were observed to be crying. During the playing of the 911 call, Deloris Sparkes, the widow of Captain Sparkes, cried out and had to leave the courtroom.

After closing arguments by defense attorney Victor Salerno and Deputy District Attorney Phillip Stirling, the jury was instructed and then retired to deliberate the fate of Miguel Angel Magallon.

On Friday, August 7, 2009, the jury returned its verdict, fixing the penalty for Magallon as death. It was almost five years to the day after the murder of Captain Michael Sparkes on August 10, 2004.

Judge Kathleen Kennedy set October 15, 2009, as the date for sentencing.

EPILOGUE – ORVIS CAMILLO ANTHONY

Criminal proceedings against Orvis Anthony had been reinstated after he refused to testify at Miguel Magallon's trial. However, his preliminary hearing testimony was used at the trial, and Magallon was convicted by the jury of first degree murder with a sentence of death.

Orvis Anthony then indicated that he wished to re-enter his guilty plea under the same terms and conditions. The prosecution agreed if he waived his custody credits. Anthony agreed, and, on September 18, 2009, he re-entered his guilty plea with a waiver of all custody credits before Judge Kathleen Kennedy. By waiving his custody credits, he lost the five years of credit that he had built up. Judge Kennedy then sentenced him to 50 years to life in prison.

SENTENCING

On October 15, 2009, Judge Kathleen Kennedy sentenced the defendant Miguel Magallon. First, she denied the defendant's motion for a new trial and for modification of the death penalty verdict. Then she made a lengthy statement about the defendant that included the following language:

Most of us go through life, and we don't try to kill anyone. And the defendant is so entrenched in that violent lifestyle by this point – I mean, having already shot someone when he was a juvenile, having executed Michael Sparkes out on the street, that a few slashings in county jail are no big deal.

I think they are a big deal. It shows his entrenched lifestyle of, you know, accepting and perpetuating violence. And it is horrible, and it is nothing to be ignored. And it is not par for the course.

He has threatened deputies repeatedly, threatened deputies with the contents of his colostomy bag. I mean, that's not normal behavior. That's not someone that is not a predator.

That is a predator. (Trial transcript, page 5405.)

Judge Kennedy then sentenced Miguel Magallon to death for fatally shooting Captain Michael Sparkes.

LESSONS LEARNED

When Captain Sparkes left his residence on the early morning of August 10, 2004, he was taking reasonable precautions to enhance his safety by taking with him a fanny pack around his waist containing his police badge, Beretta handgun, and cellular telephone. During the robbery, he was able to return fire. However, when he used his cellular phone to make a 911 call, he gave the 911 operator the wrong location of Avalon and Artesia when, in fact, he was at Avalon and Redondo Beach Boulevard. He could hear the sirens a short distance away while he was laying in the alley bleeding to death.

Officers should always be aware of their location. When I was a reserve officer for the Los Angeles Police Department, my training officer would sometimes stop the car and ask me if I knew where we were. I was always conscious of my location so I could properly respond not just to my training officer but, more importantly, to handle any situation that may arise in or out of the patrol car.

There are tactical lessons for law enforcement officers that can be derived from the Sparkes case:

- If you are an off-duty or retired officer in a public place, carry a concealed handgun along with your badge or identification card.

- Also carry at least one spare magazine.
- Be practiced on the efficient drawing of your weapon and credentials.
- Practice by firing the same handgun you carry off-duty or retired, including fire-and-movement drills.
- Mentally practice a variety of "what if" scenarios.
- Know your location just as you would if you were on duty.
- If you perceive a potential threat, determine if you must engage immediately based on your location and locations of innocents.
- If you do not need to immediately engage, surreptitiously call 911 and leave the line open, or cause someone else to do so.
- Be aware of the dangers of the arrival of on-duty officers when you have a gun in your hand.
- Attempt to implement time/distance/cover while drawing your weapon and preparing to engage.
- If an imminent deadly threat emerges, know that you do <u>not</u> have to wait to shoot until the armed suspect points his gun at you or shoots.
- If wounded, not all wounds are fatal. Continue to engage. Willpower beats fire power. Finish the fight. Stop the threat.

CONCLUSION (COMMENTARY OF STEVE COOLEY)

The death of Captain Michael Sparkes was the first time that the murder of an officer and the subsequent successful prosecution of the case was concluded during my administration. This case is testimony to the importance of having a specialized unit like CAPOS or its equivalent in any jurisdiction where it is feasible to do so. In any event, written policies, procedures, and protocols should be in place to guide these cases from the initial investigative phase through a successful prosecution.

CAPTAIN MICHAEL L. SPARKES
Los Angeles County Police Department

- *January 10th, 1951*
  - Born in Chicago, Illinois
- *November 19, 1975:*
  - Joined the Los Angeles County Police Department
- *April 1, 2000:*
  - Promoted to rank of Captain
    - *Commanding officer of police services at Harbor-UCLA General Hospital*
- *August 10, 2004*
  - End of watch

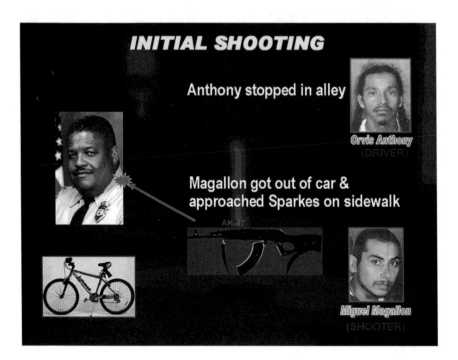

INITIAL SHOOTING

Anthony stopped in alley

Orvis Anthony
(DRIVER)

Magallon got out of car & approached Sparkes on sidewalk

AK-47

Miguel Magallon
(SHOOTER)

THEY TURNED INTO ALLEY AND CIRCLED THE BLOCK

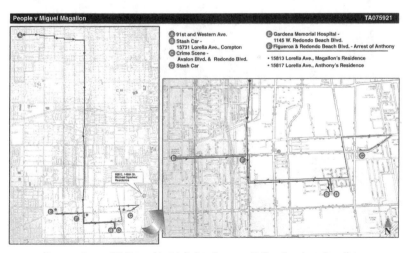

Prosecution exhibit used in trial showing proximity of various locations

LOCATION OF BADGE, GUN & PHONE

Crime scene at the intersection of Avalon Blvd and
Redondo Beach Blvd

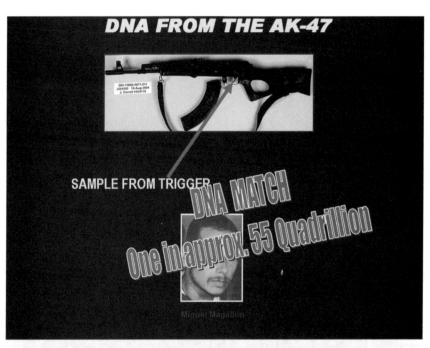

DNA FROM THE AK-47

SAMPLE FROM TRIGGER

DNA MATCH One in approx. 55 Quadrillion

Miguel Magallon

INTERIOR OF ANTHONY'S CAR HAD BLOOD

DNA MATCH One in approx 315 trillion

Miguel Magallon

Michael Sparkes Jr. at the funeral of his father

CHAPTER 8

Liberty

Los Angeles Police Department

K-9 Unit

"Warriors to the End"

LOS ANGELES POLICE DEPARTMENT'S K-9 UNIT

"There is no hunting like the hunting of men. And those that hunt armed men long enough, and like it, never care for anything else thereafter." This is the motto of the Los Angeles Police Department's K-9 Unit, taken from the works of Ernest Hemingway. It is located on a plaque at the Metropolitan Division, where the K-9 Unit is located.

The idea for a K-9 Unit in LAPD originated in 1979 when a rapist in the West Los Angeles area was breaking into the homes of women who lived alone and raped them. One early morning, West Los Angeles patrol officers responded to a "rape in progress" call. Upon arrival, they observed the suspect exiting a window, and they engaged in a lengthy foot pursuit. The officers eventually contained the suspect in a large perimeter. They now had to search the perimeter for the suspect, but LAPD at that time did not have a K-9 Unit. The officers requested a Beverly Hills Police Department K-9 unit to search for the suspect, and this K-9 Unit conducted a systematic search and located the individual. LAPD Chief Daryl Gates was embarrassed that his department had to use another agency's K-9 Unit to locate a suspect who was terrorizing the community. He decided that LAPD should have its own K-9 Unit.

The LAPD K-9 Unit was established in September 1980 as a one-year pilot program with two search dogs. The new K-9 Unit was required to show that using dogs to search for felony suspects would increase officer safety, shorten the time in searching for felony suspects, and increase the percentage of finding suspects who had concealed themselves. The achievements of the two search dogs were so impressive that the one-year trial program was declared a total success. The K-9 Unit expanded and became a permanent part of the LAPD.

Chief Gates was very proud of the Unit. He knew each K-9 team and the names of each handler and police dog. They were welcome in his office at any time. Chief Gates spoke at some training days, and, on one occasion, he volunteered to put on the "sleeve" to be a suspect during training.

Today, the K-9 Unit is one of the field platoons of the Metropolitan Division and is deployed at the direction of the Commanding Officer of the Metropolitan Division. The K-9 Unit is supervised by a Lieutenant Officer-in-Charge with five K-9 sergeants, a K-9 Chief Trainer, and sixteen police officers as K-9 handlers. K-9 teams respond to assist field and detective operations on a city-wide basis, seven days a week, 24 hours a day. K-9 teams also assist with emergency calls for service including "officer needs help", "assistance", or "back-up" calls.

INTRODUCTION (COMMENTARY OF STEVE COOLEY)

It is impossible to talk about a police dog without mentioning the dog's handler. Officer John Hall was the handler for Liberty. During my career as District Attorney, John and I became very good friends.

I first met John Hall on January 18, 2002. I was in the courtroom of Judge Larry Paul Fidler to watch the sentencing proceedings for former Symbionese Liberation Army member Kathleen Soliah. The Symbionese Liberation Army was a revolutionary group that was in existence from 1973 to 1975 which operated in the San Francisco and Los Angeles areas. Their major claim to fame was the kidnapping of heiress Patty Hearst in February 1974, but they were involved in other revolutionary activities, one of which almost took the life of Officer John Hall.

On August 21, 1975, at about 11:00 p.m., Los Angeles Police Officer John Hall and his partner, James Bryan, pulled their marked police vehicle into the parking lot of an IHOP restaurant in Hollywood. Officer Bryan parked the patrol car in a parking stall in front of a large window that looked into the restaurant. The officers entered the restaurant and got something to eat. While the officers were inside the restaurant, Kathleen Soliah and two other SLA members placed a bomb under the police vehicle. The bomb was set to explode when the police car moved, which would close two contacts on a clothespin and cause the bomb to explode. Fortunately, as the police car left the parking space, the contacts on the clothespin failed to make contact by 1/16 of an inch. Had the bomb exploded as intended, it would have killed Officers Hall and Bryan and caused death or serious injury to numerous persons in the restaurant.

In September 1975, Kathleen Soliah went underground. She was finally located in June 1999 in St. Paul, Minnesota under the name of Sara Jane Olson. She was married to a physician and the mother of three daughters. She eventually entered a guilty plea to two counts of possessing bombs with the intent to kill police officers, and she was now before Judge Fidler for sentencing. I attended the sentencing hearing.

At the sentencing hearing before Judge Fidler, the defense called friends and family of Soliah/Olson who stated that she was now a law-abiding and productive member of society who had been rehabilitated and no longer posed a threat to society. The prosecution then called John Hall as a witness. He recalled that the restaurant that night had many men, women, and children inside who would have been killed or seriously injured had the bomb exploded. If he had died in the explosion, he would have left a wife and a three-month-old daughter. His two other children and one of his grandsons would not have been born.

I had heard of John Hall by reputation, but we had never met before that date. I was very impressed with him that day. In my opinion, John Hall's statement placed the sentencing into its proper perspective, that Soliah/Olson was being sentenced for committing serious terrorist acts. Judge Fidler sentenced the defendant to two consecutive terms of ten years to life in prison on the two counts to which she had pleaded guilty.

OFFICER JOHN HALL

John Hall was born in Portland, Oregon in May 1947. His family moved to Northern California when he was three years old. He graduated from Saint Bernard High School in Eureka, California and attended College of the Redwoods, a junior college in Humboldt County. In the fall of 1967, he was drafted into the United States Army. He spent one year in Vietnam and served in the 4th Division, 1/10 Cavalry along the Laos-Cambodian border. The Tet Offensive was in full operation, and both sides sustained heavy casualties. Due to the depletion of his company, he went from a private first class to a sergeant in four months.

Hall returned to where he grew up and worked in the logging industry during the day and attended junior college in the evenings. He got married in May 1970 and, a year later, he and his wife moved to Los Angeles.

Hall was accepted into the Los Angeles Police Department and began his Police Academy training in June 1971. After graduating from the Academy, he was sent to Hollywood Division where he completed his probation. He was assigned to Hollywood Division as a patrol officer on August 21, 1975, when the SLA bomb was placed under his police vehicle. For his first ten years as a police officer, he was assigned to patrol units, foot beats, special problem units, major crimes violators, and the Detective Bureau.

In the latter part of 1980, a K-9 Unit was being formed within the Los Angeles Police Department. They were recruiting good officers rather than officers who liked dogs. Two police officer friends of John Hall's had joined the unit in the early months of 1981, and they called him and asked if he was interested in hunting down felony suspects with a search dog. By June 1981, Officer Hall was in the K-9 Unit and being trained with his first dog, Chas. For the next 17 years of his career, until his retirement on May 19, 2002, Hall worked with four different dogs, hunting down every type of felony suspect involving crimes ranging from murder to auto theft.

While Officer Hall was the "partner" to Chas, he was given Liberty to train. Liberty was a female Rottweiler who was born in Denmark in July 1983. Liberty joined Officer Hall's family when she was an eight-week-old puppy, and she was raised in a K-9 car with Chas. From a very early age, Liberty displayed an aptitude for police work. When Chas was injured in early 1987 in a fight with a felony warrant suspect, Chas had to be retired. Liberty then became Officer Hall's regular partner.

The K-9 teams were trained in obedience, protection, and searching for human scent. Training the team could take from three months to as long as nine months to complete. Once the K-9 team passed a very difficult certification, they were required to continue to perform at that high standard at all times. They were continuously tested and observed by the trainers and supervisors of the K-9 Unit.

LIBERTY

Liberty and Officer Hall were partners for about two years. Liberty lived with Hall and his family, and the dog got along well with Hall's wife and three children. Liberty was also a big hit whenever she was taken to visit a school as part of a public relations program. During the two years that they were partners, Liberty was credited with participating in 115 arrests and more than 250 searches.

One of the searches was especially notable because Liberty tracked down the killer of an LAPD officer.

In June 1988, LAPD Officer James Beyea responded to a burglar alarm at a closed business, where he confronted the suspect. There was a struggle, and the officer was shot and killed with his own weapon. The suspect then ran off. A large perimeter was established to search for the killer. Officer Hall and Liberty were called to the command post and began a search of the area. About an hour into the search, Liberty picked up a scent at a vacant residence and gave a high alert indicating that someone was in the attic of the vacant house. Officer Hall then called the command post for additional flashlights and an attic mirror. Using the lights and the mirror, he scanned the attic but saw no one. Officer Hall entered the attic and saw Bobby Steele lying on his back about 10–15 feet away. Officer Hall ordered Steele to put his hands up, but Steele reached for Officer Beyea's gun. Officer Hall then fired one round that entered the suspect's head and killed him. The gang member/suspect was dead, and the officer's gun was recovered. Liberty and Officer Hall had performed well in hunting down the killer of a police officer.

MARCH 22, 1989

On March 22, 1989, at approximately 9:10 p.m., a West Traffic motor officer attempted to stop a vehicle for a traffic violation. The two occupants of the vehicle refused to stop, and a pursuit ensued. A second motor officer joined the pursuit. The pursuit terminated at Bledsoe Avenue near Washington Boulevard when the vehicle came to a sudden halt, and the two occupants ran into an alley. One of them fired a round from a handgun at a pursuing officer, striking the windshield of his motorcycle. The two suspects continued to run off, and they disappeared from view. It was later determined that the vehicle was stolen.

Responding patrol units established a perimeter around several blocks of the area. Because the suspects were believed to be hiding within the perimeter and were known to be armed and dangerous, Metropolitan K-9

Units were requested to respond to the scene to assist in the search for the suspects.

Along with other K-9 units, Officer John Hall responded to the command post with Liberty. A search team was formed consisting of Officer Hall, Liberty, and three other police officers, and they were assigned to search a sector within the perimeter. Shortly after the search began, Liberty alerted at the fence that separated the rear yards of 4111 and 4117 Bledsoe Avenue, indicating that she had picked up the scent of a possible suspect. Two of the officers remained in the rear of 4117 Bledsoe Avenue to ensure that the suspects could not flee in that direction. Officer Hall, Liberty, and the remaining officer then entered the rear yard at 4111 Bledsoe Avenue.

Liberty then ran to the open garage door and displayed a full alert, indicating that a suspect was either in the garage or had recently been there. Officer Hall illuminated the interior of the two-car garage with his flashlight and observed that the garage had been divided by a partition into a one-car garage and a storage room. The partition contained a door that provided access into the storage room. Liberty entered the main part of the garage, conducted a search pattern, and indicated that no one was there. Liberty then entered the storage room through the door in the partition and disappeared from view.

Suddenly Liberty began barking, indicating that she had located a suspect in the storage room. From the east side of the doorway, Officer Hall first illuminated with his flashlight the west side of the room and observed that it was clear. As he moved to the west side of the doorway to illuminate the east side of the room, he heard a gunshot and saw Liberty fall to the floor, apparently wounded. Almost immediately, Officer Hall saw the muzzle flash of a second shot that struck him in the left forearm, breaking bones. Officer Hall dropped his flashlight and the only illumination in the room came from muzzle flashes and from an LAPD Air Support Division helicopter overhead, which was flashing lights that entered the room through a window. From about five feet away, the suspect continued firing at Officer Hall while the officer returned fire with his 9-mm pistol. During the exchange of gunfire, Officer Hall observed that Liberty, even though wounded by gunfire, continued to engage the suspect. None of the subsequent rounds fired by the suspect struck Officer Hall, but the suspect fell to the ground apparently incapacitated. Officer Hall was then able to retrieve Liberty and move her outside the garage, where he requested medical care for her.

Officer Hall realized that the suspect in the garage, without being handcuffed, might still be a deadly danger to anyone entering the garage. Although wounded and in severe pain, he was able to reload his 9-mm pistol by placing the weapon between his knees and inserting a fresh magazine with his good hand. He borrowed a flashlight and proceeded to lead his team back into the garage. Suddenly, a second suspect burst from the storage area and, thinking that he was being attacked again by the first suspect, Hall fired his weapon and brought the man down. Both suspects died from their injuries.

Officer Hall then bent down to cradle Liberty in his arms, yelling, "Liberty! Liberty!", but she was not responding. Many police officers tell their partners that if they are killed in the line of duty, their bodies should not be left lying on the ground or in the street while an investigation was being conducted. Officer Hall wanted to give his canine partner that same consideration, and he asked fellow K-9 Officer Joe Vita to take her to a veterinarian. Officer Vita understood and took Liberty to a vet who determined that she died from a bullet that had torn through an artery in her neck.

Officer Hall was taken to UCLA Medical Center for treatment of shattered bones and bullet fragments in his left wrist. Liberty had most likely saved the life of Officer Hall. Had she not engaged the suspect as he was shooting at Officer Hall, the suspect's shots would have had greater accuracy, and Officer Hall would have been more seriously wounded and probably killed.

OFFICER JOE VITA'S ACCOUNT

Officer Joe Vita was a member of the LAPD's K-9 Unit, and he played an important role in the events on March 22, 1989. After his retirement from the LAPD, he became an investigator for the District Attorney's Office. He became the president of the Los Angeles District Attorney's Investigators Association. He occasionally worked as part of my security detail, and he provided me with the following account of the events of March 22, 1989.

On the evening of March 22, 1989, an LAPD motor officer had observed two males in a vehicle with no seat belts. As he attempted to stop them to conduct a citation investigation, they fled, initiating a pursuit. A second motor officer joined the pursuit and caught up with the other officer as the pursuit terminated. The vehicle came to an abrupt stop, and, as one of the suspects exited the vehicle, he fired a shot at one of the motor officers. The shot struck the windshield of his motorcycle. The two suspects ran off, and a perimeter was established to contain the area where the suspects were last seen running.

LAPD K-9 handlers Joe Vita, John Hall, and Mark Mooring responded to the scene with their police dogs. Officer Vita started with his dog, Belker, on one block, and Sergeant Mooring started across the street of the next block where the suspects were last seen by the motor officers. Officer Hall with his dog, Liberty, searched the other side of the block that Officer Vita had started, split by the wall that separated the houses. As Officer Vita entered a back yard, Belker alerted and started to run along the back wall. Officer Vita observed fresh muddy footprints onto a Jacuzzi cover located adjacent to the wall separating his search area from Officer Hall's search area. Officer Vita radioed to Officer Hall, "Belker has alerted on my side, and we have fresh footprints on top of a Jacuzzi cover. It looks like he jumped to your side." Officer Hall replied, "Roger Joe."

As Officer Vita continued to search that yard, he could see that the yard on Officer Hall's side had a detached garage that was in the back of the yard adjacent to the wall near the Jacuzzi with the footprints. As Officer Vita directed Belker's search, he heard a series of shots ring out from the other side of the wall. Officer Vita advised his team to get down and hold their positions.

There was a pause in the gunfire, and then a second series of gun shots rang out. Officer Vita whispered to his team to hold their positions until they heard from Officer Hall. They waited for seconds, but it seemed like forever. Suddenly he heard words from Officer Hall that he would never forget. "Joe, come help my baby," came over the radio. Officer Vita told his team to remain in their positions and to hold Belker tightly. Officer Vita ran and jumped over the wall into the middle of a backyard, alongside a darkened garage which had a long driveway heading to the street. As he ran around the corner of the garage, he could see the air unit above Officer Hall illuminating the area. Officer Hall was seated on the ground at the apron to the driveway with Liberty seriously wounded. Officer Vita noticed that Officer Hall was holding his wrist but was focused on Liberty. Officer Hall yelled over the noise from the air unit, "Get my baby to the hospital!"

At that moment, a uniformed patrol sergeant pulled up next to them on the street. Officer Vita ran up to him, yanked open the driver's door, pulled him by his shirt, and said, "I am taking your car." A uniformed patrol officer helped Officer Vita lift Liberty into the back seat of the car. Officer Vita hit the lights and siren and was off to the West Los Angeles Veterinary Medical Center at Santa Monica and Sepulveda Boulevards. He had the telephone number memorized in case he needed it in an emergency. Officer Vita advised that he was en route with a police dog who had been shot, that he had less than a five minute ETA, and to have them meet him in front. As Officer Vita pulled up to WLA Vet, he observed several persons in white lab coats and a gurney. They lifted Liberty from the back seat and brought her to the operating room.

Officer Vita stayed with Liberty in the operating room. Liberty had taken a round to the neck that hit the carotid artery, and she had lost a lot of blood. The doctor was unable to save her. Had the wound been just half an inch in either direction, Liberty could have gone home to the comforting arms of Officer Hall and his family.

While Officer Hall was in a hospital bed waiting for surgery to remove bullet fragments from his arm, the K-9 handlers were called at their homes and told to report to the hospital to receive a debriefing of what had occurred. After the debriefing was completed, the officers joined Officer Hall in his room. While the entire unit was in the hospital room, Chief Daryl Gates entered to check on the injured officer. Officer Hall and Chief Gates spoke briefly and then they were quiet. Chief Gates then turned to the handlers in the room and in an emotional voice gave the order to have Liberty buried – an honorable burial with all the respect that she deserved for saving Officer Hall's life. Chief Gates stated, "She is a true hero." Officer Hall called Officer Vita to his side and stated, "I want you to give Liberty her final ride." Officer Vita then returned to the West Los Angeles Veterinary Center to pick up Liberty. Following the Chief's orders, the K-9 handlers gave Liberty her last ride in the K-9 car to her final resting place. The funeral was made complete when the Air Support Division responded and conducted the "Missing Man Flyover" from overhead in honor of their fallen officer. These warriors then buried one of their own.

EPILOGUE – LIBERTY

Police Chief Daryl Gates ordered the lowering of flags at police stations throughout the city on March 24, 1989, to honor Liberty. A police spokesman stated that the lowering of flags at the stations was mandatory when an officer dies in the line of duty. However, it was believed that this was the first time that flags were flown at half-mast in honor of a dog.

On March 31, 2009, Liberty was added to the California Police Dog Memorial known as Faithful Partner. The memorial is located on the University of California, Davis campus and is dedicated to police dogs that have died in the line of duty.

The Los Angeles Police Department has a "Liberty Award" that is named after Liberty and is presented for a dog or horse who died in the line of duty.

EPILOGUE – OFFICER JOHN HALL

In 1990, Officer John Hall was awarded the Medal of Valor for his actions on March 22, 1989. The Medal of Valor is the highest honor that the Los Angeles Police Department bestows to one of its officers. The award stated:

Officer Hall displayed extraordinary courage and bravery in direct confrontation with armed suspects. Despite his painful wound, he placed his fellow officers and the community above his own safety. His heroic actions upheld the finest traditions of the Los Angeles Police Department and are recognized by awarding the Medal of Valor to Officer John D. Hall.

(COMMENTARY OF STEVE COOLEY)

Officer Hall retired in May 2002 after serving almost 31 years with the Los Angeles Police Department. The District Attorney of Los Angeles County is allowed to select two law enforcement officers from outside the Bureau of Investigation as security personnel. I used that provision to hire John Hall in May 2003 as part of my security team. He was one of four full-time peace officers who provided security for me and my family. He was part of my security detail for almost ten years and retired from the office at the same time that I completed my third term as District Attorney. We are close friends, and we often talk about his favorite partner—a female Rottweiler named Liberty.

LESSONS LEARNED

This chapter describes two examples in which suspects fired shots at police officers. In both examples, the police established a perimeter in which the suspects were believed to be hiding. There is no greater danger for a police officer than to search for an armed suspect who has already fired a shot at officers and who is willing to use deadly force to avoid an arrest. In these situations, the use of a police dog to locate the suspect will greatly reduce the danger to the officer.

The shooting of Liberty has become part of a training exercise for the LAPD. The theme is that when confronted by an armed suspect, the officer must stay in the fight. When engaged in a shootout with a suspect, it is important to stay in the fight even after having been wounded, such as Officer Hall and Liberty did in this case.

LIBERTY

Los Angeles Police Department
Partner John Hall

Date of Birth: July, 1983 (Denmark)
Date Appointed: April 29, 1986
End of Watch: March 22, 1989

A Dog Named Liberty Dies Heroically on Duty

By Richard Varenchik
Citizen Staff Writer

"There is no hunting like the hunting of men. And those that hunt armed men long enough, and like it, never care for anything else thereafter." — The motto of the Los Angeles Police Department's K9 Unit, from the works of Ernest Hemingway.

Liberty was like that. She loved the hunt. "She was always out in front," said Los Angeles police officer John David Hall.

Hall, 41, has lived in the Santa Clarita Valley for 16 years. He is assigned to the LAPD K9 Unit, where his most recent "partner" was Liberty, a 95-pound, 5-year-old Rottweiler.

Liberty lived with Hall and his family. The dog got along well with

Continued on Page 8

Liberty's official picture

Partner Killed

Continued from Page 1

Hall's wife and three children. And Liberty was a big hit with the kids whenever she was taken to visit a school.

But she really came alive when it was time to work. Liberty participated in 115 arrests and more then 250 searches during the two years she worked with Hall.

"She was a working-class dog," said Hall's wife. "She was bred for police work."

So Liberty was happy to get out of the house and go to work March 22, when Hall was called to Culver City to help in the search for two car thieves. The two men had been chased, crashed their stolen car and ran off into the night after firing shots at pursuing officers.

When Hall arrived in Culver City he was told that the two men had run off in different directions. Hall and Liberty were given a section of houses to search. As usual, Liberty was out in front as she and Hall walked off into the darkness.

As they approached an open garage behind a home, Liberty "alerted" — her head and nose up in the air, sniffing. Hall watched as the dog slowly searched through the boxes and other items that cluttered the garage.

Then Liberty walked through a small door in a partition that separated the main garage from an added-on section. She began to bark — a bark Hall had heard many times before. "I've got your suspect" was what the bark meant.

Hall moved forward toward the little doorway, his pistol in his right hand, supported by his left hand which held his flashlight.

As Hall looked in the doorway a police helicopter was circling overhead, bathing the garage in a flickering, twitching light. The police officer saw Liberty standing in front

of a man who was trapped, his back against the rear wall. (Hall later learned the man was armed with a nine-shot, .22 caliber revolver.)

Two flashes lit up the inside of the garage as Hall heard two shots ring out. "Liberty yelped and went down. The second shot hit my left wrist. The flashlight went out of my hand," Hall said.

Suddenly, Liberty got up from where she lay bleeding on the floor and lunged at the criminal. "She grabbed him by the leg and jerked him all over the place," Hall said. "He shot five more times and missed all five. I shot him."

Liberty walked out of the garage and fell to the ground. Hall ran out to her when the second suspect, who the police officer had not seen, came bursting out of the garage. Thinking he was being attacked again by the first suspect, Hall fired and brought the man down. Both suspects died from their wounds.

Hall bent down to cradle Liberty's head in his hands and arms. "was yelling at her, 'Liberty! Liberty!' She wouldn't respond," Hall said.

As other officers arrived Hall shouted at once to take Liberty to a veterinarian. The vet pronounced her dead from a bullet that had torn through an artery in her neck.

Hall was taken to UCLA Medical Center for treatment of shattered bones and bullet fragments in his left wrist. When Chief of Police Daryl Gates came in, Hall asked for one favor. "Anything you want," Gates said. "I want another Rottweiler," Hall replied.

But in Hall's mind, there will never be another Liberty. "She was my partner. She was my friend. She saved my life," he said.

"She was a hunter. That was her destiny. She was always out in front."

Police Department

Awards the

Medal of Valor

to

John D. Hall

At 9:15 p.m. on March 22, 1989, the call went out: "Officer needs help — shots fired." Patrol units quickly set a perimeter and called for "K-9" units to search for "armed and dangerous" suspects. Officer John D. Hall and his rottweiler police dog, Liberty, responded.

Officer Hall and Liberty formed a search team with three patrol officers. Within minutes, Liberty "alerted" near a backyard fence, and headed toward an open garage. Here, she went into "full alert", indicating that a suspect was inside.

Officer Hall and Liberty cleared the garage area and moved to the storage area of the garage. In the darkness, Liberty went out of sight through a storage-room door. The dog barked at the hiding suspect. A shot rang out, the bullet hitting Liberty. As Officer Hall entered the storage-room, another shot was fired, hitting him in the left arm. In the darkness, Officer Hall fired his weapon at the suspect's muzzle flashes only five feet away. Through the glimmer of light from the LAPD helicopter's searchlight, the officer could see Liberty regain her feet and continue attacking the suspect, disrupting his aim. Finally the suspect collapsed from Officer Hall's fire.

Officer Hall took Liberty outside and requested medical assistance for her. Realizing that the suspect was still a possible threat until handcuffed, he reorganized his search team to return to the garage. By holding his pistol between his legs he reloaded with one hand. With a borrowed flashlight placed under his left armpit, he led his team back to the structure.

As they approached, a second suspect came out. Ordered to place his hands on his head, he suddenly reached for a gun on his right side. Officer Hall fired until the suspect fell to the ground.

Officer Hall displayed extraordinary courage and bravery in direct confrontation with armed suspects. Despite his painful wound, he placed his fellow officers and the community above his own safety. His heroic actions upheld the finest traditions of the Los Angeles Police Department and are recognized by awarding the Medal of Valor to Officer John D. Hall.

_____
Mayor

_____
Chief of Police

_____
President, Board of Police Commissioners

District Attorney Steve Cooley with personal security detail John Hall (LAPD retired) and Ernie Halcon (San Fernando PD retired). Hall and Halcon were life-long friends. Halcon had lent Hall a back-up gun several days before the shooting of Liberty.

POLICE DOG PRAYER

OH ALMIGHTY GOD,
WHOSE GREAT POWER AND ETERNAL
WISDOM EMBRACES THE UNIVERSE,
WATCH OVER MY HANDLER WHILE I
SLEEP. PROTECT MY HANDLER FROM
HARM WHILE I AM UNABLE TO DO SO.
I PRAY,
HELP KEEP OUR STREETS AND HOMES
SAFE WHILE MY HANDLER AND I REST.
I ASK FOR YOUR LOVING CARE BECAUSE
MY HANDLER'S DUTY IS DANGEROUS.
GRANT MY HANDLER YOUR UNENDING
STRENGTH AND COURAGE IN OUR DAILY
ASSIGNMENTS.
DEAR GOD,
PROTECT MY BRAVE HANDLER, GRANT
YOUR ALMIGHTY PROTECTION,
UNITE MY HANDLER SAFELY WITH THE
FAMILY AFTER THE TOUR OF DUTY HAS
ENDED.

I ASK NOTHING FOR MYSELF.

AMEN.

UNKNOWN

TitleTown
PUBLISHING

Visit www.titletownpublishing.com to see more upcoming titles.

Blue Lives Matter 2
In the Line of Duty

by Cooley & Schirn

If you've enjoyed this copy of Blue Lives Matter: In the Line of Duty, you'll be happy to know that this is only the first book in a series of books by Hon. Steve Cooley and Robert Schirn that gives readers an in-depth look at the cases that involve line-of-duty deaths in America. For more information visit www.bluelivesmatter thebook.com

YES, MA'AM!
Running the Thin Blue Line

by Officer Susan Bickett

Yes Ma'am! is the true story of female cop trying to make it in a man's world. Officer Susan Bickett (Samantha Bennet) started her career with The Green Bay Police Department in 1994 and served 22 years with the department, 18 of those years on the streets of Green Bay. Here, Officer Bickett shares her fac tual memoirs about life on the street and the courage it took to live through it.

TRUE BLUE III
Police Stories by Those Who Have Lives Them

by Sgt. Randy Sutton

Lieutenant Randy Sutton's fascinating collection of stories and memories, solicited from law enforcement officers across the country, offers a broad and insightful look at the many facets of police life: courage, exhilaration, frustration, loss, and even humor, from the everyday to the career-defining moments on the job. Told by the cops that lived them, these stories show what it truly means to protect and serve.

Spring 2018

Summer 2018

Fall 2018

additional titles for purchase at www.titletownpublishing.com

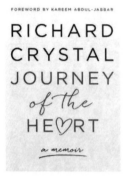

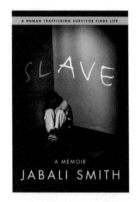

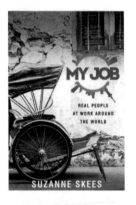

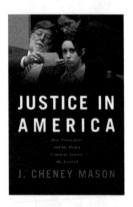

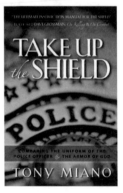

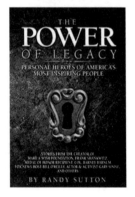